Revelations

Revelations

Personal Responses to the
Books of the Bible

VIKING
CANADA

VIKING CANADA

Published by the Penguin Group

Penguin Group (Canada), 90 Eglinton Avenue East, Suite 700, Toronto, Ontario, Canada
M4P 2Y3 (a division of Pearson Penguin Canada Inc.)

Penguin Group (USA) Inc., 375 Hudson Street, New York, New York 10014, U.S.A.
Penguin Books Ltd, 80 Strand, London WC2R 0RL, England
Penguin Ireland, 25 St Stephen's Green, Dublin 2, Ireland (a division of Penguin Books Ltd)
Penguin Group (Australia), 250 Camberwell Road, Camberwell, Victoria 3124, Australia
(a division of Pearson Australia Group Pty Ltd)
Penguin Books India Pvt Ltd, 11 Community Centre, Panchsheel Park, New Delhi – 110 017, India
Penguin Group (NZ), cnr Airborne and Rosedale Roads, Albany, Auckland 1310, New Zealand
(a division of Pearson New Zealand Ltd)
Penguin Books (South Africa) (Pty) Ltd, 24 Sturdee Avenue, Rosebank, Johannesburg 2196,
South Africa

Penguin Books Ltd, Registered Offices: 80 Strand, London WC2R 0RL, England

First published in Canada by Penguin Group (Canada),
a division of Pearson Penguin Canada Inc., 2005
Originally published in Great Britain by Canongate Books Ltd,
14 High Street, Edinburgh EH1 1TE, 2005

1 2 3 4 5 6 7 8 9 10   (FR)

Introduction to *Revelations* copyright © Richard Holloway, 2005
Please see pp 399–403 for copyright holders for each Introduction to the Books of the Bible

Manufactured in Canada.

LIBRARY AND ARCHIVES CANADA CATALOGUING IN PUBLICATION

Revelations : personal responses to the books of the Bible / edited by Richard Holloway.

Anthology of introductions from books in the Pocket canon series.
ISBN 0-670-06440-8

1. Bible—Introductions. I. Holloway, Richard, 1933- II. Title: Pocket canon.

BS475.3.R49   2005   220.6'1   C2005-903156-5

British Library Cataloguing in Publication Data available

Visit the Penguin Group (Canada) website at **www.penguin.ca**

CONTENTS

CONTENTS

CONTENTS

CONTENTS

Richard Holloway

Introduction to Revelations

It was a long time ago when I was asked by my bishop which version of the Bible I would like as an ordination present. Presciently, I chose the King James version. Dated June 11 1960, and inscribed by the Bishop of Glasgow and Galloway, it lies before me on my desk as I write these words. It is a handsome edition printed on India paper, with a supple leather cover, yet I hardly used it during my forty years in the ministry. To explain why, I have to make a bit of a digression.

The ancient Greeks made a useful distinction in their use of written texts. Some writings they called *logoi*. These were factual or reasoned accounts of some discipline or other, such as science or mathematics. But they had a second kind of writing they called *muthoi*. The classic example of a *muthos* or myth would have been one of their stories about the gods. Unfortunately, this is why the word myth gets misunderstood. It has become synonymous with something that's not true, something false, like those old Greek gods: just a bunch of myths, we say.

But consider this. I have on my bookshelves a volume of poems by Ted Hughes called *Tales from Ovid*. Ovid was a Roman poet who wrote around the time of the birth of Christ. Hughes has translated a long poem by Ovid called *Metamorphoses*. It was an account of how from the beginning of the world bodies had been magically changed by the gods into other bodies. Hughes says that, in his poem, Ovid took 'a wide sweep through the teeming underworld of Romanised Greek myth and legend'. Hughes' book is great poetry in its own right, and it is packed with insights about how humans still transform or metamorphose themselves by greed or self-love, hatred or lust. Reading it, we discover that these ancient myths are bang up to date in the way they open up to us the mysteries and sorrows of our own nature. So here's an interesting paradox: we can still read those ancient Greek myths today and find new depths of meaning in them; but we are unlikely to read ancient Greek science with profit now, because their take on factual reality has been superseded by modern knowledge, which is truer to the 'facts of the universe' than the Greeks could possibly have been in their time. In other words, the value of factual discourse turns out to be transient; while myth or imaginative discourse turns out to be enduringly useful.

The holy books of religion, including the Bible, clearly belong in the category of *muthos* rather than of *logos*. Unfortunately, many religious leaders ignore or misunderstand that distinction today. They want their scripture to have the status not of myth and poetry, but of science; they want it packed not with meaning, but with fact. Tragically, they fail to realise that a community's myths are more enduringly useful than its science. More significantly, they fail to realise that the endless reiteration of brute fact, unseasoned by colour or sorrow, is deeply boring to the average listener. Anyone who has tried to analyse the tedious genius of the bore will discover that their reverse-charisma has a great deal to do with their endless rehearsal of *facts*. Whether it is the minutely detailed recital of an office conflict or an intricate description of the versatility of a recent software purchase, their narrative style invariably destroys the will to live in the average listener. The speech of the true bore lacks tragic depth and comic width, precisely because, like the speaking clock, bores are locked into the numbing repetition of facts. In short, they lack mythic resonance, they do not realise that *the letter killeth, but the spirit giveth life*.[1] That is why when we read, as an ancient myth, the account of the expulsion of Adam and Eve from the Garden of Eden we continue to be impressed by its contemporary validity as a picture of the power of discontent to destroy human happiness. But if we are told we have to understand it as a description of a historical event, we know immediately the claim is false and are likely to dismiss the story's importance: and we miss the depths of meaning that a different

---

[1] The Second Letter of Paul to the Corinthians 3.6.

reading of the text will afford us. Like thousands of preachers before me, in the years when I was expounding the Bible I preferred modern translations because they gave it the false gloss of factual discourse; whereas the majesty of the King James version would have been a far better way of introducing my listeners to the dark beauty and tragic depth of ancient myth.

Ironically, we have reached a stage when it is unbelievers who are more likely to champion the great traditional versions of the Bible, such as the King James, while believers are more likely to resort to the banalities of modern translation. This is because unbelievers, if they read the Bible at all, are likely to read it as a constellation of myths that continue to express the height and depth of human existence; whereas believers are more likely to try to read it as an information manual, a sort of users' guide to the universe. In my experience, when you let go of the Bible as explanatory *logos*, you get it back as depthless myth. That is why, when I quote it in my writing and lecturing now, it is the King James version I use.

I do so for two reasons. First of all, I want to emphasise the fact that we are dealing with an archaic text here. I don't want people to fall for the assumption that the Bible is a contemporary document that can be doctored to affirm the equal value of women in society or suggest that God is relaxed about same-sex love. I want to feel its cultural offensiveness as well as its tragic sublimity full in my face. The other reason I use it is that I believe the

King James version is itself an extraordinary human achievement, and part of that achievement lies in what I can only describe as the politics of divinity. In his magnificent account of the writing of the King James Bible, Adam Nicolson points out that the wily Scottish monarch who commissioned it had some definite intentions in mind. In the sixth of his sixteen instructions to the translators James wrote: 'Noe marginal notes att all to be affixed, but only for ye explanation of ye Hebrew or Greeke Words, which cannot without some circumlocution soe breifly and fitly be expressed in ye Text'. Nicolson points out that behind that instruction lay James' long and bitter experience of theological conflict in Scotland. He wanted the text, as far as possible, to do its own thing and not to be made to dance to the tune of rival interpreters. Nicolson quotes a sixteenth-century text on the art of rhetoric that described circumlocution as 'a large description either to sett forth a thyng more gorgeously, or else to hyde it'. He goes on to write: 'The words of this translation, then, could embrace both gorgeousness and ambiguity, did not have to settle into a single doctrinal mode but could embrace different meanings, either within the text itself or in the margins.' Later on he continues: 'There is no need, though, to choose between these things, and that avoidance of choice is, in the end, the heart of the King James Bible. It does not choose. It absorbs and includes . . . Unlike the churches themselves, the words of this Bible remain alive, a way of speaking and a form of language which is still a vehicle of meaning in circumstances when little else can be.'[2] That is a better description of the enduring power of myth for humanity than anything I am likely to come up with. And it is why the King James Bible will go on being read by unbelievers long after it has fallen out of use in the churches.

It is significant that when the publisher at Canongate was approaching people to introduce the individual books of the Bible, it is from a secular group of writers that the introductions came, the kind of people who wrestle with myth every day of their lives. I can still remember the launch of the first series of Canons in St James Piccadilly in the autumn of 1998. Fay Weldon, Blake Morrison and A.N. Wilson were there; and so was Nick Cave. Will Self couldn't come, which saddened me, because I thought his introduction to *Revelation* was the most intriguing of the bunch. Louis de Bernières was also there, and thereby hangs a tale. The lovely old church was packed to the gallery, and by the end of the evening I had figured out that there were three different groups of people there. It was obvious that a lot of discerning young people had come along to see and hear Nick Cave. It was also obvious that many people had come to hear the famous novelists ranged before them. But before we really got going it became clear that we had also been invaded by a group of religious demonstrators, whose target was the author of *Captain*

---

[2] Adam Nicolson, *Power and Glory*. HarperCollins. London 2003, 77, 241.

Correlli's Mandolin. Louis de Bernières had been asked to write the introduction to the great *Book of Job*, and he had fulfilled the task with mordant relish. In his summary he had concluded: 'There are many episodes in the Bible that show God in a very bad light, such as when He commands Abraham to sacrifice his son Isaac, or when He commands Saul to slaughter the Amalekites, and one cannot but conclude from them either that God is a mad, bloodthirsty, and capricious despot, or that all this time we have been inadvertently worshipping the Devil.'[3] That was too much for Paul Slenert, an English solicitor of intense evangelical convictions: he tried, unsuccessfully, to halt publication of the Canons on the ground of blasphemy. I don't think he was there that night, but there was certainly a group of passionate evangelicals present, and they made their opinions noisily obvious. To be fair to them, they made their protests and added to the gaiety of the occasion by singing hymns from the gallery, before walking out and shaking our godless dust from their feet. Apart from its ritualistic predictability, their protest was significant. Since evangelical Christians assert their ownership of and interpreters' rights over the Bible, they couldn't just disagree with Louis de Bernières or offer another interpretation of the role of the divine trickster in the sufferings of Job: they had to assert the primacy of their own view and the wrongness of everyone else's. If *Revelations* is anything, it is a

---

[3] *Revelations*, 96.

complete demolition of this blinkered and partisan view of the Bible. It shows that the best way to get to the layers of meaning in a great text is not to ask propagandists or special pleaders to explain it, but to get writers to bring their own passion and insight to the task. That, in abundance, is what you get in this volume.

Here, to start at the beginning, is what E.L. Doctorow says about *Genesis*: 'If not in all stories, certainly in all mystery stories, the writer works backward. The ending is known and the story is designed to arrive at the ending. If you know the people of the world speak many languages, that is the ending: The story of the Tower of Babel gets you there. The known ending of life is death: The story of Adam and Eve, and the forbidden fruit of the Tree of the Knowledge of Good and Evil, arrives at that ending.' He also reminds us that all writers are plagiarists, so he goes on: 'Another venerable storytelling practice is the appropriation of an already existing story. Otherwise known as adaptation, it is the principle of literary communalism that allows us to use other people's myths, legends, and histories in the way that serves ourselves . . . Here in *Genesis*, the ancient scribes have retooled the story of the Flood recounted earlier in Mesopotamia and Sumer, including the vivid rendition in the Epic of Gilgamesh. Yet though the plot is the same, the resounding meanings are different, as befits an adaptation.'[4]

---

[4] *Revelations*, 19.

But the most compelling part of this book for me has been the revelation of the passion and sorrow of the Hebrew vocation throughout history, captured vividly by David Grossman in his introduction to *Exodus*: 'This may be the principal anomaly of the Jewish people's identity, in Israel as in the diaspora. It may be the secret of the people's endurance and vitality, but it doubtless also makes it constantly vulnerable to tragedy in a world that is all definitions and borders. The *Book of Exodus*, the grand story of the childhood of the Jewish people, sketches the primordial face of that people as it is being formed and, as we now know, describes what will be its fate throughout thousands of years of history.'[5] That was why I was particularly moved when A.S. Byatt, in her introduction to the *Song of Songs*, reminds us that this haunting piece of erotic poetry is associated with the holocaust through the poetry of Paul Celan. She writes: 'And in quite another world, the Song inhabits some of the greatest and most terrible poetry of our time, the poems in German of Paul Celan. The figure of Shulamith, whose name occurs only once in the Bible, appears in many forms in his work. His riddling poems about terror and loss, about the Holocaust and Israel, mourn both the Rose of Sharon, and, specifically, "my sister, my spouse", the lost and destroyed.' Celan placed the Shulamith of the *Song of Songs* in his devastating poem *Death Fugue* in what Byatt calls 'a repeated,

---

[5] *Revelations*, 60.

chanted juxtaposition with the doomed Margaret of Goethe's *Faust*.

> *Dein goldenes Haar Margarete*
> *Dein aschenes Haar Sulamith*
>
> *(Your golden hair, Margareta,*
> *Your ashen hair, Shulamith).*[6]

Byatt shows in her essay how a great text lives beyond itself into the future; in this case the terrifying future of the Jewish people. No wonder Mordecai Richler ends his introduction to *Job* by inviting God to choose another people: 'According to the Jewish calendar more than 5000 years have passed since God declared us a Holy people, chosen to be special. Enough is enough. As we enter into the new millennium, possibly he might consider favouring others with his love.'[7] According to the sequel to the Old Testament, that's exactly what God did, when he abandoned his aged spouse Israel and went off with a new love, the Christian Church. Even if you don't want to take sides in the quarrel, it's hard not to feel sorry for the one who got dumped, especially when you read some of the boastful assertions of the new love, especially in the letters she had ghost-written by her opportunistic pal from Tarsus. Even so, the note

---

[6] *Revelations*, 168–169.
[7] *Revelations*, 131–132.

of tragedy and loss comes through here as well, especially in the great parable of judgement at the end of the *Book of Matthew*. And it takes a novelist like A.N. Wilson, haunted by his own struggles with faith, to get it pitch perfect: '. . . perhaps the most haunting passage in the entire New Testament is that parable in the final discourse of *Matthew* when Jesus predicts that the King will welcome the chosen into his kingdom. They are those who have seen him, not in his glory, but as poor, naked, hungry, in prison and in need. Neither the blessed, nor the damned, in this tale, understand during their lifetimes, that in so far as they responded to the depths of human need in others, they had responded to God. It is in the context of this story that we begin to understand the sense in which this book is true. By the stern test of that parable and of this Gospel, most of us will feel like the rich young man. We will go away sorrowful, deeply conscious of our inability either to understand the Gospel, or to live up to its precepts, or to have the humility to accept Divine Grace. Yet, though we are sorrowful, and though we go away, we shall never read this text without being, in some small degree, changed.'[8]

It's no wonder that Alasdair Gray tells us that the unknown authors who lie behind the books of the Old and New Testaments made 'their God the strongest

---

[8] *Revelations*, 237.

character in world fiction'.[9] Coming from a master storyteller, that is no reductionist sneer: it is an act of powerful approbation, which is why he ends his contribution by warning us that the Old and New Testaments teach us that we should all reform our ways for the sake of our children.[10] *Whoso readeth, let him understand.*[11]

[9] *Revelations*, 181.
[10] *Revelations*, 187.
[11] *Matthew* 24.15.

THE OLD TESTAMENT

THE FIRST BOOK OF MOSES, CALLED GENESIS

In the beginning God created the heaven and the earth. And the earth was without form, and void; and darkness was upon the face of the deep. And the Spirit of God moved upon the face of the waters. And God said, 'Let there be light': and there was light.

(1:1–3)
authorised King James version

E.L. Doctorow

The King James Version of The Bible, an early-seventeenth-century translation, seems, by its now venerable diction, to have added a degree of poetic lustre to the ancient tales, genealogies, and covenantal events of the original. It is the version preachers quote from who believe in the divinity of the text.

Certainly in the case of *Genesis* 1–4, in which the world is formed and populated and Adam and Eve are sent from the Garden, there could be no more appropriate language than the English of Shakespeare's time. The King James does not suffer at all from what is inconsistent or self-contradictory in the text any more than do the cryptic ancient Hebrew and erring Greek from which it is derived. Once you assume poetically divine authorship, only your understanding is imperfect.

But when you read of these same matters in the contemporary diction of the English Revised Bible, the Jamesian voice of Holy Scripture is not quite what you hear. In plain-spoken modern English, *Genesis* – especially as it moves on from the Flood and the Tower of

Babel, and comes up in time through the lives of Abraham, Sarah, Isaac, Rebecca, and then to the more detailed adventures of Jacob and Rachel and Joseph and his brothers – seems manifestly of the oral tradition of preliterate storytelling out of which the biblical documents emerged, when history and moral instruction, genealogy, law, science, and momentous confrontations with God were not recorded on papyrus or clay tablets but held in the mind for transmittal by generations of narrators. And so *Genesis* in the English Revised Version is homier – something like a collection of stories about people trying to work things out.

The contemporary reader would do well to read the King James herein side by side with the English Revised. Some lovely stereophonic truths come of the fact that a devotion to God did not preclude the use of narrative strategies.

If not in all stories, certainly in all mystery stories, the writer works backward. The ending is known and the story is designed to arrive at the ending. If you know the people of the world speak many languages, that is the ending: The story of the Tower of Babel gets you there. The known ending of life is death: The story of Adam and Eve, and the forbidden fruit of the Tree of the Knowledge of Good and Evil, arrives at that ending. Why do we suffer, why must we die? Well, you see, there was this Garden. . . . The story has turned the human condition into a sequential narrative of how it came to be; it has used conflict and suspense to create a moral framework for *being*. And in suggesting that things might have worked out another way for humanity if the fruit had not been eaten, it has, not incidentally, left itself open to revision by some subsequent fantasist who will read into it the idea of original sin. Artistry is at work also in the blessings the dying Jacob bestows on his twelve eponymous sons. Each blessing, an astute judgement of character, will explain the fate of the twelve tribes led by the sons. A beginning is invented for each of the historical tribal endings the writer knows. Never mind that we understand from the documentary thesis of Bible sources – for it is, after all, the work of various storytellers and their editors – that different sons are accorded hands-on leadership by their father according to which writer is telling the story. Character is fate. And life under God is always an allegory.

Another venerable storytelling practice is the appropriation of an already existing story. Otherwise known as adaptation, it is the principle of literary communalism that allows us to use other people's myths, legends, and histories in the way that serves ourselves – Shakespeare's reliance on Hollinshed's Chronicles, for example, which should have, in honor, disposed him to share his royalites. Here in *Genesis*, the ancient scribes have retooled the story of the Flood recounted earlier in Mesopotamia and Sumer, including the vivid rendition in the Epic of Gilgamesh. Yet though the plot is the same, the resounding meanings are different, as befits an adaptation. Noah is unprecedented as the last godfearing, righteous man on earth . . . who may nevertheless drink a bit more wine than is good for him. And the God of *Genesis* is a Presence beyond the conception of the Sumerian epic.

The cosmology of *Genesis* is beautiful and, for all we know, may even turn out to be as metaphorically prescient as some believers think it is. One imagines the ancient storytellers convening to consider what they had to work with: day and night, land and sea, earth and sky, trees that bore fruit, plants that bore seed, wild animals, domesticated animals, birds, fish, and everything that crept. In their brilliant imaginations, inflamed by the fear and love of God, it seemed more than possible that these elements and forms of life, this organization of the animate and inanimate, would have been produced from a chaos of indeterminate dark matter by spiritual intent – here was the story to get to the ending – and that it was done by a process of discretion, the separation of day from night, air from water, earth from sky, one thing from another in, presumably, a six-day sequence culminating in the human race.

Every writer has to be awed by the staying power of the *Genesis* stories that have passed through the embellishing realms of oral transmission and the literate multilingual cultures of thousands of years. They are a group effort but not at all afflicted with the bureaucratic monotone that would be expected to characterize written collaborations. One reason for this may be the wisdom of the later scribes in leaving intact on the page those chronicles they felt obligated to improve upon. As a result we get more than one point of view, which has the effect, in the depiction of human character, of a given roundness or ambiguity that we recognize as realistic. Consider Jacob for example, who will wrestle with God or His representative and be named Israel, after all, but is impelled twice in his life to acts of gross deception – of his brother, Esau, and of his father, Isaac. Or the lovely gentle Rebecca, who as a maid displays the innocent generosity that the servant of Abraham seeks, offering him the water from her water jar, and then seeing to his camels . . . but years later, as the mother of Jacob, shrewishly assists her son in depriving Esau of his rightful patrimony.

In general, family life does not go all that smoothly for the founding generations. Beginning with Cain and Abel and persisting to the time of Joseph, brothers seem – like the brothers in fairy tales – to be seriously lacking in the fraternal spirit. Wives who are not themselves sufficiently fertile foist slave women on their husbands for purposes of impregnation, and then become jealous of those women and have them sent away. There seem to be two stations of wife, high and low – Hagar and Leah being examples of the low – and the anger and resentment this creates is palpable. Overall, the women of *Genesis* may be subject to an exclusively biological destiny as childbearers – theirs is a nomadic society that to survive must be fruitful – and the movable tent kingdoms in which they live may be unquestioningly paternalistic, but the modern reader cannot help but notice with relief how much grumbling they do.

It is in the pages of *Genesis* that the first two of the three major covenants between God and humanity are described. After the Flood, God assures Noah that He will not again lay waste to all creation in a flood. The sign of this covenant will be a rainbow in the clouds. Later, Abraham is commanded by God to resettle in Canaan, where he will be assured that he will eventually prevail as the father of many nations. Circumcision is the way Abraham and his descendants are to give sign of keeping this covenant. It is only in the next book, *Exodus*, that the final element of the covenantal religion, the Ten Commandments, will be given through Moses to his people. It is here that God will be identified as Yahweh and a ritualized sabbath – a simulation of God's day of rest after the Creation – is to be identified as the sign.

Apart from their religious profundity, this graduated series of exchanges between God and man have to remind us of the struggle for human distinction or identity in a precarious, brute life. This was the Bronze Age, after all. The Abrahamic generations were desert nomads, outlanders, who lived in tents while people such as the Egyptians lived in cities that were the heart of civilization. The territory that Abraham and his descendants were called to was abuzz with Amorites and other tribes of ethnically diverse Canaanites. Under such difficult circumstances it is understandable that the Abrahamic nomads' desire to be a designated people living in a state of moral consequence would direct them to bond with one God rather than many gods, and to find their solace and their courage in His singularity, His totality. But that they did so was tantamount to genius – and a considerable advance in the moral career of the human race.

For finally, as to literary strategies, it is the invention of character that is most telling, and in the *Genesis* narratives it is God Himself who is the most complex and riveting character. He seems at times to be as troubled and conflicted, as moved by the range of human feelings, as the human beings He has created. The personality of God cannot be an entirely unwitting set of traits in a theological text that declares that we are made in His image, after His likeness. There is an unmistakable implication of codependence. And it is no doubt some of the incentive for the idea expressed by the late Rabbi Abraham Joshua Heschel that the immanence of God, His existence in us, is manifest in the goodness of human works, the *mitzvot* or good deeds that reflect His nature. 'Reverence,' says the rabbi, 'is the discovery of the world as an allusion to God.' And so in reverence and ethical action do our troubled, conflicted minds find holiness, or bring it into being. Recognizing the glory of God is presumably our redemption, and our redemption is, presumably, His.

Thor Heyerdahl

As part of the Bible, *Genesis* has been translated into more languages, and read by more people, than any other text written since script began. Script was developed about five thousand years ago, as a means of perpetuating human memory. But by that time most of man's past was already forgotten, for our hominid ancestors have lived on this planet for more than two million years.

The historic period in any part of the world is reckoned from the time script was introduced locally. Any written text describing events from earlier periods must be based on generations of human memory, and oral traditions are therefore necessarily more fragmentary and questionably accurate the further back we go. Furthest back they generally peter out into mere names in royal genealogical lines which, all over the world, from the written Nordic sagas of Iceland to the oral tribal traditions throughout Polynesia, merge with demi-gods and deities. In most of the great early civilisations of the Middle and Far East and in Mexico and Peru, the ruling families claim supernatural descent directly from the sun.

Not so in *Genesis*. And not least for this reason it stands out conspicuously among all written records describing prehistoric events. In *Genesis'* description of the origins of human life, there is a clear distinction between the first mortal and sinful human beings, and the omnipotent power which hovers as an invisible spirit over the emptiness until it sheds light on the material world and fills sea and land with creatures able to see and be seen.

Two thousand years ago *Genesis* was familiar to Jesus of Nazareth, and six centuries after him the prophet Mohammed frequently quoted from his teachings as well as from *Genesis'* story of creation and the other books of Moses. *Genesis* is therefore a basic religious text shared by Hebrews, Christians and Muslims. In consequence, the three monotheistic faiths all share the same god.

Genesis, like most of the other 65 independent books in the Bible, is obviously composed of texts obtained from different sources, at different times. Abraham and his descendants are the first to be devoted much text in *Genesis*. So much, that it is obvious that by this time script had taken over from oral tradition. Abraham is recognised as a historic person who emigrated from Ur in Mesopotamia about four thousand years ago, by some calculated to about 1800 BC.

Abraham and his kin were devout worshippers of their own one and only God, for whom they built altars and made blood sacrifices – rituals that were customary among their contemporaries who worshipped many gods. But Abraham's God was part of their daily life and spoke to his people with advice and promises both in daytime and in dreams. Nevertheless, their moral conduct followed ethical laws no more than that of people today. The patriarchs and their relatives aimed to accumulate wealth in the form of livestock, and descendants in the form of sons, and they attained their aims through mutual tricks and deceit. *Genesis* makes no attempt to portray Abraham and his kin as anything other than ordinary, sinful people. Abraham pretends that his wife Sarah is his sister and offers her to Pharaoh to obtain security in Egypt and great wealth in carefully numbered herds of camels, cattle, goats and sheep. Then he offers the same deal to the king of the Philistines, but the king sends her back, for God has revealed the trick to him in a dream. To help her husband have more sons, Sarah lets Abraham sleep with her maidservant, Hagar. Abraham might have feared that his blood offerings of beasts and birds to the divine Creator were not enough so, instructed by God, he ties up his son Isaac on an altar, planning to stab him with a knife and submit him as a burnt offering. Isaac survived because he was exchanged with a ram.

Later, Isaac imitated his father when he went to the land of the Philistines: he introduced his wife Rebecca to the people as his sister, but the king looked out of the window and recognised the trick from the former visit of his father. Rebecca in turn cheated Isaac by helping her son Jacob obtain, through fraud, the birthright from his brother Esau. Jacob fooled his blind old father and bought the birthright from his starving brother for a bowl of soup. He then resorted to two sisters and their maids to obtain twelve sons, who would also end up in Egypt after attempts at fratricide and forgery. Even allowing for certain changes in moral codes, this part of *Genesis* continuously reveals human nature in all its weaknesses.

The story of Lot, Abraham's nephew who accompanies him on his long trek into the Promised Land, is no more flattering. His two daughters made him drunk with wine two nights in succession, and in turn they seduced him to give him children. Such revelations about venerable patriarchs are not suggestive of divine authorship or that the book is dictated by close members of Abraham's own family. They testify rather to the honesty and bluntness of one or more authors who demonstrate an unbiased interest in preserving the facts as they became known to them.

The prehistoric lineage of Abraham's ancestry, from his father Terah back to the legendary Noah, consists only of a large number of names obviously recorded while oral traditions were still tribal treasures handed down through numerous generations of family elders. That the authors demonstrate considerable knowledge of names of tribes and places in Mesopotamia increases the scientific/historical value of this section. Contact with the twin-river country was obviously maintained long before the Babylonian captivity of Abraham's descendants in 586 BC. Abraham made his servant swear by the Lord that he would not let Isaac marry any of the Canaanites, but go back to Mesopotamia for a bride from his own country.

Since *Genesis* considers life on earth extinguished but for the survivors aboard Noah's ark, we can see the authors' need to bring all people, including Abraham's own ancestry, together as descendants of Noah's three sons, Shem, Ham and Japheth. Such a presumed narrow relationship between all humans created problems for genealogists due to the admitted diversity between the vast number of unrelated languages – hence the famous allegory about the Tower of Babel. This allegory is the only instance in what is otherwise a genealogical list of names, which traces Abraham's line back to one of Noah's sons, Shem. Shem was blessed by the Lord for covering up his drunken father, who was sleeping naked. Ham was cursed by the Lord because he did not do it, and Japheth was forgiven because he helped. All those who are not Jews, descend from either Ham or Japheth.

This classification of the whole of humanity into three branches – simplified and symbolised by the names of these three brothers – could easily be discarded altogether as a tale, but it might be an indicator of whom Abraham's early kin considered relatives and whom they considered strangers. What gives some credibility to the origin of this old Mesopotamian genealogy is that the Jews, descendants of Shem, mention only unknown persons in their own lineage up to Abraham, whereas the list of Ham's descendants, who remained in Mesopotamia, includes such famous names as Nimrod, hailed as 'the mighty one on Earth' and founder of Babylon, and Ashur, the founder of Nineveh and king of the Assyrians. They even admit that Ham's descendants, the Canaanites, later spread abroad as far as Gaza. As sons of Japheth, the Philistines were clearly set apart in the same category as all foreign peoples.

Give and take names from generations lost and forgotten, and the probability of other mistakes in the name lists, this orally preserved section of *Genesis* cannot be ignored by historians and archaeologists trying to reconstruct an important epoch in the lost human past.

When we go further back in time along Abraham's genealogy, Noah marks a new transition in style and story in *Genesis*. He takes us from oral tradition to legend. Noah is clearly a legendary figure although described, like Abraham, as purely human, getting drunk and living among normal animals rather than dragons and monsters. He even imagines his own God as rather human, enjoying the sweet smell rising from the burnt offerings on his altar. Children relish the wondrous fairy tale of Noah's ark riding the flood with all the animal species in the world, while adults wonder how he found them all and set them free on Mount Ararat, the highest peak in the Middle East. Yet this story has survived scorn and ridicule as sacred literature in the Bible, because it is not meant as a fairy tale, nor is it a myth, but a legend. Legends are usually formed around a base of ancient knowledge.

The legend about his early ancestors surviving a flood sent by the Creator to punish mankind, was brought along by Abraham from his original home, Ur in Mesopotamia. In Ur, archaeologists from the University of Pennsylvania discovered a buried library of 35,000 inscribed Sumerian clay tablets when they excavated the ziggurat, or stepped pyramid of Nippur in 1929. On one of these tablets was written the original version of the flood story; it had been hidden from sight for more than a thousand years when Abraham left the country. We recognise the main story, although Noah and God have Sumerian names, and this older version is more realistic in its details.

In this Sumerian text, the god in the sky who wants to drown sinful mankind is Utu, the Sun-god, and the pious king he tells to build a ship is Ziusudra. Ziusudra, however, was simply instructed to bring his family and domesticated animals on board, not all the wild species. And the ship did not land on an inland mountain peak, but on the low island of Dilmun, identified as the modern Sultanate of Bahrain in the gulf outside Ur. From Dilmun island in the gulf, the descendants of Ziusudra travelled by boat to the mainland, and founded Ur as their capital.

We recognise the sacred number seven which is so important in the Hebrew flood legend, for the Sumerian flood-wave lasted seven days and seven nights, 'and the big ship was tossed about on the waters'. When the flood abated and the Sun-god reappeared, Ziusudra prostrated himself on the ground and generously offered an ox and a sheep from the livestock he had saved. Noah 'took of every clean beast, and of every clean fowl, and offered burnt offerings on the altar'.

The Sumerian version was recorded on a clay tablet, which was a means of preserving important events in local history by the scribes in Mesopotamia in the third millennium BC. Centuries later the Sumerians were obliterated as a nation, and eventually the rule of Mesopotamia moved away from the coast to the inland Assyrian capitals of Ashur and Nineveh on the upper banks of the River Tigris. They preserved the main elements in the universal flood story, but adapted the landing to their own territory so that the vessel came ashore on a peak in Upper Kurdistan. It was their version of world history that was taught in Ur when Abraham came of age, and that explains why the Jews had Noah land on Mount Ararat, the highest peak in that part of the world, whereas the Muslims land him on El Judi in the same area.

The texts of *Genesis* and the Koran survived, but, like the Sumerian account, the Assyrian version of the flood was forgotten until found on a clay tablet in 1872 when the vast library of King Assurbanipal was excavated. In this Assyrian version it was the Ocean-god Enki who told the pious king Utu-Nipishtim to tear down his reed house and build a ship to save both mankind and animals. Enki tells him how to mix the right proportion of pitch, asphalt and oil to waterproof his reed ship. This explains the original text about Noah's ark in *Genesis*, stating that the ark was built from reeds, in typical Assyrian fashion. Omitted in earlier translations, it was included in the *New English Bible*, where God says, 'Make yourself an ark with ribs of cypress, cover it with reeds, and cover it inside and out with pitch.'

Noah's ark returns to the realm of reality and

embodies valuable scientific hints when we learn that it was built as a genuine Sumerian *magur*, an ocean-going reed ship, and landed on a low island rather than on a mountain peak. Whereas the original Sumerian text had the royal family bring only their livestock onboard, as depicted on so many Sumerian seals, the Assyrians added that they brought both the livestock and 'the beasts of the field'.

Clearly, the flood height was greatly exaggerated in *Genesis*, as it followed the Assyrian version in having the waters rise until the ship landed on a mountain peak. But this detail, inherited from the Assyrian story, can be discounted because of contradictions within the same Assyrian text. The Assyrian epic admits that the original storyteller sailed to the island of Dilmun to get his information from the mouth of the immortal king who survived the flood. Why sail to Dilmun in the gulf if the king landed on a peak inland? And in *Genesis* the height of the floodwater is actually given: 'Fifteen cubits upward did the water prevail.' Fifteen cubits is thirty feet. How could this land a boat on a mountain peak?

The archaeologist Leonard Wooley who excavated the Sumerian library in Ur actually found evidence of a flood that had buried Lower Mesopotamia in mud just before the Sumerian period. The flood-wave was estimated by him to a height of twenty-five feet. The homogenous mud layer deposited was three metres thick and covered the remains of an earlier settlement, while the Sumerians had built their city on top of it.

There is good reason to believe that the original flood

legend from Ur is based on an actual catastrophe. It would be as foolish to dismiss it as a fable, as to accept it in its final form without looking for the original version. There is every reason to accept that a story surviving for thousands of years as a religious belief among changing civilisations is based on a kernel of reality.

The part of *Genesis* prior to the deluge story brings us back, by way of a few names of kings supposed to have lived before the flood, to purely mythical times. Myth, as opposed to legend, is a pure product of mind not meant to be taken literally. Myth can be, but is not always, a fable. Myth among the world's great early civilisations was a means of simplifying and clarifying information too complicated to explain except through allegories. The Bible is full of such examples, and in the New Testament, Jesus used parables in most of his messages.

Genesis opens with a parable. We underestimate people who had invented scripts and gave us our astronomical calendar system, if we think they literally referred to one couple and six days in the parable about Adam and Eve. In both the Hebrew and Arab texts, the word used for 'day' is *yom*, and in Arabic *yom* also means a period of indefinite length. Long before Albert Einstein's theory of relativity, the ancient scribes of the Bible expressed their own view of the relativity of time by writing that 'one day [is] with the Lord as a thousand years, and a thousand years as one day'. (*Corinthians* II: 3:8). In the parable of creation, time was obviously measured in the days of God.

It is a common mistake among those of us who belong to the technological generations to assume that man's brain capacity and intelligence have increased with the progress of civilisation. There is no foundation for such an assumption. If we assume, like most intellectual readers, that *Genesis* was written by our human equals and not by a supernatural hand, we can only marvel at the concurrence between the chronology in *Genesis* of events during the six pre-human days of God and the sequences proposed by Charles Darwin and modern evolutionists.

In the beginning there was nothing, say the authors of *Genesis*. And out of nothing an invisible omnipotent spirit created everything. 'Let there be light', said the spirit of God on the first day of creation, and lit up a hitherto non-existent universe.

In the beginning there was nothing, say modern scientists. And out of nothing everything was created by a tremendous 'Big Bang'. How something could explode before there was anything is not explained. Technically there could be no 'bang' before the evolution of the first ear. It would therefore seem that a silent spirit leaves a better image of the invisible creativity that lit up the universe than a big bang that nobody had set off and nobody could hear.

The second day, according to the allegory in *Genesis*, our planet was without form, a mere abyss of water. And the planet was covered with water until the spirit of God separated 'the waters above' from the waters below.

This is a most amazing statement. It is difficult to understand how the early scribes could know what we know today, that, when our planet took form, it became totally covered with a world ocean. Water evaporated and rose to a certain distance above the surface as a sea of clouds, with a cargo of water, able to sprinkle down again into the same sea.

It is difficult for any scientist to explain how all these transformations could have happened. First, everything created out of nothing, next a ball of fire covered by water, whereupon this water started rotating as a *perpetuum mobile* all by itself. According to generally accepted physical law, nothing can start changing or moving without an outside impulse, and a *perpetuum mobile* is accordingly an absolute impossibility. There must have been an invisible outside impulse, one omnipotent and able to overcome impossibilities. And how could water cling to all sides of a rotating round ball without splashing off into space? *Gravity,* we say, and camouflage our ignorance with another invented word as empty as the Big Bang. Gravity works on everything from metal to water and flesh, and must be a power located in minimum space exactly in the centre of planet earth since it draws the ocean as well as the floating continental plates towards the same point from all sides.

On the third day, according to *Genesis,* dry land rose from the sea. Plants grew up from seeds that appeared by themselves in the ground, and each of them carried their own seeds to propagate the species.

With microscopes, science has discovered the chromosomes within that define the 'programme' for the production of the species. But the producer of the programme does not show up under the microscope, nor does the power stronger than gravity that pushes plants and tree trunks up from the soil. By calling it *osmosis*, we think we know this power small enough to hide in a seed and strong enough to push tons of timber and fruit into the air.

The fourth day was the first with full daylight on Earth, according to *Genesis*. Not until then did the sun and the moon appear visible in the firmament, and the difference between day and night began.

This late appearance of sun and moon in *Genesis* is puzzling as they are usually worshipped as creators in other early civilisations. But it reflects the image of a sky such as the early scribes must have visualised after the first appearance of land above the sea. A single volcano can blacken the sky and turn day into night after a major eruption. It is easy to imagine that no daylight could have reached planet Earth until the end of the formative period, due to vapour, smoke and ashes emitted from volcanoes and a boiling ocean. Hence the late appearance of the sun and moon in the human world.

On the fifth day, according to *Genesis*, living creatures began to move about in the ocean. The waters brought forth an abundance of species, large and small, that began to swim, and some grew wings and took off into the air.

Science confirms that life began in the ocean. First as a simple living cell that split and split again, until it changed into myriads of marine species with specialised limbs and organs, some had fins so long that they changed into winged reptiles and the ancestry of feathered birds. Darwin proposed a gradual evolution through the survival of the fittest. Others now believe in rapid changes through mutation.

But what 'decided' that there should be any change in the dead world the Big Bang had created? And why were the changes meaningful and super-ingenious? The ocean was totally sterilised on a ball of fire.

The parable in *Genesis* is no more incredible than scientific reality.

On the sixth day the Creator terminated his creation on our planet, according to the text in *Genesis*. The spirit of God that day brought forth all that could crawl and walk on dry land. Only then was the stage set for an environment able to sustain man. The Creator, still invisible, decided to make man in his own image. In 'our' image, according to the words in *Genesis*, for He created man as one male and one female. The scribes of *Genesis* did not visualise the Creator as an old man in a long gown. His self-portrait was a young and naked couple, the symbol of love.

God rested on his seventh day. He blessed it, content with the work He had done.

In a second version of *Genesis*, obviously with a different authorship, man was formed out of the dust and mist that rose from the earth. In fact, there was nothing else for the Creator to start evolution with. Man was created through evolution from dust in the ocean made alive by rays from the sun.

The parable of the expulsion from the Garden of Eden has been interpreted and misinterpreted in many ways, possibly due to ambiguity in translations. It would be an underestimation of the wisdom and allegorical style of the authors of antiquity to think that they wrote of a man and woman tempted by a snake to eat an apple. 'Adam' symbolises early man, and the naked couple in the garden is an image of early 'mankind' living in nature. The temptation was the wish to be godlike by eating allegorically from the tree of knowledge – 'of good and evil', says the Hebrew text. In old Hebrew 'good and evil' is a way of saying 'everything'; there is no allusion to knowledge of the difference about what is right and what is wrong.

Whatever they learned by eating from the tree brought them misfortune and drove them away from the natural environment that had nourished them. They began covering their nakedness first by sewing leaves together and then by dressing in clothes of skin. Outside the garden, men had to toil for their daily bread and women gave birth in pain.

The first descendants of the earliest humans are symbolised by Cain, the tiller of the soil, and Abel, the keeper of the sheep. They represent the farmers who planned for organised subsistence by cultivating plants, and the nomadic shepherds who domesticated beasts. These were the two distinct groups of human society typical throughout the Biblical period. Although offering to the same God, hostility made Cain slay Abel, whereupon he immigrated to a foreign country where his son,

Enok, founded the first city. In three generations the allegory about early humanity brings us from the first naked food-gatherers up to the first city-builders and the beginnings of civilisation.

Genesis deserves attention as the most remarkable piece of literature ever written.

Steven Rose

In the Beginning

For me it wasn't *Genesis* at all but *Berashis,* in the Old Hebrew pronunciation with which the *Torah* – the five books of Moses, or *Chumash* – were chanted section by section in a ritual which took the entire synagogue year, Saturday by Saturday. And I sat at the back of the *shul* with the other boys, explaining why the Biblical version of creation had now been firmly put in its place by modern science. So when, aged eight and with a copy of Darwin's *Origin* and a chemistry set, I felt able to declare my atheism, I ceased to pay any attention at all to the Bible – either my bit, the so-called Old Testament, or the New. Not that I could really read Darwin then – that was to come much later – but I grasped, however childishly, his symbolic power as an alternative to the Bible story. If science was right, religion could not be, and I preferred white coats to black hats. The lab coat was to provide its route out of the close and foetid familial embrace, cloaked as it was in religious ritual. And so it has remained for me for the following half century. Did the editors of this series of volumes of the

King James realise that I was an ex-orthodox Jew, an atheist and a biologist to boot when they suggested that I write this introduction? Yes, they said, and that's why we asked you. So now, nudging sixty, I have read King James's *Genesis* for the first time.

Of course, in a sense none of us ever reads it for the first time; so much of the Biblical account, and its sonorous English text, is familiar. Its stories are of course central to Jewish, Christian and indeed Islamic traditions, but perhaps surprisingly its claims as to who we as humans are, and our complex relationships to nature – including our own, human nature – underlie many of the presuppositions of our assumedly post-religious, rationalist and reductionist modern science, however forcefully we dismiss the Biblical version of creation. So the militant atheism of my youth has been tempered by a recognition that science too has its problems. White coats, as much as priestly robes, crucifixes and *mogen davids*, can be bloodstained.

The Creation, Eden, Adam and Eve, the Fall, Cain and Abel, the Flood and Noah's Ark, Babel's tower, Abraham and the sacrifice of Isaac, Jacob and his ladder, Sodom and Gommorah, Joseph with his Coat of Many Colours – and with Potiphar's wife – Pharoah's dream of the seven fat and seven lean cattle. The images speak to us through centuries of painting, sculpture, novels and poems, to say nothing of mountains of learned commentaries and exegeses. And all within 65 pages (in the standard editions of the Bible). A miracle of terse story telling – yet these familiar episodes form only part of a text full of tales of murder, incest and adultery and of apparently God-sanctioned tricks, by father on son and son on father, brother on brother, nephew on uncle. Seemingly random collections of often elliptic stories interspersed with columns of obscure images whose interminable detail almost drowns the rest. Creation may have taken God six days; the text deals with it in 31 short paragraphs. By contrast the complex sagas of the travels, loves and lusts of cunning Jacob and later of his virtuous and put-upon, but ultimately successful, son Joseph take up virtually half the book.

For modern fundamentalists who take each sentence literally, as in the days when Archbishop Ussher could calculate from the lineages that the Creation could be dated precisely to 4004 BCE, these diverse and disjointed episodes continue to occupy many Casaubon-years of study and analysis. If we see them as modern Biblical scholars do, as accretions of early Mesopotamian and Egyptian myths and sagas, read into a single and reasonably coherent narrative in order to provide a history for a particular group of initially nomadic, later sedentary shepherds and pastoralists, non-believers like me would do better to pass them by, and focus instead on those themes which still have resonance today. What follow then are my personal reflections – though reflections which owe unacknowledged debts to many contemporary philosophers, sociologists and scientists – on the central themes of those 65 pages.

I write as a biologist, but I am not concerned here to take issue with those who argue for those travesties of science called Creationism, nor with those who send me learned tracts proving that Noah's flood really occured and that the remains of an ark (big enough doubtless to hold exemplars of all of the upwards of 14 million known species of life on earth – two of each of the unclean and seven of the clean, presumably plus survival supplies of appropriate food) have been discovered by archaeologists on Mount Ararat. I am content to leave such disputations to others. Nor do I need to 'prove' the fact that species have evolved, albeit by a multitude of mechanisms of which Darwinian selection is but one, or to reflect on the limited state of genetic knowledge and selective breeding practices which led to Jacob's spotted sheep. Instead, I focus on the vision of the world and humanity's place within it offered by the story of the Creation, Eden and the Fall.

First and foremost, the Creation itself. In the beginning, *Genesis* tells us, God created the heaven and the earth, a creation from nothingness, a nothingness not perhaps so conceptually different from that offered by modern cosmology's Big Bang. Nor, for that matter, is the sequence of creation, culminating in that of humans, so different from that proposed by modern cosmology, if we ignore the timescales. If we today have better grounds for believing that provided by cosmologists rather than the Biblical account, we should also not forget that the basis for scientific knowledge remains doubt, not certainty. It is just that as scientists we are allowed to answer questions like 'What came before the Big Bang?' by saying 'We don't know' rather than 'God did it.' For some this statement of ignorance rather than faith may be threatening; I myself don't find it so.

After heaven and earth, light and dark, plants and animals, comes the creation of humans – in chapter 1, male and female together, in chapter 2 the more familiar version in which, as in so many other of the world's creation stories, man is created out of clay (the dust of the earth) and the breath of God, and only later woman as a companion and helpmeet. Making objects from clay was one of the earliest of human technologies and analogising the act of human creation to that of the potter begins a tradition of attempting to understand living processes via technological artefacts which continues today. A modern-day God would perhaps take a computer and breathe consciousness into it.

And creating Eve after Adam – as opposed to the earlier versions, in which Adam and Lilith were co-equal – establishes the hierarchy of the genders which persists – despite the feminist challenges – to the present day. As Milton puts it in *Paradise Lost*, Adam's task is to serve God, Eve's God through him. Further, and unequivocally, God gives Adam dominion over all other living creatures by inviting him to name, to control and to own them. This belief in humanity's right to tame and dominate Nature, to transform the world according to our perceived need, has been largely if not entirely unquestioned until recent times by the various religions of the Book. Belief in this right has also been central to Western science from its origins in the protestant and emergent capitalist societies of north-western

Europe in the 17th century up until today's secular society. Read anyone from Francis Bacon to James Watson, the co-discoverer of the structure of DNA, and the unquestioned technological imperative shouts from every page. Hence perhaps the attempts amongst the present-day ecology movements, with their contrasting ethos in which humans live harmoniously with Nature, to seek support from the traditions of other, non-Western, religious forms.

Placing humanity as the culminating point of God's handiwork, rather than as merely the end of one recent twig on a branching evolutionary bush is the hubris most modern science rejects, it is true (I ignore those who argue for progressive evolution, or anthropic principles). In *Genesis*, humans are chosen and breed, then hunters conflict with gatherers (Cain and Abel), then, because God is troubled by the growing strength and lack of respect shown by such humans ('Giants in those days') all bar Noah and his family are destroyed, requiring the world to be repopulated. The unequivocally single origin for all of the many human tribes is one that the consensus of modern anthropology and archaeology shares, our common ancestress, the so-called Mitochondrial Eve. Less clear is the Biblical claim that there was originally but a single human language, and that only the threat to heaven presented by the builders of the tower of Babel resulted in a fearful and jealous God confounding the Babel-builders' goals by confusing their tongues. Once again, there is a contemporary debate amongst linguists and psychologists over whether there was a universal human 'language instinct', which echoes Babel's message.

And finally, amongst the new generations of humans, the children of Jacob called Israel are singled out. Why Jacob's and not Esau's? God's arbitrary will expressed through Jacob's complicit trickery? I find *Genesis* to be full of such seemingly motiveless and often unjust Godly acts. If believers find useful ethical values to be drawn from these stories, I must leave it to those who read the Bible as allegory to make their own case.

The other great theme on which my reading of *Genesis* centres is that of the Fall. Adam and Eve live in tranquility in Eden until Eve is tempted by the serpent to eat of the tree of the knowledge of good and evil. With that bite comes consciousness (soul?), and of course, God's expulsion of Man and Woman from the garden lest they also eat of the tree of life and become like gods. Instead, they must labour to live, and she must labour to give birth. The implications of this story have shaped both theology and the unspoken assumptions which have been incorporated into much of modern philosophical and biological thinking. The issues relate to predestination and determinism, to free will and to original sin. Was the Fall inevitable – that is, determined? Are most of us born sinners, and only a fortunate few in a state of Grace? Maybe even as born sinners we can attain Grace?

The centuries of theological disputes around such questions have also taken a contemporary form. Evolutionary psychologists argue that why we do what we do, for good or evil, is fixed by our selfish genes, which, by acting in their own 'interests', have shaped our evolutionary past, even if humans can transcend the 'tyranny' of their genes. The Christian origins of this claim and its echoes of Milton, three centuries earlier, are clear. We have eaten of the tree of the knowledge of good and evil, and we have free will. God creates men free to choose good or evil. If they did not have the choice, how could they freely serve God by eschewing evil? God knows that they will be tempted by the serpent, Satan, choose wrong, and fall, but nonetheless the choice is theirs.

This dichotomising, between body and soul, determinism and free will, gene and organism, lies deep within our Judaeo-Christian tradition, so deep that it seems natural, inevitable. Scrutinising *Genesis* with a secular eye helps us understand the roots of these dichotomies. Perhaps we need to look at our own assumptions from outside, from other theological and philosophical traditions, to see that they are not thus inevitable, that freedom is implicit in the nature of living processes, so that the concept of free will, with all the paradoxes it brings in its train, is a part not of our biological, but of our problematic religious inheritance, as children of the Book.

THE SECOND BOOK OF MOSES, CALLED EXODUS

And the Lord said, 'I have surely seen the affliction of my people which are in Egypt, and have heard their cry by reason of their taskmasters; for I know their sorrows, and I am come down to deliver them out of the land of the Egyptians, and to bring them up out of that land unto a good land and a large, unto a land flowing with milk and honey.'

(3:7–8)

authorised King James version

David Grossman

Into the swirl of events at the beginning *The Book of Exodus* – the tale of the bondage and oppression of the children of Israel and the growing enmity between the Israelites and Egyptians – seeps another, more personal and poignant story: a Hebrew child is born and his mother, who would save him from the death decreed for all sons by Pharaoh, lays him in a basket of bulrushes and sets the basket in the Nile. There, among the reeds, the daughter of the King of Egypt finds him. Pharaoh's daughter knows instantly that he is 'one of the Hebrews' children', but nevertheless decides to raise him as her son; she is the one who gives him his name, Moses.

How enchanting the entwining of this winsome tale with the tempestuous, epic myth of the birth of a nation. In a sense, this is the fabric of the entire book, an almost illusive weaving of fairy tale with strict legal and religious code: the warp – rods that turn into serpents, a vicious, cruel king, a land blighted by a plague of frogs; the woof – the giving of the law on Mount Sinai, the moment at which a people becomes welded to its destiny.

Reading *The Book of Exodus* is charged with tension: between the miserable, 'childlike' state of the children of Israel, a people physically and spiritually enslaved, and the exalted role God has chosen for them, heedless of the pace of their spiritual and moral development. Perhaps this is the truly demanding journey made by the children of Israel in *The Book of Exodus*: from clan to nation, from slavery to freedom.

II

Here in my study in Jerusalem, in Israel, in 'the promised land' to which the Jews have returned time and again from exile, I think about my forefathers, the children of Israel, during those first days after the maelstrom that uprooted them from Egypt. They are in the desert, and the desert is empty. They are being led, like an immense herd, to an unknown destination. What can they cling to? They escaped bondage in Egypt, but also abandoned their daily routine, their habits and customs, a familiar place and the social interactions and hierarchies that had become fixed over the course of generations. Suddenly everything is new and strange. Nothing can be taken for granted. What had appeared to be the end of the road, now appears to be its beginning. Somewhere in the heavens hovers the spirit of a God who seems to be benevolent; yet they, who have seen how He dealt with the Egyptians, know how unpredictable, brutal and fierce He can be.

Stunned, they stride onward, as if in a void. They follow their leader, a man who never lived among them, who from the time he was weaned lived in the king's palace and then in Midian. He tells them they are at long last free men, but perhaps free is the last thing they feel or want to be. Every day brings new experiences, new religious regulations and laws, and strange food – enough for one day – that falls from the skies.

If they have any spirit left they will realize that a miracle has befallen them, that they are privileged to have been given the chance to reinvent themselves, to be redeemed. If they dare, they can fashion a new identity for themselves. But to do so they must fight the ponderous gravity of habit, of anxiety and doubt, of inner bondage.

Maybe their hearts swelled at times – the expansive, dramatic landscapes of Sinai could have awakened unfamiliar feelings in the hearts of those who had for generations lived the choked lives of slaves in the confines of huts. Suddenly the body could try broader, more daring movements. Perhaps an ancient memory, thousands of years old, flickered, of their forefathers wending their way toward Egypt across this very desert on a journey of which only shards of legend remain. Perhaps their carrying the body of Joseph, son of Jacob, to burial in the land of Israel made tangible for them the abstract promise of return to their country; return to the place where Joseph was a child, and Jacob before him lived; return home.

In addition, a new factor entered their lives: calendar time. God determined the cycle of their days, sealing the week with the Sabbath (*Exodus* 16:23). Since the six days of creation this concept of the 'week' had hovered over the *Torah*, yet only now does it become clear to the reader that this concept was apparently known to God alone. Now He imparts it to His people. Can we, who were born within calendar time, fathom the impact this conceptual change must have had on human beings? Did it strengthen their sense of the circular, the cyclical, the monotonous? Or did time suddenly seem to be just another dimension of the desert in which they were trapped?

Not only did God create the 'circle of the week', but He designated holidays and festivals, setting the new year at Passover to emphasize its historic, religious and national significance. What did the children of Israel feel about God's having inscribed them in the historical consciousness of generations to come, while they themselves were but the dust of men, bewildered and frightened? Did they know they were only one step on the road to another, more exalted existence? At the end of a long day's wandering, as they sat by a dying fire, did a bitter, tragic silence fall as they realized, vaguely, that they were but putty in God's hands, their tortured existence destined to become a 'history' and a religion, an 'epic' tale, and their ability to comprehend this tale no more than that of letters to comprehend a book?

III

In *The Book of Numbers* (14:18 ff), God decrees that the entire generation of those who fled Egypt – a defiant generation that consistently refused to believe in God wholeheartedly and with complete faith – will be destroyed in the desert and not brought into the promised land. Yet the *Zohar*[1] calls this generation the 'generation of knowledge'; some envy its having witnessed God's wondrous acts during the exodus from Egypt, and its presence at the giving of the law on Mount Sinai. Nevertheless, throughout their history the Jewish people have conceived of the 'desert generation' as a lost, transitional generation, rootless and lacking identity and faith, a generation tossed in the 'chasm' between past and future, consumed by anxiety regarding its destiny. According to ancient Jewish legend, on the eve of *Tisha B' Av*[2] during the sojourn in the desert, the children of Israel would dig themselves graves and lie in them, rising in the morning to see who had remained alive.

Even today, the Jewish people read in the Passover *Haggadah* that 'in every generation, each individual is bound to regard himself as if he personally had gone forth from Egypt'. This is a direct summons to the people of Israel to examine the essential components of their identity.

It is difficult to grasp just how crucial those forty

---

[1] A commentary on the *Five Books of Moses*, the *Zohar* is a fundamental work of Judaism's mystic teachings (trans.).

[2] The ninth day of the Hebrew month of *Av* is observed by fasting, prayer and mourning in commemoration of the destruction of the first and second Temples, and other calamities that have befallen the Jewish people on that date (trans.).

years in the desert were to the formation of the Jewish people as a people. During those years, the lines of its 'national character' were drawn through the crucible of slavery and 'victimhood' and the ensuing phenomenal propensity for redemption and rejuvenation. Moreover, a complex pattern of contradictory emotions was formed: pride, indeed arrogance, over being 'the chosen people', tempered by a sense of having been banished, even cursed – the price of such mysterious chosenness; comfort and security in the knowledge of being the people of Yahweh, tempered by a fear of that same invisible and fickle God, Himself seemingly buffeted by internal storms rife with contradiction; and a taste for wandering, branded on the consciousness during the wandering in the desert, tempered by an intense longing for a 'promised land' where – and only where – existence could at last be merged with identity, and a zest for living could be freed.

Wandering is also searching, and longing always gives rise to new ideas and abstract thought. Gradually, searching and longing affect the dormant consciousness of this people that for generations had been subjugated, tethered to physical distress and hardship, become ossified. Searching and longing leave a unique mark on this people, reflected in its ideological motivation, its penchant for the abstract and talent at keeping an entire reality alive in its imagination, its aspirations and yearnings and, above all, its ability to be revitalized by the power of a dream, to use a dream to rise above real affliction.

IV

The people of Israel was formed as a result of a commandment to wander to a new place. God said to our forefather Abraham, 'Get thee out of thy country, and from thy kindred, and from thy father's house, unto a land that I will show thee' (*Genesis* 12:1). While at that time many tribes and peoples wandered constantly in search of sustenance, such wandering was never an end in itself – a national end in itself – as it was for the Jewish people, and as it is presented in the Books of *Genesis* and *Exodus*.

In retrospect, it seems that during those years in the desert these two contradictory elements – the urge to wander and the longing for a 'place' – became forces so integral to the soul of the Jewish people that it is difficult to know which is stronger. Perhaps this is one reason why for centuries the people of Israel have been mired in the same dilemma, lacking a sense of inner conviction: are they a people of place, or a people of time? That is, can the people of Israel live in a country with traceable, permanent borders and a distinctly national (or any other) 'character', or are they doomed, inherently, to seek out a 'borderless' existence of perpetual movement, of alternate exile and return, assimilation and individuation, restoration and change generation after generation, forever eluding definition and vulnerable to surrounding forces that would fortify or destroy them by turn?

Perhaps this also explains why for centuries other peoples have been so eager to determine just what a

'Jew' is, hemming him in to some 'definition' or other based on distinct characteristics, confining his fields of commerce or even penning him into a ghetto, as if to make him comprehensible, easy to monitor.

After all, this is also a description of the utter, onerous foreignness of one people among many. Indeed, from the harsh and violent exodus from Egypt to God's insistence on the separateness of this people and His exclusive 'possession' of it, *The Book of Exodus* brings into sharp relief the unique status of the Jewish people: its ability to quickly uproot itself, as if cutting itself out along an ever-present dotted line, coupled with a trenchant need to mingle with others, to become lost in them and thereby, paradoxically, to distill its identity, to define itself for itself.

This may further explain the necessity to the Jewish people of spending those forty years in the desert, almost completely cut off from other peoples and identities. Those years served as a lengthy cocoon stage, the final one before the Jewish people was hatched into its history, giving it time to formulate its identity solely through internal dialogue and an acceptance of its essential components, through countless occurrences, crises and climaxes.

V

More than any other of the *Five Books of Moses*, *The Book of Exodus* lays the foundation for the sense of 'epic', of myth, that has dogged the Jewish people since the exodus from Egypt, until the present. This is a most complex, disturbing feeling; perhaps it has contributed to Jewish existence having become, in the eyes of other peoples, an immense 'drama' – too immense – that cannot be confronted without being turned into a symbol or metaphor for something else. In other words, that existence is never just an existence, the Jews never just a people among peoples. This attitude is so entrenched, so ancient that it is difficult to know whether it resulted from the historic fate of the Jews or was 'projected' onto them and determined their fate. It burdens the 'Jew' by ascribing him either a heavy load of sentimental ideals or a refutably demonic character. The Jew is stretched between these two extremes, suffering from them, of course, but also surely finding solace in the equally ancient sense that his suffering and wandering has 'meaning', that a hidden author's intent will at some point lend the whole story significance.

It is no less interesting to ponder the extent to which the Israelis of today, citizens of a sovereign, free, strong Israel, are impaired by a perception of themselves as a 'symbol' of something else – one they may not really, truly want to give up. To what extent does this warped self-perception cause them to fall short of their aspiration to be at long last a people living in its country, a people that has fully internalized its sovereignty and might, and that is capable of conducting a life of minutiae, of concessions, of practical compromises with its neighbours, a normal people, a people like any other?

As one who was born in Israel and has lived there all his life, I read *The Book of Exodus* and wonder how it is that even today, and even by its inhabitants, Israel is still called 'the promised land'. That is, not 'the land that was promised' or 'a land of promise', but the land that is still promised, and that, even after the return to Zion, has not yet been fulfilled, and whose people have not yet fully realized their potential. It would seem that the disenfranchisement of the 'desert generation' still casts its spell within Israel, fifty years after the State's establishment.

This 'eternal promise' carries with it the hope of growth and a potential for almost limitless freedom of thought, and flexibility of perspective, regarding things that have become fossilized in their definitions. However, it is inevitably tainted by the 'curse of the eternal', a latent, deep-seated sense of inability to ever achieve fulfilment, and a concomitant inability to address fundamental questions of identity, of belonging to a place or of that place's permanent borders, vis à vis its neighbours.

This may be the principal anomaly of the Jewish people's identity, in Israel as in the diaspora. It may be the secret of that people's endurance and vitality, but it doubtless also makes it constantly vulnerable to tragedy in a world that is all definitions and borders. *The Book of Exodus*, the grand story of the childhood of the Jewish people, sketches the primordial face of that people as it is being formed and, as we now know, describes what will be its fate throughout thousands of years of history.

Translated from the Hebrew by Marsha Weinstein

THE BOOKS OF
RUTH AND ESTHER

. . . whither thou goest, I will go; and where thou lodgest, I will lodge: thy people shall be my people, and thy God my God: where thou diest, will I die, and there will I be buried: the Lord do so to me, and more also, if ought but death part thee and me.

(Ruth 1:16–17)
authorised King James version

Joanna Trollope

At first glance, it would seem natural, perhaps, to pair off the books of *Ruth* and *Esther* since they are the only two books in the Old Testament with women as their central characters, their heroines. At even a second glance, it might be tempting to see the two stories as applauding the courage and fortitude of women, a kind of remarkable early accolade to feminism. But a third glance reveals the reality. These two stories may *star* women, but only against the conventional biblical background of supreme male power; and if the women are celebrated, it is merely because of their ingenuity in exploiting that power. We are dealing it seems, with traditional, accepted romantic heroines – except that we are not. Love may come into both stories, lust even, but the loyalties the women in these stories show is most fiercely directed in the one case to another, older woman, and in the second case, to a race, to a people. If these women had merely been feisty examples of romantic femininity, they would not have taken such a hold as they have, on Jewish and Christian minds and hearts down the ages. It is their breadth and their differences that have given them their enduring power.

There are thirty-nine books in the King James Old Testament, from the first book of Moses, called *Genesis*, to *Malachi*. In most bibles, this works out at about a thousand pages. And for the first five hundred pages, we know roughly where we are; not just following the revelation of God's will and purpose for mankind, but also pursuing the extraordinary story of the rise and fall of the nation of Israel, from the call of Abraham to the point in the fourth century BC when the Jews eventually emerged as a distinct religious community settled in a tiny corner of the Persian Empire.

So far, so reasonably manageable. But after the book of *Nehemiah*, the pattern disappears. The continuity of the story fragments and diffuses into something-different and less accessible – into the (very broadly speaking) literature of the Hebrew people, into their prophecies and poetry, their wisdom and stories. Instead of reading the books of the Old Testament in sequence, we can read them individually. They aren't exactly random but they aren't, because of their separate natures, in narrative or development of thought order, either.

Some books, like those of the prophets, illuminate the history that has gone before as well as foretell the future. Some, like *Psalms*, from which hymns were used in Temple services, describe the nature and mood of Jewish worship after the exile of its people. And some – *Ruth* and *Esther* among them – are stories that, for various reasons, plainly became interwoven into Jewish life and faith, into its attitudes as well as its rituals.

Like all stories – at least stories that endure – the stories of *Ruth* and *Esther* are metaphors. At one level they are simple narratives – one romantic, one dramatic – but at another they are illustrations, or images, of human behaviour, human attitudes, human arbitrariness, human trial and error, human failing, human (with divine assistance) triumph. We may not be able to identify with the time and place, but in some way, however small, we can identify with some aspect of the human condition.

They are also in violent contrast to one another. *Ruth* is a story of simplicity and gentleness; *Esther* one of hatred and savagery. Both books were of course written pre-Christ, but only the book of *Ruth*, with its quiet virtues, its extolling of compassion and tolerance and honourable conduct, found favour with later Christian thinking. The name of God is invoked, called upon and blessed. *Esther*, on the other hand, never even mentions the name of God. Yet both have their place, and particular point, in this rich and amazing history of a remarkable people and their remarkable faith.

The book of *Ruth*, in the authorised version, now sits between *Judges* and the first book of *Samuel*. The Greek translators put it there because there is reference, in the first chapter, to the story having taken place 'in the days when the judges ruled'. It could have been written before the Exile (598 BC), it could have been written some time after, but its exact date is nothing like as important as the question raised by the mere fact of its inclusion in the first place. It's a charming story, certainly, with an equally charming, peaceful, pastoral setting, among the Bethlehem barley fields at harvest time (a welcome relief after all the blood and thunder of *Judges*). But it's also something more significant and more muscular because it suggests that not all Jews of the period believed in the remorselessly tough racial laws that followed their return from exile – the ban on mixed marriage, the segregation of their people from any other, the open hostility to foreigners.

Ruth, you see, is not a Jew. She is a Moabitess. She marries a Jew who has come to live in Moabite country and, after his death, makes her immortal speech to her Jewish mother-in-law, Naomi: 'Whither thou goest, I will go; and where thou lodgest, I will lodge; thy people shall be my people and thy God my God; where thou diest will I die and there I will be buried: The Lord do so to me and more also, if aught but death part thee and me' (1:16–17).

Naomi takes Ruth home to Bethlehem. To sustain them both, Naomi sends Ruth out to glean barley after the reapers – a privilege accorded to widows and the poor – in a kinsman's field. 'Whose', demands the immediately interested kinsman, 'damsel is this?' Soon, after some delicate moonlight manoeuvrings, she is his, Moabite or not. And soon again, she, as his wife, bears him a son. The son is named Obed. Obed was the father of Jesse who in turn was the father of the great king, David. And the great King David – honoured almost as much as Moses – was the grandson, not just of Obed, but naturally of his wife too, who was a Gentile. It is as if the storyteller of *Ruth* is saying, gently but firmly, either that even the blood of the great king was diluted or – more likely – that God's chosen people must make room for others who truly wish to join them, such as Moabites and other Gentiles.

This tiny hint of racial intolerance is the only link between the tender book of *Ruth* and the fierce book of *Esther*; both the Jewish canon and the Christian church have expressed huge reluctance in accepting *Esther*, and Martin Luther bluntly wished it had never been written.

Their repugnance isn't hard to understand. It's a horrible story, a tale of hatred and massacre and revenge, and at the heart of it stands the beautiful Jewish consort of the Persian king, Xerxes I, remorselessly defending her people. In fact – again unlike Ruth – it hardly seems a suitable Biblical story at all.

It is, instead, like something from the *Tales of the Arabian Nights*. Xerxes, ruling a seething court in an opulent palace – the architecture and furnishings are described in lavish detail – is displeased at some minor (and understandable) disobedience on his wife's part. So he commands the land to be scoured for beautiful virgins and, of all of them, Esther, the foster-child and cousin of a Jew named Mordecai, finds supreme favour and becomes queen, without disclosing her religion. But the king's vizier, Haman, is deeply offended that Mordecai 'bowed not, nor did him reverence', and orders him to be hanged, as a punishment, and also that all Jews around shall be slaughtered as a warning against further contemptuous behaviour.

Only the queen, revealing her race to the besotted king, saves the day. And that should be the happy ending. But it isn't. Haman is hanged on his own gallows and the Jews rise up and massacre everyone who had intended to massacre them. Then they have a party in celebration, two days of 'feasting and gladness'. And, down the ages, that party has continued in these 'days of Purim', a festival when the Jewish people celebrate relief from their enemies '. . . the month which was turned unto them from sorrow to joy, and from mourning into a good day . . . days of feasting and joy, and of sending portions one to another, and gifts to the poor' (9:22).

I have read both books over and over. I can see every reason – Jewish, Christian, humanitarian – for including the book of *Ruth*. But the book of *Esther* is another matter altogether. It incorporates everything that we all know fights strenuously against all the charities and harmonies we strive to achieve. But perhaps, on reflection, that is the point of it – it is a fascinating, glittering, gaudy, alarming reminder of how we can be, how we too often are. *Esther* is darkness in a beguiling mask of light.

THE FIRST AND SECOND BOOKS OF SAMUEL

And it came to pass in an eveningtide, that David arose from off his bed, and walked upon the roof of the king's house: and from the roof he saw a woman washing herself; and the woman was very beautiful to look upon. And David sent and enquired after the woman. And one said, 'Is not this Bath-sheba, the daughter of Eliam, the wife of Uriah the Hittite?'

(2:11:2–3)
authorised King James version

Meir Shalev

'Ruddy, and Withal of a Beautiful Countenance'
Of the three main characters in the *Book of Samuel*, only
two died. King Saul, a tragic, haunted figure, fell on his
sword at Mount Gilboa. Samuel the prophet, a benighted
religious zealot, is brought back from the dead once,
then sinks into oblivion forever. Aside from the two
books at hand, the books that bear his name, he left
nothing worth pining for. But David, king of Israel – as
we children of Israel are fond of singing – lives and
breathes.

Three thousand years after the death of David we
still wait for him to reappear, we read the psalms attributed to him, we even let him participate in political
discussions on the future of the Middle East. But like
another ruddy, charming, shrewd war hero – Odysseus
– David, too, has a deep, personal side, emotional and
spiritual. Today, three thousand years later, it is far more
interesting than his politics or liturgy.

Like many other Israelis, I met King David. I was
nine at the time, and my father took me to the valley

of Elah, between Shochoh and Azekah. Ceremoniously planting himself in the middle of the valley, he announced that here David had killed Goliath. He read me *I Samuel 17* and instructed me to pick up five pebbles; when I touched the smooth, rounded stones, I – a short, bespectacled boy – felt as though I were clasping Excalibur and fighting off all the evil Goliaths of the world.

The victory over Goliath is not David's first appearance on the Biblical stage. It was preceded by the prophet Samuel's visit to Bethlehem, where David was anointed king. In the finest tradition of fireside stories, Samuel saw before him a young man who 'was ruddy, and withal of a beautiful countenance, and goodly to look to' (1:16:12) and underestimated him. Samuel saw with his eyes, but the Lord, who saw into the heart, said: 'Arise, anoint him: for this is he' (1:16:12).

We next meet David when he comes to play for Saul. Here he is described with more impressive, magnanimous adjectives: '. . . [he] is cunning in playing, and a mighty valiant man, and a man of war, and prudent in matters, and a comely person, and the Lord is with him' (1:16:18). Without reservation, this is a description of the perfect man: he is wise, handsome, brave, an artist favoured by God. No wonder his star rises, no wonder he ascends higher and higher, and no one – friend or foe – can resist his charm, his might, or his wisdom.

All five of these characteristics – courage, wisdom, artistic ability, beauty, and good luck – will be manifested at one stage or another of David's life; this is obvious.

But often the Bible requires a closer reading, even a creative understanding of the text.

Although not apparent on first reading, I am referring to one of David's most basic characteristics, which may result from the combination of the five traits listed above. That is, his ability to kindle love in the heart of another. On the wings of this love David ascended to lofty heights.

'And Jonathan Loved Him as His Own Soul'

The reader of the chronicle of David will discover that the world 'love' is used extensively in the *Book of Samuel*: 'And David came to Saul, and stood before him: and he loved him greatly'; '. . . the soul of Jonathan was knit with the soul of David, and Jonathan loved him as his own soul'; 'And Michal Saul's daughter loved David'; '. . . for Hiram was ever a lover of David'; 'But all Israel and Judah loved David . . .'

Not one Biblical figure was the object of as much love as David. But closer inspection reveals an additional phenomenon: every time the verb 'love' is connected to David's name, the love is directed at him, but does not emanate from him to another. Saul, Michal, Jonathan, Hiram king of Tyre, the people of Judah and Israel – all of them loved David, but who did David love? At the linguistic level, David did not love even one person – the verb 'love' is never used to describe *his* relation to anyone.

To return to the lovers of David, King Saul loved him and wanted his life at one and the same time. His children Jonathan and Michal, loved David fully and entirely, with out reservation or score-keeping. In particular, this is ascribed to Jonathan. I do not see the relations between them as homosexual but they do seem to be 'soulmates'. One way or the other, Jonathan, like his sister Michal, loved David 'as his own soul' and, like her, betrayed the interests of both Saul's lineage and himself because of that love.

In his famous lamentation over the death of Saul and Jonathan, David says: 'I am distressed for thee, my brother Jonathan: very pleasant hast thou been unto me: thy love to me was wonderful, passing the love of women' (2:1:26). It is interesting that he says 'thy love to me' rather than 'my love to thee' or 'our love'.

David's lamentation over Saul and Jonathan is a political and literary masterpiece. It expresses not only his grief, but also his perception of leadership. In effect, it is so polished and calculating that the reader is liable to think that David is either hiding his emotions or perhaps has none. But was David lacking in emotion? Absolutely not.

His terrible pain over the death of his son Absalom, with his horrifying, unpolished wail that rends the heart of the reader even today: '. . . would God I had died for thee, O Absalom, my son, my son!' (2:18:33) – these words testify to immense depths of soul and emotion. But strangely enough, the word 'love' is absent even from David's relation to Absalom, and to his children in general. This is odd, because the text provides a picture of a devoted father, concerned and coddling, sometimes in excess, as with Amnon, Absalom and Adonijah, his unsavoury and debased sons, whom he refused to scold. The verb 'love' is absent from his relation to them, whereas it is prevalent in the descriptions of other Biblical fathers' relations with their children.

'Went . . . Along Weeping'

In the description of David's relationship to women, the writer refrains from using the specific word 'love', and here, too, this is in contrast to other relationships between men and women in the Bible: Isaac loved Rebekah, Jacob toiled for Rachel for seven years, 'and they seemed unto him but a few days, for the love he had to her' (*Gen.* 29:20). Of Samson it is said: 'he loved a woman in the valley of Sorek, and her name was Delilah' (*Jud.* 16:4). Amnon said of himself: 'I love Tamar, my brother Absalom's sister' (*Sam.* 2:13:4). Elkanah preferred Hannah to Peninnah, 'for he loved Hannah' (*Sam.* 1:1:5). Of Ahasuerus it is said: 'And the king loved Esther above all the women' (*Esther* 2:17), and King Solomon, emotional profligate that he was, 'loved many strange women' (*Kings* 1:11:1).

David, unlike all of them, did not love his women but rather made use of them: in Abigail he found an ally, and one who gave him a private lesson in eliminating opponents. Michal was his ticket into the royal family. And Abishag and Bath-sheba served to fulfil much more basic needs. He, of all people, though famed in this regard, did not love a single woman.

This is never more noticeable than in regard to

Michal, Saul's daughter. She is the first woman who loves him, and she is the tragic figure, the one who suffers most from lacking his love. David enters her father's palace as a victorious and handsome hero, he rises to greatness in his court and his army, he amazes Michal when he clasps a sword or plucks a harp, he brings her father two hundred Philistine foreskins to win her. Both Michal and Jonathan succumb to his charm. Both of them sacrifice their interests and those of their family for him. Both shield him, spy for him, save him from their father's hand – and neither wins reciprocal attention from him.

Like Jonathan, Michal, too, betrays her father for her beloved, and the climax is on the same night when she warns him: 'If thou save not thy life tonight, tomorrow thou shalt be slain' (*Sam.* 1:19:11). She lets David out through a window so that he can flee the palace. The next time the two meet, David will be married to other women, and a brief, lone, sad verse will tell what befell Michal after the escape of her husband: 'But Saul had given Michal his daughter, David's wife, to Phalti the son of Laish, which was of Gallim' (*Sam.* 1:25:49).

After the death of Saul, David reigned in Hebron and demanded his wife back. He said then to Abner, Saul's captain of the army: 'Thou shalt not see my face, except thou first bring Michal Saul's daughter, when thou comest to see my face' (*Sam.* 2:3:13). Thus Michal was taken from her second husband, who was devoted to her heart and soul. This is described in a heart-rending verse:

'And her husband went with her along weeping behind her to Bahurim. Then said Abner unto him, Go, return. And he returned' (*Sam.* 2:3:16).

Did Michal return to a loving embrace? No. David did not ask for Michal's return out of love and longing. He wanted her back as one who retrieves property and honour, primarily because of his political interests. Michal was the daughter of the previous king and David, who at this time was reigning only over the tribes of the south, wanted to expand his rule over all Israel.

And not only that. Six additional women have already come to roost in David's harem, and they have six little princes – it is easy to imagine Michal's feelings about the new situation. This poor woman, who sacrificed for David her loyalty to her father and the love of her second husband, wanders now as a shadow among the walls of the king's palace in Hebron, and the rift between the couple is not long in coming. It happens during the celebration of the bringing of the Lord's ark up to Jerusalem: 'And as the ark of the Lord came into the city of David, Michal Saul's daughter looked through a window, and saw king David leaping and dancing before the Lord; and she despised him in her heart . . . And Michal the daughter of Saul came out to meet David, and said, "How glorious was the king of Israel today, who uncovered himself today in the eyes of the handmaids of his servants, as one of the vain fellows shamelessly uncovereth himself!"' (*Sam.* 2:6:16–20).

Michal invests all of her anger and frustration in this bitter, derisive statement, but David's response is many times more cruel and harsh, and she discovers another aspect of his personality: 'It was before the Lord, which chose me before thy father, and before all his house, to appoint me ruler over the people of the Lord, over Israel: therefore will I play before the Lord' he says, and adds in scorn, 'and of the maidservants which thou hast spoken of, of them shall I be had in honour' (*Sam.* 2:6:21–22).

And the Bible, in its reserved way, concludes this bitter argument with a laconic, pithy, yet succinct statement that evokes sadness and thought: 'Therefore Michal the daughter of Saul had no child unto the day of her death' (*Sam.* 2:6:23).

'A Woman of Good Understanding, and of a Beautiful Countenance'

The lack of love appears again in the relation of David to his other women. Of Ahinoam, Eglah, Maacah, Haggith and all the rest, we know nothing. But of his second wife, Abigail, the wife of Nabal the Carmelite, an entire, breathtaking chapter is devoted, *I Samuel 25*.

In many senses, Abigail is David's soul sister. David is the only man in the Bible described as 'prudent in matters, and a comely person' (*Sam.* 1:16:18); Abigail is the only woman in the Bible ascribed these two traits – with a similar phrase: 'Of good understanding, and of a beautiful countenance' (*Sam.* 1:25:3). The reader of *I Samuel 25* can sense how charming and wise this woman is, quite like David himself, and at the same time – how wily and dangerous.

David meets Abigail when he comes up from the desert in order to kill Nabal, her husband. She comes out to meet him, softening his wrath with gifts, and gives him a lesson in politics that will be implemented many times in the future: a leader must not kill his opponents with his own hand. He must make sure that the eradication is accomplished by others.

'As the Lord liveth, and as thy soul liveth' she says to him, 'seeing the Lord hath withholden thee from coming to shed blood, and from avenging thyself with thine own hand' adding, 'now let thine enemies, and they that seek evil to my lord, be as Nabal' (*Sam.* 1:25:26). And indeed, within several days Nabal has died under mysterious circumstances, and David has hastily married the attractive widow.

Also from this tale, which contains elements of blood, sex, politics, and violence, the basis of love is lacking – and not by accident. From the beginning the relations between the two were based on a deal. Abigail, so it seems, did away with her husband – a coarse, violent, and stupid man – and won a husband many times more excellent. David has eliminated a very powerful enemy, and repaid her for her assistance. Abigail does not again appear on centre stage, but her spirit and ideas continue to hover over the chapters of the *Book of Samuel*. From that day forward, David never kills an opponent or foe with his own hand. This is especially notable when Joab son of Zeruiah kills Abner, a relative of Saul and captain of his army, who was the primary potential threat to David's early reign.

In a similar fashion David also rids himself of Saul's sons, whom he hands over to the Gibeonites who had a long association with Saul's tribe, the sons of Benjamin; and David, in his way, knew how to take advantage of this. David's permanent henchman was always Joab son of Zeruiah. It was he who killed Abner, he who killed the captain of the mutinous army of Absalom, as well as Absalom himself. It was he who arranged the elimination of the king's most famous victim – Uriah the Hittite, the unfortunate husband of Bath-sheba. But in this case three things indicate change in fortune: the one – Joab acts on a written order of David, who for once is imprudent. The second – God responds severely. And the third – alongside the story of adultery and murder, the first cracks in David's apparent armour of perfection and good fortune become apparent.

'From the Roof He Saw a Woman Washing Herself'
The story of David, Uriah, and Bath-sheba takes place against the background of David's war against the Ammonites. This is thought-provoking because, in this war, as in the murder of Uriah, David acts for the first time with less logic and wisdom.

In contrast to his previous wars, which were primarily wars over existence and independence, here David goes to war for the dubious reason of honour. The king of Ammon has humiliated an Israeli diplomatic emissary, and David sees in this a just and worthwhile *causus belli*. Similarly, the murder of Uriah is the first time in which David eliminates a man who is not his political rival, but rather a good and loyal soldier whose only crime is being the husband of a woman the king desires. The same intoxicating and additive charm with which he has been blessed, of arousing love in the heart of another, proves that such charm might pave the way for him who possesses it, but destroys his soul and morality over the years.

This is, then, the first time in which hasty rather than rational elements are involved in David's actions. Until this incident, the king fully justified the description, 'prudent in matters'. Henceforth begins his great decline: from heights of glory and success to mistakes and failures whose culmination is an ignominious old age.

And so, Joab readies the army of Israel for a siege of Rabbah in Ammon, and David sits in Jerusalem. 'And it came to pass in an evening-tide, that David arose from off his bed, and walked upon the roof of the king's house; and from the roof he saw a woman washing herself; and the woman was very beautiful to look upon. And David sent and enquired after the woman . . . And David sent messengers, and took her; and she came in unto him, and he lay with her; for she was purified from her uncleanness: and she returned unto her house. And the woman conceived, and sent and told David, and said, "I am with child." And David sent to Joab, saying, "Send me Uriah the Hittite"' (*Sam.* 2:11:2–6).

David's intention was that Uriah sleep with his wife, and the pregnancy be attributed to him. This incident, the most infamous and dramatic of all of the king's love affairs, again reveals his inability to love. After he has quenched his desire for Bath-sheba, he no longer has any interest in her. Now he plans to extricate himself from the situation in which he finds himself. But Uriah refuses to go up to his house. So David presents in his hand a signed letter. In the letter, which was intended for Joab, captain of the army, the order is given to place Uriah 'in the forefront of the hottest battle . . . that he may be smitten, and die' (*Sam.* 2:11:15). The Bible, typically, does not say whether Uriah knew he was carrying his own death warrant, but it is very detailed in everything pertaining to David's punishment: the death of Bath-sheba's son, and the mutiny of Absalom. From here on, as I noted before, he declines ever further.

David suffers a miserable old age, of mental flaccidity and physical feebleness; there is no longer even a hint of the five good traits that were attributed to him in his youth. Not courage, not wisdom, not beauty, not musicianship, and not the supportive hand of God.

'But the King Knew Her Not'

Of what was David thinking during that chill Jerusalem winter, as he lay in the warm embrace of Abishag the Shunammite? The text, as usual, does not say. We get to read only the journalistic chronicle, which in this case is fairly sensationalist: 'King David was old . . . and they covered him with clothes, but he gat no heat. His servants said unto him, "Let there be sought for my lord the king a young virgin . . . and let her lie in thy bosom, that my lord the king may get heat." So they sought for a fair damsel . . . and found Abishag, a Shunammite, and brought her to the king. And the damsel was very fair, and cherished the king, and ministered to him: but the king knew her not' (*Kings* 1:1:1–5).

The familiar and always relevant question – to what extent can one delve into the private life of a leader – receives here a surprising answer: it is permissible to plumb depths that even modern newspapers agonize over descending to. But the motivation is different. The Biblical author is not reporting on the king's love life because of considerations of circulation and sales, but because this information concerns the functioning of David as a leader. King David is a man in whose life sex and politics have already mingled. He is a man whose ability to arouse love has already degraded his soul. He is a man who has already committed adultery and murdered because of his desire. If now he is in bed with the loveliest maiden in Israel, and does not sleep with her, it is a sign he is in very bad shape.

The Jewish joke tells that when Abishag returned to Shunam, the village from which she was taken to the palace, her friends asked her how it was. Abishag said: 'Now I understand the difference between, "it was an honour" and "it was a pleasure".' But our sages, in contrast, did not find anything humorous in the king's impotence, but adopted the purifying and apologetic approach that is characteristic of many of their other interpretations. It is said that David did not sleep with Abishag because she was forbidden to him, and when the young woman expressed her disappointment and puzzlement, the old king slept with Bath-sheba in front of her, until Bath-sheba 'wiped herself with thirteen cloths'. It is also said there that 'even in David's hour of infirmity, he observed the eighteen seasons' (that is, he was sure to perform his conjugal duties with all eighteen of his wives).

But the plain meaning, it seems, was different. Near the description of David's physical weakness are described the mental details and their political consequences: Adonijah son of Haggith and Solomon son of Bath-sheba, David's sons, are fighting over the inheritance. The court is divided and Adonijah crowns himself king while his father is yet alive. In other words, not only does David 'not know' Abishag, but he is also unaware of all that is happening around him.

In *I Kings*, we learn that Nathan the prophet and Bath-sheba take advantage of the king's weakness and bring about the coronation of Solomon, Bath-sheba's son. This is a most stunning matter, since Nathan the prophet is the man who told David the parable in which Bath-sheba was the poor man's ewe lamb, and it was he who shouted the harsh reprove of David: 'Thou art the man.' That is the power of corruption. It is no wonder that the *Book of Chronicles*, which was written many years after the events described in it transpired, invests great effort in eradicating David's love life from history.

The compiler of *Chronicles* wanted to clear David, to ignore his emotional world, to cleanse him of his own personality and to leave in our hands only his religious-political shell. But the guardian-angel of history and the editors of the Bible wanted otherwise. Despite the censorship of *Chronicles* and despite the generations of sanctimonious and apologetic religious commentary that followed in its footsteps, the *Book of Samuel* – informative, revelatory, and courageous – has not been erased from our chronicles or our consciousness.

And see what a wonder: in spite of everything written there, we still love David, we still contemplate him, we still long for him and wonder about the riddles and contradictions of his personality. Three thousand years after his death, David, king of Israel, lives and breathes. Three thousand years after his death, David still arouses love.

Translated from the Hebrew by Marsha Weinstein

THE BOOK OF JOB

When I lie down, I say, 'When shall I arise, and the night be gone?' and I am full of tossings to and fro unto the dawning of the day. My flesh is clothed with worms and clods of dust; my skin is broken, and become loathsome. My days are swifter than a weaver's shuttle, and are spent without hope. O remember that my life is wind: mine eye shall no more see good.

(7:4–7)

authorised King James version

Louis De Bernières

The Impatience of Job

One would naturally assume that a book of the Old
Testament must have been written by an Israelite, and
indeed the earliest rabbinical tradition asserts that Moses
was the author of *The Book of Job*. In the past Christians
readily accepted this notion, which is why, for example,
one finds Isaak Walton referring to it whilst discoursing
on the alleged patience of the angler. In fact there are
literary parallels to the story in Persian, Sumerian,
Akkadian and Babylonian, and in the Biblical version
there appear to be several allusions to Ugaritic myth.
Some of the unique or rare words in the text are possibly
Edomite. There exists an apocryphal 'Testament of Job',
and there is even an amusing tale about Job and his
wife in the Islamic tradition. It would seem, then, that
the story is a variant on an ancient folktale, that may
indeed be as old as the patriarchs, but could have been
composed by anyone from any of the interlocking
mosaic of cultures that existed in the region between
2000 and 700 BCE. God, in the story, is not omniscient
(He asks Satan what he has been up to), there is no

clear belief in the afterlife, and Satan is still one of God's courtiers. This means that if the tale is Jewish, it would have to date from before the exile in Babylon.

There may have been at least three authors of the book, since Elihu's intervention, and the long and wonderful poem about the inaccessibility of wisdom are almost certainly interpolations, but whoever the main author was, he was a great poet. The original is very terse, but since Hebrew requires half the number of words needed in English, no English translation could hope to do justice to it. Furthermore, no-one knows exactly how Hebrew poetry was stressed or scanned, and so for us the quality of the verse will depend upon the force, aptness and beauty of expression; the reader of *Job* will be struck mostly by the skill of the author in repeating the same thoughts in new ways that are continually refreshing and illuminating. It has to be said that one gains very little new information from each speech, and anyone looking for snappy action and exciting new events would certainly be better off hiring a video, the point being that this is really a long and beautiful poem about divine justice, rendered in the forms of narrative, dialogue, hymn, lament, proverb, and oracle. The compilers of the King James version in this volume did not have the benefit of modern scholarship, and so their rendition is often confused and inaccurate, but they have nonetheless managed to contribute their sonorously fair share of poetry to the English language. Chapter 14 stands independently as a moving lament for the human condition: 'Man that is born of a woman is of few days, and full of trouble. He cometh forth like a flower, and is cut down . . .'.

Elsewhere we find the proverbs: 'The price of wisdom is above rubies' and 'The fear of the Lord, that is wisdom', and the memorable words adapted by Handel for his *Messiah*: 'I know that my redeemer liveth, and that he shall stand at the latter day upon the earth; and though after my skin worms destroy this body, yet in my flesh shall I see God.' It may be unfortunate that this is a hopeless mistranslation of the original verses, which are not about redemption and resurrection at all, but it is still great writing.

The book is in fact very largely about faith, however, and particularly about the issue of theodicy – whether or not one can have faith in the goodness and worthiness of an omnipotent creator who is apparently responsible for creating evil, and tolerating the suffering of the innocent. Whereas Job's attitude is profoundly felt and deeply personal, his four comforters take a more detached and philosophical line, but it is important to remember that God and Satan are the only two who really know what is going on.

Satan is portrayed as an affable but astute fellow who is on terms of familiarity with God; when the latter asks him where he has been, Satan casually replies 'From going to and fro in the earth, and from walking up and down in it.' When God invites Satan to admire Job's uprightness, Satan very acutely points out that God has made sure that Job has had an easy ride of it, 'but put forth thine hand now, and touch all he hath, and he will curse thee to thy face.' God accepts the challenge, with the proviso that Job himself must not be physically harmed, whereupon Satan destroys Job's oxen, sheep, camels, servants and children. Job's equanimity survives these trials, and Satan points out to God that an attack on Job's person is more likely to do the trick. God gives his permission, and Job is struck down by a revolting combination of foul diseases. At this point Job does indeed turn against God, and Satan is heard of no more, having won his wager. The quantity of shekels involved in this bet is not recorded, but no doubt Satan spends them whilst going once more to and fro in the earth, and walking up and down in it, his conscience eased by the thought that he has merely been obeying orders from a superior.

Job's comforters are possibly the most irritating characters in all of literature, and Job more than once tells them that they are completely intolerable. Elihu is the last, and is the most annoying of all of them, since he announces that all the others have been beside the point, whilst he, although the youngest, has the conclusive arguments. He then says nothing interesting or original, in the manner of sententious bores the world over. He says that God rescues people repeatedly, that it is up to God to choose what happens, that Job must have done something wrong, because God is righteous, that God is beyond our capacity to comprehend, and that God does not do evil.

To be fair to young Elihu, he was probably not in the original story, but the other self-righteous prigs certainly were. Each has three speeches, and Job replies to them in turn. Eliphaz says that God only punishes the wicked, that God saves and protects, that we cannot know God's plans, that Man is naturally vile and unclean in God's eyes, that God punishes sinners in their own lifetime, and that Job must therefore be a rebel and a sinner. His concluding comment is that none of us make any difference to God one way or the other.

Bildad asserts that God does not pervert justice, that we are ignorant of the real state of things, that God will not reject the upright, that we are punished for forgetting God, and that Job must therefore be evil and Godless. His final thought is that we are nothing, before God's omnipotence.

Zophar says that God knows what the reality is, and that therefore Job must be guilty of something. The mirth of the wicked is brief, he says, and God brings them down.

That phrase about the 'patience of Job' could not be further from the mark. Job is, for all but three of the forty-two chapters, exasperated by his comforters, reduced to abject misery by his afflictions, and disillusioned and furious with God. 'The defiance of Job' would have been a far more apposite figure of speech to have passed into the language. His comforters have all the usual inane, pious, platitudinous, facile morsels of cod-wisdom at their fingertips, but it is Job who has all the passion, and all the grasp of the real paradoxes implicit in the idea of theodicy. Job tells his comforters that his argument is with God, and not with them, and that, if they are just trying to curry favour with God, then the latter will surely see through them. He says that in their position he would talk the same rot. He even accuses them of behaving like God, and persecuting him unjustly. Readers, of course, are in the privileged position of knowing that all the arguments of the comforters are either false or completely beside the point, since God's assault on Job is nothing whatsoever to do with just punishment, it is to do with an interesting bet between Himself and one of His friends.

There is an amusing vignette, wherein Job's wife advises him to curse God and die, whereupon he says, 'Thou speakest as one of the foolish women speaketh.' Before long, however, he is indeed cursing God and wishing for death, and no doubt Mrs Job (whose name was said to be 'Sitis') derives some quiet satisfaction from this. Chrysostom proposed that Mrs Job might have been Job's 'greatest scourge of all', but this would seem to reflect the former's peculiar preoccupations rather than anything one can find in the story. Job is very like the character of Philoctetes in the play of Sophocles, abandoned on an island whilst his foot rots, and his sentiments are very much those of Jesus on the cross, who cries out, 'My God, My God, why has thou forsaken me?' There is also a remarkable but probably coincidental resemblance between Job's declarations of innocence and the speech of the dead before Osiris in the Hall of Righteousness, as inscribed in the Egyptian 'Chapters of Coming Forth by Day' (*The Book of the Dead*).

Job reproaches God, saying, 'They are tricked that

trusted.' He avows ignorance of any wrongdoing on his part, and he demands how is one supposed to have a sensible argument with God when the latter is omnipotent, invisible, unaccountable, and unjust? It is futile asserting one's right when God is both adversary, judge, and executioner, and why does God take vicious action against that which he has created? God is an oppressor, He is incapable of human sympathy; behind a smiling face He hides an evil heart. Job asks why we bother to serve God; the wicked prosper, He does nothing to help the desperate ('God thinks nothing amiss'). Job's despair is so well depicted that we get a distinct and lasting impression of his character, the most notable feature of which is his absolute refusal to disengage his intelligence, be a hypocrite, or give up his case. He is not going to be cowed even by fear of God or by the untrue accusations of his friends. This makes Job a very modern figure (in literature if not in real life), one who asserts his individuality and integrity in the face of all conventional wisdom or arbitrary power. He is, in other words, a classic existentialist hero.

At the end of the tale there is a theophany, God speaks out of the whirlwind, and demonstrates, to His credit, that he finds the comforters as tiresome and obnoxious as Job does. He reproves them: 'My wrath is kindled against thee . . . for ye have not spoken of me the thing that is right, as my servant Job hath.' It is rather startling to find God thus admitting somewhat disarmingly to all of Job's indictments, but it is true even so that He comes out of this story as the most morally tarnished. The comforters may emerge from it looking stupid (which they are), but God does so looking like an unpleasantly sarcastic megalomaniac. Instead of answering Job's charges of injustice and heartlessness, God devotes 129 verses to a magnificently irrelevant and bombastic speech about His own accomplishments and abilities; it is as if He knows perfectly well that He has abused His power, but does not wish to address the issue. God boasts about two of his favourite and most impressive creations, Behemoth and Leviathan, but at no point does He clear up the mystery that we call 'The Problem of Evil'. We are left with Job holding the field philosophically, with no-one to deny that God finds nothing amiss, and would not care even if He did.

It is true that God restores Job to good health and good fortune, but He absentmindedly does not restore to life the servants or the children killed off in chapter 1; they get no justice. Not only do we have a God, therefore, who is a frivolous trickster, but one who even botches up the reparations when He decides to make them. There are many episodes in the Bible that show God in a very bad light, such as when he commands Abraham to sacrifice his son Isaac, or when He commands Saul to destroy the Amalekites ('. . . Utterly destroy all that they have, and spare them not; but slay both man and woman, infant and suckling, ox and sheep, camel and ass'), and one cannot but conclude from them either that God is a mad, bloodthirsty, and capricious despot, or that all this time we have been inadvertently worshipping the Devil.

In the modern age in the West there has been a great falling off of religious faith, because although Jesus Christ and a deluge of sophistical theology did much to improve God's image for a few centuries, Job is still winning the argument, and *The Book of Job* is still insidiously subversive. If God is omnipotent, we cannot blame anything on the Devil, and if God is no help, we have to do His work for Him. He has still failed to appear in court, and we construe His absence either as non-existence, hubris, apathy, or an admission of guilt. We miss Him, we would dearly like to see Him going to and fro in the earth and walking up and down in it, but we admire tyranny no longer, and we desire justice more than we are awed by vainglorious asseverations of magnificence.

Charles Frazier

Have pity upon me, have pity upon me,
O ye my friends;
for the hand of God hath touched me. (19:21)

As a piece of writing, the great *Book of Job* strikes me as
somewhat similar to watching people thresh grain with
a herd of horses: it is all kinds of things trying to go in
many different directions at once. Among these are a
desperate plea for ultimate justice, an examination of
how the individual relates to force and authority, an
eloquent and affecting cry of despair, a great and healing
song of the power of Creation, and a turgid philosophical drama patched together with a framing device
that apparently includes leftover bits of a considerably
more ancient Mesopotamian happy-ever-after folktale.
Most strikingly, it tells what a fearful and sorrowful thing
it is to fall into the hands of a torn and discordant God.

Mark Twain, in his late bitter years, wrote frequently
about the Bible. He called the Old Testament's account
of God's doings 'perhaps the most damnatory biography

that exists in print anywhere.' Twain catalogs the offenses: 'He was an unfair God; he was a God of unsound judgment; he was a God of failures and miscalculations; he was given to odd ideas and fantastic devices.'

To be sure, the *Book of Job* is filled with such behavior. The plot, frail as it is, hinges on a troubling bet between God and Satan – depicted not as real enemies but as affable adversaries. Satan is rather less the Prince of Darkness here than a folkloric trickster figure, slyly but pointedly challenging power and authority. The wager, a test of Job's faith, requires the murder of all Job's ten children and countless servants, the theft and arson of all his vast holdings. This is a measure of destructiveness that even God – at the very least an accessory to these crimes – later calls 'without cause.'

God initiates the action, dangling Job in Satan's face, saying, 'Hast thou considered my servant Job.' He calls Job 'perfect,' holds him out as an example of 'an upright man, one that feareth God.' Satan very reasonably takes the implied challenge, arguing that the prosperous Job has little reason for fear, since he has always been protected by God: 'But put forth thine hand now, and touch all that he hath, and he will curse thee to thy face,' Satan says.

God – apparently forgetting his own omniscience in the heat of the moment – falls for this trap and gives Satan almost free rein to test his theory, restraining him in but one regard: 'Only upon himself [Job] put not forth thine hand.' So Satan pours down tornadic winds, marauding Sabeans and Chaldeans, and the fire of God from Heaven. Job responds much as God expects: he tears his clothes, shaves his head, and falls on the ground to pray, saying, among other things:

the Lord gave, and the Lord hath taken away; blessed be the name of the Lord. (1:21)

Kierkegaard, in his *Discourse on Job*, makes much of that pair of lines, and he appears to have lost interest at this point, choosing to see Job as a story of unquestioning faith in the face of adversity. Satan, on the other hand, is not yet ready to call the game. He suggests that one's property is one thing, 'But put forth thine hand now, and touch his bone and his flesh, and he will curse thee to thy face.' With God's blessing Satan then smites Job with boils from crown to sole, leaving him sitting in an ash heap scraping his sores with a potsherd. Job's wife's best advice at this most recent downturn in fortune is that he should 'curse God, and die.' Job, though, insists on some accounting. What did he do to call down such weight of calamity? Not a thing that he can figure. As stand-in for mankind under constant attack – both physical and spiritual – until woe overbrims our frail vessels, Job demands an explanation for his fate, some justice, an assurance of cosmic fairness. Lacking that, he demands at the very least a chance to yowl his fear and despair at a God that by all the evidence of his actions holds man in contempt and the strictures of justice that bind civilized cultures in weak regard.

For the arrows of the Almighty are within me,
the poison whereof drinketh up my spirit:
the terrors of God do set themselves
in array against me. (6:4)

At Enfield, Connecticut, in 1741, Jonathan Edwards delivered the most famous of American sermons, 'Sinners in the Hands of an Angry God.' Edwards's violent, unknowable God, like the one in the *Book of Job*, expresses much of His power through boundless and easily provoked rage. This is the way Edwards recommends we consider such a Deity:

How awful are those words, *Isaiah* 63:3, which are the words of the great God: 'I will tread them in mine anger, and trample them in my fury; and their blood shall be sprinkled upon my garments, and I will stain all my raiment.' It is perhaps impossible to conceive of words that carry in them greater manifestations of these three things, viz., contempt, and hatred, and fierceness of indignation. If you cry to God to pity you, He will be so far from pitying you in your doleful case, or showing you the least regard or favor, that instead of that He will only tread you under foot; and though He will know that you cannot bear the weight of omnipotence treading upon you, He will not regard that, but He will crush you under His feet without mercy; He will crush out your blood and make it fly, and it shall be sprinkled on His garments, so as to stain all His raiment. He will not only hate you, but He will have you in the utmost contempt; no place shall be thought fit for you but under his feet, to be trodden down as mire in the streets.

In the city and suburban churches of the current version of America, God is really not much that way at all anymore. On the rare occasions I attend such churches, I am struck with the overriding conviction of pastor and congregation that to the extent God is angry at anyone, it is certainly not with people remotely like you and me. God's dark moods have lifted. He is love, and our flaws are really quite understandable and totally forgivable. So minor indeed that, honestly, personal change – at least of any radical or inconvenient kind – is not in order, not the least bit called for.

It is only when I am driving in the rural bits of the country – the regions – that I find any remnant of the old mad God of Edwards and Job, and that confined to the extremes of the AM band where vestigial spittle-spewing preachers rant the breathless and urgent message that God might very well despise us all, and with good cause. It is easy to ridicule such men, to find them humorous or, worse, quaint. But it may be a dangerous proposition to dismiss their views out of hand. Look about you; go to and fro in the world, walk up and down in it like Satan in the *Book of Job*; make a fair report and then try to present a convincing argument against them.

When I say, My bed shall comfort me,
my couch shall ease my complaint;
Then thou scarest me with dreams,
and terrifiest me through visions;
So that my soul chooseth strangling,
and death rather than my life. (7:13–15)

In my line of work it is often incumbent upon me to read the great spiritual texts of our many people. I am fondest of the Buddhist writings, and also those of various shamans and visionaries and anchorites and desert fathers. All useful in their own ways. I have not, however, read the *Book of Job* since I was perhaps twelve, when I was, for a brief time, Methodist. Each month I took from a stand in the church foyer a copy of *The Upper Room*, a booklet of suggested daily Bible readings with suggested interpretations. The cover of it was always an artistic rendering of a biblical event, done in rich saturated colors like Caravaggio or Dell Comics. My Bible had a black leather zippered cover with my name stamped in gold letters, and for a bookmark I used a cross twisted from a palm frond. It was the height of the Cold War, and I read the Bible with a certain superstitious consistency every night before turning out the light and tuning in to WLAC's fifty thousand clear watts through the earphone of a gray plastic Zenith transistor radio.

I had trouble sleeping. We lived in a cup of Appalachian valley that lay as the crow flies only a short way from Oak Ridge, a place all my teachers assured me was a first target for Soviet nuclear attack. Some of my friends had bomb shelters buried underneath their houses. You reached them through twisting tunnels, as if visiting the tombs of pharaohs. Inside were canned goods, jugs of water, reading matter. All the things you'd need when you got to the other side. We did not have a shelter.

Sometimes as I lay awake listening to Stax and Chess R&B – John R and Daddy Gene emphatically naming the tunes and reading mail-order offers for Ernie's Record Mart and a thousand baby chicks – I was convinced that this night was the night it all would fall. The siren down at the town fire station would sound, and then before I even had time to get out of bed, the whole broad sky out the window would flash up bright as the flame at the tip of a welder's torch toward which one dare not look.

My bedroom window opened out onto our neighbor's house. It was a log cabin with pale plaster chinking between the dark logs. It sat under a big black walnut tree, and the man that lived alone in it was a sweet old drunk who woke every morning at four no matter what shape he was in or what hour the sun rose. If we locked our keys in our house he would come over with a hammer and a screwdriver and make a single delicate tap and the door would spring open. When, long before dawn, he turned on his lights, it seemed to me that the night watch had changed and I could go to sleep. Old Doug was awake behind his yellow windows, and not much bad could happen.

Therefore I will not refrain my mouth;
I will speak in the anguish of my spirit;
I will complain in the bitterness of my soul. (7:11)

So there sits Job, on the wrong side of God, scraping his boils with a sherd, wondering what he did wrong. And saddled with such a wife. Then three old friends – Bildad the Shuhite, Zophar the Naamathite, and Eliphaz the Temanite – show up to sit with him. They do not, however, commiserate with him; they argue at great length that despite the severity and apparent injustice of his afflictions, he must have had it coming. They're not sure why, but there has to be a reason. Undeserved suffering cannot be. William Blake, in plate X of his *Illustrations of the Book of Job*, shows these men kneeling, their staring faces close together in expressions of self-righteous condemnation, all bearing a great family resemblance to demons. They all point at weeping Job with the fingers of their hands held in creepy, incantatory gestures.

In Blake's reading of *Job*, despair seems to come – if not wholly, at least significantly – from isolation, a devastating inturning that finds visual expression in several ways. One is a lonely set-apartness in the relation of Job to other human figures in the plates; they turn from him, space themselves away from him, hide their faces from him. They draw away; he pulls into himself. Or the other way around. When they do look at him, they mock and scorn and condemn. Most affectingly, Job's isolation is evident in the odd and troubling resemblances of God, Satan, and Job – as if Blake were suggesting that Job has fallen so far in upon himself that he has created a God and a Devil in his own image.

It is at this point in the narrative that Job – utterly ruined, all his vast holdings and the people he presumably loved yanked from him – begins speaking powerful poems cursing his personal existence. 'Why me, Lord' is a good question, and one we've all cast out at one time or another to an unresponsive universe. But Job fashions the simple query into some of the greatest and most terse expressions of despair and soul weariness we have. Job's laments are as blunt and stripped in their pain as Delta blues. I'd like to think there's influence there, to imagine Charlie Patton sitting down with a huge limp Bible flapped open on his lap to chapter 3 of *Job* and then switching to his guitar and making up 'When Your Way Gets Dark' or 'Down the Dirt Road.' I'll just point out, rather at random, some personal high points of Job's blues: 'My face is foul with weeping, and on my eyelids is the shadow of death' (16:16); 'My days are swifter than a weaver's shuttle, and are spent without hope' (7:6); 'My soul is weary of my life' (10:1); 'My days are past, my purposes are broken off, even the thoughts of my heart' (17:11); 'For now shall I sleep in the dust; and thou shalt seek me in the morning, but I shall not be' (7:21).

It is some reimbursement, at least, with everything you have taken from you, everything you desire denied you, everything you fear come to pass, to have language of such force and simplicity at your command as both weapon and balm.

Hast thou perceived the breadth of the earth?
Declare if thou knowest it all. (38:18)

One of the central questions the *Book of Job* asks is:
How might man and Deity communicate in order to
settle the issues Job raises? Job offers logic as a path.
'Surely I would speak to the Almighty, and I would desire
to reason with God,' he says (13:3). It is tempting to
view God's entrance in a whirlwind and his subsequent
boastful listing of his creative accomplishments, his
power and authority as dodging the question, a victory
of force over reason, of fear over all else. The Almighty
supports such a reading when He asks, 'Hast thou an
arm like God? Or canst thou thunder with a voice like
him?' (40:9).

But his long speech also offers hope for an alternative reading, one that proposes quite a different channel
of communication than the one Job recommends. What
God holds out for consideration is Creation, all that is
the world, its bigness and smallness, its infinite detail, its
differing statements of motif and theme, their complex
variations and repetitions, beauty and terror intermixed.
It is a construct so finely made that even its wild and
violent and enormous elements – Leviathan is an example
God offers with particular pleasure – contain in their
details the smallest and most delicate elements, for the
eyes of the monster are 'like the eyelids of the morning'
(41:18). God is also rightfully pleased with the concept
and execution of water in its various forms, rain and dew
and ice and frost. His pride is the understandable pride

of the artist who has succeeded in creating a whole world. The detail of horse anatomy, he feels, worked out particularly well: 'The glory of his nostrils is terrible' (39:20).

Blake seems to have liked this line too, for in plate XIV – his illustration of this bit of the text – one of the details of Creation he chooses to include are four horses, nostrils flaring. Blake's God stares out from this frame, just missing eye contact with the viewer, an oddly stricken expression on His face, but His arms are stretched out to encompass ranks of jubilant angels, stars, beasts and humans, mountains and rivers, birds and plants and creeping things. Look at it all, God seems to be saying. Don't trouble me with reason; what you need to know is there in the art and the mystery and ultimate unknowableness of my elegant design. Love it and fear it. Submit to it.

> For the thing which I greatly feared
> is come upon me, and that
> which I was afraid of is come unto me. (3:25)

A number of years ago I read the account of Black Elk, an old Sioux visionary and a friend of Crazy Horse. He lived to see catastrophes to his people at least the like of Job's. They lost as close to everything as you can and not just be extinct. He lived on past his particular apocalypse, to be another exile in the twentieth century. In telling his story, he dwells in great detail on a time in his earlier life when he had become consumed with fear, 'afraid of being afraid.' He then had a powerful vision that featured the four quarters of the earth, the weathers of the sky, animals and man. In other words, all of Creation. The great lesson of this all-encompassing vision was the conviction that we should not fear the universe. I remember writing the line down in a lost notebook along with a poem by Stephen Dunn and some lines from a Thomas McGuane novel expressing what struck me as somewhat the same ideas.

Not fearing the universe is a useful and comforting attitude if you can sustain it. And with varying degrees of success, I've tried to do it many times. Once I was lost in the Bolivian cloud forest, the damp brow of mountain between the Andes and the Amazon. I had walked down from a barren eighteen-thousand-foot pass, and gradually my map and the land came more and more to disresemble one another. And then fairly suddenly the trail was gone. My one companion waited by a river for me to scout a route.

I walked a mile or so, contouring around a heavily treed hillside and over a ridge, and then I came to a high cliff. Stretched out far beneath my feet was the Amazon basin. I could see for what must have been a hundred miles before the jungle faded into haze. There was not a road or clearing or feather of smoke, just unmarked green treetops. It was a sensation similar to lying on your back in a Cherry County, Nebraska, field and looking up into the moonless night sky. So to say, the legendary indifference of nature to man's individual existence was much in evidence. I sat on a rock for a long time looking out, and one of the word-strings I remember crossing my mind was, Do not fear the universe. I remember that it helped. And that is about all that you can ask of words.

I thought them again after two days of bushwhacking, when in the dark I stumbled through a banana grove and cutters came out from their camp and stood with machetes in their hands, the thick blades backlit in the glare of pressurized gas lanterns. As it turned out, the men were as scared of me and my thrashing as I was of them. They had warm beer in liter bottles, and they showed me where to camp. I slept by a black river and the night was so quiet I could hear the rocks in the riverbed moving against each other in the current.

It is easy enough when the universe behaves in such a benign way not to fear it. But the *Book of Job* and its God of the whirlwind are of a different turn of mind. They say – also usefully – 'Yes, sometimes do.'

Benjamin Prado

Job or, The Pain With No Solution

The *Book of Job* is the part of the Bible in which it proves most difficult to be on God's side. Its subject is that of injustice and its doctrine comprises a series of questions without answers which makes it a fascinating yet incomprehensible text. Why does the just man suffer? Why are goodness and uprightness punished with pain and poverty? Why, if the Lord sees everything and controls everything, do righteous people suffer, the virtuous live loaded down with misfortunes and the innocent die before their time? If we look at the other side of the coin the prospects are even more gloomy. Why do the wicked prosper? Why aren't the cruel stopped? While they sank into the snow of Siberia what did Stalin's victims think about Divine Justice? When the prisoners of Auschwitz looked upwards what did they see, Heaven or Hell? The *Book of Job* is in many ways God's Achilles' heel because it sets out the questions but hides the answers. It's the bull's eye for those who doubt, the point at which the bulwarks of faith threaten to give way; still more, it's within Job's pages that the Scriptures contradict themselves in an incongruous way, annihilating ferociously the central idea that Good deserves the love of God and Evil deserves his wrath. And all this just on account of a wager.

At the beginning, Job is described as a man who is 'blameless and upright, one who feared God and turned away from evil'. So we're faced with a real star, someone without weaknesses, the Frank Sinatra of believers and one who would think the Almighty would give him everything in return, from robust health to a far-off and gentle death. But at that moment Satan turns up to formulate a strange theory: it's precisely Job's flawless existence that makes him seem suspicious, hypocritical and guilty until proven innocent. Lucifer says that Job is full of solidarity because he has too many possessions, upright because his character has been formed by good fortune and generous because his prosperity allows him to be, but that he would renounce God as soon as luck and prosperity turned their back on him. The Lord responds promptly to this taunt, and decides, on the one hand, to use Job like a laboratory rat and on the other, to behave just like those cowboys in the movies who first gamble away their horse (and then their wife) in a desperate game of cards. In a single day Job's seven sons and three daughters die, his camels and his livestock are stolen, robbers put his servants to the sword, his house is consumed by fire and his land, once again, becomes barren. But from the lips of Job – who can't have been a very good father – come only the following words: 'Jehovah gave and Jehovah has taken away.' That is to say, he behaves as if the only thing that Napoleon had said on his way to exile on the island of Elba had been: 'It was a real pleasure discovering Russia.'

But all this is insufficient to defeat the Devil or to convince God. Lucifer says that Job remains upright because, despite losing everything, he himself hasn't been touched; he says that if his skin and bones were harmed, his faith would evaporate. Once more he is authorised to injure Job, whose pointless sufferings and headlong fall undoubtedly contain the seed of works such as *The Trial* by Franz Kafka or Samuel Beckett's *Malloy*. If there's one thing in particular that moves us in Kafka's novel, as we see how his protagonist – a man who's just as flawless as Job, although a lot poorer – is arrested, cornered and finally murdered like a dog, it's precisely the fact that his torment is inexplicable and not connected with any kind of ideology. If there's one thing that we remember about Beckett's book, it's the way in which the world changes around the character who is collapsing. Instead of feeling compassion or offering help, it becomes more hostile and less charitable as he gradually sinks further down in the mire. The same happens with Job: on seeing him humiliated his friends feel not pity but disgust. Unfortunately, that's a pattern that has been repeated down to the present time.

The second strange thing about the *Book of Job* is the way in which its protagonist – who seems to anticipate and modify in line with his own situation Saint Thomas Aquinas' precept, according to which faith is courage of spirit – rebels obstinately against arbitrariness, displaying an inner strength with which he opposes the undeserved violence that God uses against him. As a matter of fact, and possibly in a more modest sense (because his resistance isn't physical but moral, and because his only act of daring consists in not wanting to move from where he is) his role is very similar to that of the heroes of Greek mythology: human beings capable of facing up to the whims of the gods and, at times, defeating them. Job is a believer but he's not docile; he respects God but he also respects himself and in fact he has more faith in his own innocence than in God's apparent vengeance. He's a kind of Ulysses who challenges everything, who takes up an embattled position against the slanders of his enemies until he seems invincible, someone who can be wounded but not defeated by the evil chorus comprising Eliphaz of Teman, Bildad of Shuah and Zophar of Naamah, surely recognisable in our world today, a place teeming with people whose main mission in life consists in pulling other people down. In fact, what Eliphaz, Bildad and Zophar do in order to convince themselves of Job's guilt is to use the same sophistry with which the Devil tricked God – only the other way around. It stands to reason, they say to one another, that if someone suffers so many misfortunes it must be because he deserves them.

This means that Job is in the firing line with everything against him, running along a tunnel that doesn't appear to have a way out. That is to say, we're dealing with a classical prototype: that of the solitary hero who fights valiantly but without any assistance against things that are much bigger than him; who is hounded merci-lessly until the point at which it seems that the rope is about to break. The general effect of the suffocating setting is reinforced by the theatrical structure of the text (somehow, I can't help visualising a film based on the *Book of Job* made by Orson Welles, with desert-like country-side, brutal close-ups of the actors and expressionist surroundings; something like his *Mr Arkadin* or his versions of *Macbeth, Chimes at Midnight* and, of course, *The Trial* by Kafka). As the accusations of Eliphaz, Bildad and Zophar follow one another or, later on, Elihu and Job's subversive attitude grows, as Job defends himself time after time against all their charges and he finally loses the patience for which he is famous, the pain and rage produced by his suffering occupy all of the space previ-ously taken up by his blind obedience and resignation.

By gradually increasing the dramatic quality of his narrative until it reaches a temperature that seems unbearable, the author of the text – which for centuries was attributed to Solomon – leads us to the edge of the abyss, to the point where everything seems lost and we are left feeling that all the hero can ask for is that the next blow will be the last. At that moment God appears to Job and his enemies in the midst of a storm, to carry out justice and draw some moral out of everything that has happened. And this is the strangest thing of all: the fact that he doesn't actually do either of these things.

Until the episode in which God appears, the parable which the *Book of Job* supposedly wants to formulate remains completely indecipherable. Why does this man (who is, as Antonio Machado would say, in the best sense of the word, 'good') receive such terrible harm as a reward for his virtues? How is it that the Devil can manipulate God so simply and how is God going to justify his wilful betrayal of someone who has always been so faithful to him? The just will be made wretched and the hands of the faithful will be broken; the most hard-working will lose their jobs and he who sows roses will harvest nettles; the night will tarnish clean hearts and he who gives alms will be brought low by poverty. That's what this place is like, a world in which things tend to turn out time after time exactly the same way: with Dostoyevsky locked up in prison at Omsk and the Tsars dancing in a ballroom in the Kremlin; with García Lorca in a common grave and Franco having tea in El Pardo.

However, the Bible and the rest of the sacred writings, from the Koran to the Hindu Brahmana and Upanishad, do not exist just to remind us of the horrors that lie in wait for us on this side of paradise, but to teach us not to pay heed to them, to leap over them, to put within our grasp a map that guides us to the sunniest part of the beyond. The fact that we can't understand the way in which the *Book of Job* fulfils this function is what makes it so amazingly different. In reality, the easiest thing is to feel defenceless in the face of this story, confused as one always is when faced with the incomprehensible; just like the characters in the film *Hana-Bi* by Japanese director Takeshi Kitano. While still mourning the recent loss of their daughter, they suffer a further blow when the wife falls ill with cancer. Throughout the film the parents repeatedly turn over the pieces of a simple puzzle, attempting to form the number five, the age at which the girl died. But they don't manage to. Their surprise and bewilderment are a moving metaphor for pain and our inability to understand it. The *Book of Job* is also, first and foremost, that same metaphor.

In the Sixties, many Spanish schools used to devote Saturday mornings to teaching their pupils the subject of religion. We children – at that time, in 1968 or 1969, we must have been between six and eight years old – used to get to the classroom at about nine o'clock and, for half an hour, we would listen as the teacher read to us or explained a part of the Bible. Then we had to draw a small square, making a drawing inside it that represented what we had been taught, and writing fifteen or twenty lines on the subject. My mother still has a couple of those drawings and while I was putting together this prologue I asked her to let me have a look at them. Inside the small vignette that went with the *Book of Job*, drawn with coloured pencils and placed, as always, at the top and to the left of the essay, there was a man attempting to run and a swamp-green devil hunting him down and stabbing him in the back. Above them is the triangle in which one would normally find the eye of God, a symbol of his infinite presence, of his boundless power to see everything; but the fact is, there's nothing there this time, the triangle appears abandoned, with no sign of life, completely white and empty. Was it because the illustration wasn't finished or because what that child understood from the *Book of Job* was the absence of God and His active part in our suffering? Perhaps it was because that day one of us had asked a question of don Lope (the old teacher in that state school) and perhaps he had answered that the purposes of the Lord are inscrutable and that the true Christian should give thanks even for pain. I now realise that these aphorisms come together to form a vicious circle: we would like to know why it's necessary to give thanks to God for the undeserved pain that He inflicts upon us, but his purposes are inscrutable, and when we look in the dictionary to see what that means, the doors close forever, in an inhuman, hermetic way: inscrutable is something that you can't understand or find out about. After that, one is frightened to continue asking because, with each word that we utter, the silence seems greater.

We have all seen on more than one occasion the God who appears to Job at the end of his book: He's one of those violent, muscular gods depicted by Michelangelo, one of those colossal beings who look a lot less disposed to forgiveness than to punishment, furious and implacable, part lion, part Arnold Schwarzenegger.

What that God does is to reproach Job for having had the temerity not to yield to Him, but to offer instead something more than resignation to the calvary allotted to him, to reject the famous inscrutability of His acts. He makes him see how insignificant he is; He mocks the arrogance implied by believing that He must give Job an explanation or in any way be accountable to him. He asks him, with a devastating grandness, if by some chance he believes himself worthy of competing with Him, if some time in his life he has done or could have done something comparable with God's magnificent creation: the oceans, the mountain ranges, the forests and the animals, night and day. Faced with this avalanche, Job reacts with humility (although I don't think he's particularly repentant), and the Almighty finally admits his innocence, gives him double his original prosperity and allows Job to live until he's one hundred and forty years old.

The final question is: why? The literary structure and the development of the storyline of the *Book of Job* are perfectly orthodox: the good man falls and falls, but he finishes at the summit again; the evil are victorious at first and divide the spoils amongst themselves only to lose in the end. What isn't very clear is its moral intention: why does God commit the monumental injustice of which Job is the victim? Is it to Lucifer, to Job or perhaps to Himself that he wants to prove something with his behaviour? And, above all, who is the winner in this strange combat? It doesn't seem to be Job. It doesn't seem to be worth gaining twice as much in exchange for having lost everything. Nor does escaping from injustice lessen the pain of having suffered it. Nor do the seven new sons and three new daughters granted to him by Jehovah eliminate the anguish felt on account of his ten dead ones.

Nor is it logical to think that God has gained something. The fact is, by allowing the destruction of Job, He works against His own desires and His only apparent motive is that of once more defeating His son, the Devil. However, the impression we are left with is that He doesn't succeed. The *Book of Job* does something different from all the others in the Bible: the one who triumphs on this occasion is Leviathan, the monster from primal chaos, the devourer of the sun. If we think about it carefully, Satan doesn't lose anything because he risks what isn't his, because he ensures that God is for a time unjust and rash, that He falls into the trap of the general who wishes to show his power by sending his soldiers to their death.

The fact that God rewards Job without explaining to him why He had previously deserted him turns this text into a blind alley, a fearful hole in the hull of the boat. Perhaps this is the correct reading of the *Book of Job*, that there's one Truth that is valid for everyone, even for God: When one starts to be unjust, one stops being invincible.

Mordecai Richler

God's straight man: was Job the butt of God's biggest joke? Or is he the ultimate example of faith?

The mischievous deity who enjoyed such sport with Job, if only to honour a wager with Satan, the stakes never explicitly stated, doesn't make an appearance until the story is almost done. Proclaimed as a Voice out of the Whirlwind, a heavenly swaggerer's roaring: 'Where wast thou when I laid the foundations of the earth?' And, pushing it some, 'Canst thou bind the cluster of Pleiades, or loose the bands of Orion?'

A case can be made against the God who approved Job's torment as the first of the ethnic cleansers. As the Hebrews stood on this side of Jordan, following forty years of wandering in the wilderness, Moses delivered unto them a message from Jehovah, to clear Cannan of its inhabitants: 'thous shalt save alive nothing that breatheth'.

Mighty, capricious, vengeful, cruel, a jealous God, Jehovah can also be seen as a prankster, the first in a long line of dark Jewish humorists, extending to Franz Kafka in our day. Long before he took Job for his patsy, he enjoyed a celestial hee-haw, Abraham serving as his straight man. 'Take thy son,' the Lord said unto Abraham, 'thine only son Isaac, whom thou lovest, and get thee into the land of Moriah; and offer him there for a burnt offering upon one of the mountains which I will tell thee of.' And Abe, the first of too many Jewish grovellers, saddled his ass and did as he was told. He built an altar, and laid the wood in order, and bound Isaac, his son, and laid him on the altar upon the wood. 'Behold the fire and the wood,' said Isaac, 'but where is the lamb for the burnt offering?' In response, a dutiful Abraham stretched forth his hand, and took the knife to slay his son. At which point, Jehovah, just possibly quaking with self-satisfied laughter, sent down an angel who said, 'Lay not thy hand upon thy son,' and Abraham lifted up his eyes, and beheld behind him a ram caught in a thicket by the horns; and Abraham went and took the ram, and offered him up in the stead of his son.

The *Book of Job*, its poetry sublime, its author or authors unknown, dated by some to before the exile in Babylon, deals with Jeremiah's complaint: 'Wherefore doth the way of the wicked prosper? Wherefore are all they happy that deal very treacherously?'

Or, as the suffering Job had it, putting a question that begs for a satisfactory answer to this day: 'Wherefore do the wicked live, become old, yea, wax mightly in power?'

This conundrum also troubled the great medieval Jewish philosopher Moses Maimonides, who was born in Cordova in 1135, and wrote in his *Guide of the Perplexed*: 'Men frequently think that the evils in the world are more numerous than the good things; many sayings and songs of nations dwell on this idea. They say that a good thing is found only exceptionally, whilst evil things are numerous and lasting.' Not only common people make this mistake, but many who believe they are wise. Al-razi wrote a well-known book, *On Metaphysics*. Among other mad and foolish things, it contains the idea, discovered by him, that there exists more evil than good. 'For if the happiness of man and his pleasure in the times of prosperity be compared with the mishaps that befall him – such as grief, acute pain, defects, paralysis of the limbs, fears, anxieties and troubles – it would seem as if the existence of man is a punishment and a great evil for him.'

Or, again, as Job put it: 'Why died I not from the womb? Why did I not give up the ghost when I came out of the belly?' We have the Lord's word for it that until he was tampered with, Job was a perfect and upright man, one that feared God and eschewed evil. He was blessed with seven sons and three daughters, as well as many loyal servants, and he owned thousands of sheep and camels and oxen. Then one day Satan, who was still one of the Lord's ground crew, took a break from 'going to and fro in the earth, and from walking up and down in it'. Looking for some amusement, he accused the Lord of bragging about a much-favoured servant whose fealty had never been tested. 'But put forth thine hand now, and touch all that he hath, and he will renounce thee to thy face.' Provoked, the Lord accepts the challenge, with the proviso that no harm is done to Job himself. So poor Job's children are killed, his servants are slain, and his sheep and camels and oxen are destroyed or stolen. But Job's faith is not shaken: 'The Lord gave and the Lord hath taken away; blessed be the name of the Lord.'

Satan, protecting his bet, convinces the Lord to up the ante: 'But put forth thy hand now, and touch his bone and his flesh, and he will renounce thee to thy face.'

With the Lord's permission, Satan 'smote Job with sore boils from the sole of his foot unto his crown,' and, even as Job sat among the ashes, his wife came unto him: 'Dost thou still hold fast thine integrity? Curse God, and die.'

Job responds, 'Thou speaketh as one of the foolish women speaketh. What? Shall we receive good at the hand of God, and shall we not receive evil?'

And then, as if Job's plight were not already sufficiently dire, there come unto him his three ironically dubbed 'comforters', easily the most insufferable trio in literature: Eliphaz the Temanite, Bildad the Shuhite and Zophar the Naamathite. And Job says, 'Let the day perish wherein I was born.'

The pompous Eliphaz suggests Job must be guilty of something. 'Remember, I pray thee,' he says, 'who ever perished, being innocent?' Rubbing salt in Job's wounds, he adds, his manner chirpy, 'Behold, happy is the man whom God correcteth: therefore despise not thou the chastening of the Almighty.'

But Job, who has never denied the words of the Holy One, will have none of it: 'My days are swifter than a weaver's shuttle, and are spent without hope.'

Next Job is rebuked by Bildad, a comforter blissfully

unaware that the Lord, understandably weary of bringing forth lightning, drawing out Leviathan with a fish hook, and performing other heavy-duty chores, finds respite in the occasional flutter, however cruel. 'Behold,' says Bildad, 'God will not cast away a perfect man, neither will he uphold the evildoers.'

In response, Job allows that the Lord performs marvellous things without number, but 'Lo, he goeth by me, and I see him not: he passeth on also, but I perceive him not.' Professing that he is blameless, a righteous man, Job ventures that the Lord destroys the perfect as well as the wicked, and will mock at the trial of the innocent: 'The earth is given into the hand of the wicked.'

Unimpressed, Zophar accuses Job of boasting. And mockery: 'Know therefore that God exacteth of thee less than thine iniquity deserveth.'

It was the Apostle James, in his letter, who urged readers to admire 'the patience of Job,' which is ridiculous. The ill-used Job is seething. Defiant. He would not be one of the most touching characters in literature, who still speaks to our immediate concerns today, had he been patient. 'The tents of robbers prosper,' he protests, 'and they that provoke God are secure.' He longs to speak to the Almighty and reason with him. And finally he has had enough of the cliché-mongering, boring Eliphaz, Bildad and Zophar, whom he dismisses as miserable comforters: 'How long will ye vex my soul, and break me in pieces with words?'

Readers may well wonder what Job might have

made of his Lord had he known his suffering was not punishment for any evil he had done, but, instead, the consequence of a frivolous bet the heavenly capo di capos had made with one of his men. Even so, he dares to ask, 'What is the Almighty, that we should serve him? And what profit should we have, if we pray unto him?' And he goes on to complain, 'I cry unto thee, and thou dost not answer me; I stand up, and thou dost not heed me.'

Having lost his wager with Satan, God appears to Job at last as a Voice out of the Whirlwind. He denounces Job's comforters and starts to brag, casting his CV in the best possible light, and then reminds his patsy that the Lord 'beholdeth everything that is high; he is king over all the sons of pride'.

Job repents, earning a good deal of vigorish. Twice as many sheep and camels and oxen as he owned before, as well as seven new sons and three new daughters. But the Lord, a sore loser, does not restore Job's innocent slain children or servants to life, and the question of why the wicked prosper is left hanging.

The villain of the *Book of Job* is not Satan, but the Lord. Whether it's Jehovah, a.k.a. Jahve ('he that is'), or Adonai for the 'ineffable name', or Eloi, as in the Gospel according to Mark, or one of the secret names known only to the most exalted cabbalists, the Almighty – before and long after he amused himself with Job – has a good deal to answer for. In Deuteronomy, the fifth book of the Pentateuch, a desert tribe of Hebrews was put on notice. The Lord loved them: 'For thou art a holy people, unto the Lord thy God: the Lord thy God hath chosen thee to be a special people unto himself, above all people that are upon the face of the earth.'

After all these punishing centuries, we might well question the Lord's professed ardour for my bunch and ask, chosen for what? Captivity in Babylon?

'By the rivers of Babylon, there we sat down, yea, we wept, when we remembered Zion.'

For the Inquisition?

O, I have been to Madrid's vast Plaza Mayor, its cobblestones nicely worn, its Herrera Towers lovely to contemplate, each portico perfection itself. The splendour indecent. For this had once been the setting for numerous *autos publicos generales,* which in those days vied with the bullfights in popular appeal. Many of the *auto-da-fé* victims were *conversos,* Jews forcibly converted but suspected of continuing to practise their faith secretly. Usually the ceremony would be held on feast days to attract as large a mob as possible. Elaborate stagings were erected on the Plaza. Windows looking out on the show went for large sums. The proceedings would begin at dawn with a procession through narrow streets, the clergy followed by those of Jehovah's Chosen who were for burning. Lighting the brand that ignited the pyre was a signal honour. First of all, however, spectators were encouraged to increase the suffering of the condemned by lighting their beards, a sport known as 'shaving the new Christians'.

Pogroms?

It was Pavolachi Krushevan who introduced 'The

Protocols of the Elders of Zion' into Russia, first publishing it in the St Petersburg newspaper *Znamya*, and later in *Bessarabets*, a daily printed in Kishinev, the provincial capital of Bessarabia. This publication, in tandem with a charge that a Christian boy had been the victim of a Jewish ritual murder, prompted the infamous Easter 1903 Kishinev pogrom, in which forty-nine Jews were murdered and hundreds more injured.

In those small-bean days the innocent still had names, not a tattoo of numbers. They could be buried in individual graves. Then the Holocaust. Jahve had declared us the Chosen, subject to his kind of loving, and then Dr Mengele, a deity of sorts in his time and place, made his own selections from among them.

Scroll of Agony, the Warsaw diaries of Chaim Kaplan, a latter-day Job, was smuggled out of the ghetto in 1942. Kaplan's entry for September 10, 1939, reads in part: 'The streets are sewn with trenches and barricades . . . The enemy of the Jews attested long ago that if war broke out, Jews would be eliminated from Europe. Now half of the Jewish people are under his domination. Why has God embittered our lives so cruelly? Have we indeed sinned more than any nation?'

Possibly the problem is that the Lord, our God, never trusted our bunch. Before laying his faithful servant Moses to rest without entering the promised land, the Ineffable Name appeared in the Tabernacle in a pillar of cloud:

Behold . . . this people will rise up, and go a-whoring after the gods of strangers of the land, whither they go to be among them, and will forsake me, and break my covenant which I have made with them.

Then my anger shall be kindled against them in that day, and I will forsake them, and I will hide my face from them, and they shall be devoured, and many evils and troubles shall befall them.

The Lord, our God, was as good as his word. All the same, there were many whose faith proved unshakeable even during the Holocaust. Included among the stories – touching or infuriating, depending on where you pay your dues – related by Yaffa Eliach in his Hasidic Tales of the Holocaust, there is an account of an SS Aktion in a small Ukrainian town. As the Einsatzgruppen were about to execute the Jews there, a Hasid stepped forward and told the young officer in charge that it was customary in civilised (sic) countries to grant a last request to those condemned to die. The officer asked the Jew what his last wish was.

'A short prayer,' said the Hasid.

'Granted.'

The Hasid covered his bare head with his hand and recited the following prayer, first in Hebrew, then in German: 'Blessed art thou, O Lord our God, King of the Universe, who hath not made me a heathen.'

Then he walked to the edge of the pit, already filled with bodies, and was shot in the back of the head.

According to the Jewish calendar more than 5000 years have passed since God declared us a Holy people, chosen to be special. Enough is enough. As we enter into the new millennium, possibly he might consider favouring others with his love. But, before passing on, it would be gratifying if he could answer Job's question:

'Wherefore do the wicked live, become old, yea, wax mighty in power?'

THE BOOK OF PSALMS

Make a joyful noise unto God, all ye lands: sing forth the honour of his name: make his praise glorious.

(66:1–3)
authorised King James version

Bono

Explaining belief has always been difficult. How do you explain a love and logic at the heart of the universe when the world is so out of whack? How about the poetic versus the actual truth found in the scriptures? Has free will got *us* crucified? And what about the dodgy characters who inhabit the tome, known as the bible, who claim to hear the voice of God?

You have to be interested, but is God?

Explaining faith is impossible . . . Vision over visibility . . . Instinct over intellect . . . A songwriter plays a chord with the faith that he will hear the next one in his head.

One of the writers of the psalms was a musician, a harp-player whose talents were required at 'the palace' as the only medicine that would still the demons of the moody and insecure King Saul of Israel; a thought that still inspires, if not quite explaining Marilyn singing for Kennedy, or the Spice Girls in the court of Prince Charles . . .

At age 12, I was a fan of David, he felt familiar . . . like a pop star could feel familiar. The words of the psalms were as poetic as they were religious and he was a star. A dramatic character, because before David could fulfil the prophecy and become the king of Israel, he had to take quite a beating. He was forced into exile and ended up in a cave in some no-name border town facing the collapse of his ego and abandonment by God. But this is where the soap opera got interesting, this is where David was said to have composed his first psalm – a blues. That's what a lot of the psalms feel like to me, the blues. Man shouting at God – 'My God, my God why hast thou forsaken me? Why art thou so far from helping me?' (Psalm 22).

I hear echoes of this holy row when un-holy bluesman Robert Johnson howls 'There's a hellhound on my trail' or Van Morrison sings 'Sometimes I feel like a motherless child'. Texas Alexander mimics the psalms in 'Justice Blues': 'I cried Lord my father, Lord eh Kingdom come. Send me back my woman, then thy will be done'. Humorous, sometimes blasphemous, the blues was backslidin' music; but by its very opposition, flattered the subject of its perfect cousin Gospel.

Abandonment, displacement, is the stuff of my favourite psalms. The Psalter may be a font of gospel music, but for me it's in his despair that the psalmist really reveals the nature of his special relationship with God. Honesty, even to the point of anger. 'How long, Lord? Wilt thou hide thyself forever?' (Psalm 89) or 'Answer me when I call' (Psalm 5).

Psalms and hymns were my first taste of inspirational music. I liked the words but I wasn't sure about the tunes – with the exception of Psalm 23, 'The Lord is my Shepherd'. I remember them as droned and chanted rather than sung. Still, in an odd way, they prepared me for the honesty of John Lennon, the baroque language of Bob Dylan and Leonard Cohen, the open throat of Al Green and Stevie Wonder – when I hear these singers, I am reconnected to a part of me I have no explanation for . . . my 'soul' I guess.

Words and music did for me what solid, even rigorous, religious argument could never do, they introduced me to God, not belief in God, more an experiential sense of GOD. Over art, literature, reason, the way in to my spirit was a combination of words and music. As a result the Book of *Psalms* always felt open to me and led me to the poetry of *Ecclesiastes*, the *Song of Solomon*, the book of *John* . . . My religion could not be fiction but it had to transcend facts. It could be mystical, but not mythical and definitely not ritual . . .

My mother was Protestant, my father Catholic; anywhere other than Ireland that would be unremarkable. The 'Prods' at that time had the better tunes and the Catholics had the better stage-gear. My mate Gavin Friday used to say: 'Roman Catholicism is the Glamrock of religion' with its candles and psychedelic colours . . . Cardinal blues, scarlets and purples, smoke bombs of incense and the ring of the little bell. The Prods were better at the bigger bells, they could afford them. In Ireland wealth and Protestantism went together; to have either, was to have collaborated with the enemy, i.e. Britain. This did not fly in our house.

After going to Mass at the top of the hill, in Finglas on the north side of Dublin, my father waited outside the little Church of Ireland chapel at the bottom of the hill, where my mother had brought her two sons . . .

I kept myself awake thinking of the clergyman's daughter and let my eyes dive into the cinema of the stained glass. These Christian artisans had invented the movies . . . light projected through colour to tell their story. In the '70s the story was 'the Troubles' and the Troubles came through the stained glass; with rocks thrown more in mischief than in anger, but the message was the same; the country was to be divided along sectarian lines. I had a foot in both camps, so my Goliath became religion itself; I began to see religion as the perversion of faith. As to the five smooth stones for the sling . . . I began to see God everywhere else. In girls, fun, music, justice but still – despite the lofty King James translation – the scriptures . . .

I loved these stories for the basest reasons, not just the New Testament with its mind-altering concept that God might reveal himself as a baby born in straw poverty – but even the Old Testament. These were action movies, with some hardcore men and women . . . the car chases, the casualties, the blood and guts; there was very little kissing . . .

David was a star, the Elvis of the bible, if we can believe the chiselling of Michelangelo (check the face – but I still can't figure out this most famous Jew's foreskin). And unusually for such a 'rock star', with his lust for power, lust for women, lust for life, he had the humility of one who knew his gift worked harder than he ever would. He even danced naked in front of his troops . . . the biblical equivalent of the royal walkabout. David was definitely more performance artist than politician.

Anyway, I stopped going to churches and got myself into a different kind of religion. Don't laugh, that's what being in a rock 'n' roll band is, not pseudo-religion either . . . Show-business is Shamanism: Music is Worship; whether it's worship of women or their designer, the world or its destroyer, whether it comes from that ancient place we call soul or simply the spinal cortex, whether the prayers are on fire with a dumb rage or dove-like desire . . . the smoke goes upwards . . . to God or something you replace God with . . . usually yourself.

Years ago, lost for words and forty minutes of recording time left before the end of our studio time, we were still looking for a song to close our third album, *War*. We wanted to put something explicitly spiritual on the record to balance the politics and the romance of it; like Bob Marley or Marvin Gaye would. We thought about the psalms . . . 'Psalm 40' . . . There was some squirming. We were a very 'white' rock group, and such plundering of the scriptures was taboo for a white rock group unless it was in the 'service of Satan'. Or worse, Goth.

'Psalm 40' is interesting in that it suggests a time in which grace will replace karma, and love replace the very strict laws of Moses (i.e. fulfil them). I love that thought. David, who committed some of the most selfish as well as selfless acts, was depending on it. That the scriptures are brim full of hustlers, murderers, cowards, adulterers and mercenaries used to shock me; now it is a source of great comfort.

'40' became the closing song at U2 shows and on hundreds of occasions, literally hundreds of thousands of people of every size and shape t-shirt have shouted back the refrain, pinched from 'Psalm 6': '"How long" (to sing this song)'. I had thought of it as a nagging question – pulling at the hem of an invisible deity whose presence we glimpse only when we act in love. How long . . . hunger? How long . . . hatred? How long until creation grows up and the chaos of its precocious, hell-bent adolescence has been discarded? I thought it odd that the vocalising of such questions could bring such comfort; to me too.

But to get back to David, it is not clear how many, if any, of these psalms David or his son Solomon really wrote. Some scholars suggest the royals never dampened their nibs and that there was a host of Holy Ghost writers . . . Who cares? I didn't buy Leiber and Stoller . . . they were just his songwriters . . . I bought Elvis.

PROVERBS

A wise man will hear, and will increase learning; and a man of understanding shall attain unto wise counsels: to understand a proverb, and the interpretation; the words of the wise, and their dark sayings.

(1:5–6)
authorised King James version

Charles Johnson

Where there is no vision, the people perish.

Of all the practical observations in that most pragmatic of texts in the Old Testament, *The Book of Proverbs*, this one sentence linking vision and life comes singing off the page as the most profound. Meditate, please, on the possibility that in life there is a *goal*, an end that makes all our worldly efforts intelligible. Carefully think it through: without a *vision*, either personal or political, the individual (or society) is 'like a city that is broken down, and without walls'. This is not simply a question for the schools, for without a comprehensive and capacious philosophy life fails. The unsentimental implication here – the basic, philosophical and secular premise – is that life can be a perilous journey. Perhaps a social minefield. (Just read today's newspaper if you need proof that the world is and has always been a dangerous place.) And any young person hesitantly starting out on this odyssey, now or in the days of King Solomon, soon discovers that his (or her) chances for survival, prosperity and happiness are enhanced a hundred-fold if – and only if – they have a good map.

Put simply, *Proverbs* is that richly detailed, many-splendored map. A timeless wake-up call. More importantly, along with its companion books, the poetic 'wisdom' literature of the Old Testament (*Job, Ecclesiastes, The Song of Solomon,* and *Psalms*), it is a two-millennium-old blue-print for the staggering challenge of living a truly *civilized* life. Culture, we realize after reading *Proverbs,* is an on-going project. We are not born with culture. Or wisdom. And both are but *one* generation deep. Achieving either is a daily task requiring as much work for the individual as an artist puts into a perfectly balanced painting, or a musician into a flawless performance. (Thus one wonders if the great bulk of human-kind can be truthfully called either cultured or civilized.) Here, in this repository of moral instruction, in its 31 chapters, 915 verses, approximately 900 proverbs, and 15,043 words, the journey that we call a life is presented as a canvas upon which the individual paints skillfully a civilized self-portrait – an offering – that will please himself and the Lord. In chapter 3, we are told, 'Happy is the man that findeth wisdom.' The Hebrew word for 'wisdom' is *chokmah.* It occurs no less than thirty-seven times in *Proverbs. Chokmah* also means skillfulness in dealing with the job that is before us – life itself – and I believe it is comparable to the Greek word *techne,* the rational application of principles aimed at making or doing something well. The reader who takes *Proverbs* to heart, who believes like the Greeks that 'the unexamined life is not worth living', is by nature a lover of wisdom: a philosopher. For that is precisely what the word 'philosophy' means (*philein*, to love – *sophia*, wisdom).

I'm aware those words – 'wisdom', 'civilized' and 'philosophy' – may sound musty and antique to modern (or post-modern) ears. As so many have said, ours is an Era of Relativism, or situational ethics, perhaps even of nihilism, an historical period in which *Proverbs* will for some readers seem right-wing and patriarchal, oppressive and harsh, dogmatic and illiberal. Many will regard its contents as obsolete for the conditions we face at the eleventh hour of the twentieth century because, above all else, we moderns value individual freedom. Unfortunately, our passion for liberty is often misunderstood as license or, more accurately, as licentiousness. Personally, as a Buddhist, I was at first wary of writing about this book, though I was raised on its vision in a midwestern, African Methodist Episcopal church. But after going over *Proverbs* a half dozen times, after opening myself to its spiritual core, which complements nicely the world's other great religious traditions, I re-discovered the gems it has offered western humanity for centuries. I saw in its gnostic truths the reason why Professor C E M Joad once defined decadence as 'the loss of an object in life'. In fact, I realized that *Proverbs* not only speaks powerfully to our morally adrift era, but describes rather well my own often benighted, rebellious-on-principle generation (the Baby Boomers) when it says, 'There is a generation that curseth their father, and doth not bless their mother. There is a generation that are pure in their own eyes, and yet is not washed from their filthiness' (30:11–12).

Chilling.

Like all rich, multi-layered digests, *Proverbs* was not the work of a day. Nor is it the product of a single author, though King Solomon, that Ur-figure among ancient wise men, is credited with having contributed two of its oldest sections (1:1 and 1:10). Several centuries after the death of Israel's king, the men of Hezekiah (700 BCE) added chapters 25 through 29 from Solomonic material. In short, the book was built layer upon layer, one tissue at a time, borrowing its synthesized instructions from many ancient sources, and did not achieve its finished form until the fourth or fifth century BCE. It favors, one might say, an old, old coin that has traversed continents, picking up something from each one as it was passed down through centuries – advice on social etiquette, philanthropy, how to choose a wife, and why children may need an occasional dose of Dr Spanker's tonic (the 'rod') – and bears the sweat and palm-oil of millions who have handled it. Bible scholar Kenneth T Aitken persuasively argues in his commentary *Proverbs* that the third section of the text (chapter 22) takes a few pages from the *Instructions of Amenemopet.*[*] That work, dating back to between 1000 and 600 BCE, was strictly a manual of professional training aimed at helping Egyptian civil servants achieve successful careers as they served the state. The sages of Israel, says Aitken, reworked some of the precepts from *Instructions* and at

---

[*] Kenneth T Aitken, *Proverbs* (The Westminster Press: Philadelphia, 1968), p. 3.

the same time re-contextualized them in a book far broader in its teachings for a triumphant life.

And these were, of course, originally *oral* teachings. They were delivered by a sage to pupils he addressed as a father would his children. His young charges were expected to memorize the proverbs until they were hard-wired into their hearts. Thus, this book was written for the ear. It relies heavily on repetition, a mnemonic device (which might weary modern eyes), and in its compositional strategies employs couplets linked by parallelisms. In his exegesis of *Proverbs*, J Vernon McGee identifies three forms of parallelisms that occur in the text: (1) *Synonymous Parallelism*, where the second clause restates the content of the first ('Judgments are prepared for scorners, and stripes for the back of the fool', 19:29). (2) *Antithetic (Contrast) Parallelism* that states a truth in the first clause, then contrasts it with an opposite truth in the second ('The light of the righteous rejoiceth, but the lamp of the wicked shall be put out', 13:9). And (3) *Synthetic Parallelism* in which the second clause develops the truth of the first ('The terror of a king is as the roaring of a lion; whoso provoketh him to anger sinneth against his own life', 20:2).[*]

Yet, for all the sophisticated architectonics in *Proverbs*, and for all the complexity of its literary pedigree, this is a book that sketches out a compelling, classic story: a pilgrim's progress. Imagine a young man (or

---

[*] J Vernon McGee, *Proverbs* (Thomas Nelson Publishers: Nashville, 1991), p. x.

woman) about to embark on life's journey. Call him –
well, Pilgrim. Then, as now, the world teemed with a
kaleidoscope of temptations, stramash and confusion.
In the bustling cities where colorful bazaars, beggers,
thieves, perfumed harlots, con-men, murderers, insou-
ciant idlers and false teachers eager to entice a young
person toward wrong-doing and sin (one hoary
meaning of which is 'to miss the mark'), all can be
found in great abundance. Indeed, these players, some
as beautiful as Satan and who say, 'Let us lay wait for
blood, let us lurk privily for the innocent', have from
time immemorial taken advantage of callow youths (as
well as given writers as diverse as Voltaire, De Sade,
Dickens, Fielding and Maugham inexhaustible material
for the *Bildungsroman*). Given a strictly materialistic
viewpoint, it follows that the world of matter, mere *stuff,*
will be dominated everywhere and in any era by those
who treat objects and others as *things* to be used for
their own pleasure and profit, and view everything
through the lens of their own limited consciousness.
Surveying this social field, we can imagine the authors
of *Proverbs* agreeing with Thomas à Kempis who, in *The
Imitation of Christ,* wearily quotes the Stoic philosopher
Seneca, 'A wise man once said, "As often as I have been
among men, I have returned home a lesser man" . . .
No man can live in the public eye without risk to his
soul . . .'*

---

* Thomas à Kempis, *The Imitation of Christ,* trans. by Leo Sherley-
Price (Penguin Books Ltd: Middlesex, 1953), p.50.

As we have seen, if our young Pilgrim is not to lose his (or her) soul on this planet where everything is provisional, if he is not to end bellied up and bottomed out, he needs a damned good map. Ethically, he should not have to reinvent the wheel each time he is confronted by a new moral dilemma. That, I believe, would be like a physicist claiming he can learn nothing from Galileo, Newton, Copernicus or Einstein because the conditions of their time differed so much from his own. But young people are notorious for forgetting instructions (ask any teacher about that), especially the 900 lessons on living delivered in *Proverbs*. What Pilgrim needs is the teaching condensed into *one* simple, bareknuckled mantra that encapsulates the pith of all the other proverbs. Anticipating just this problem, the *Proverbs* authors provide that axiom in the very first chapter: 'The fear of the Lord is the beginning of knowledge: but fools despise wisdom and instruction.' From this one antithetic parallelism, this stern and admonishing couplet – moment by moment mindfulness of the Most High – all else in *Proverbs* follows with Mandarin exactitude and the necessity of a logical proof. Pilgrim is counseled to 'Commit thy works unto the Lord, and thy thoughts shall be established' (16:3), for the authors of this text understood the irrefragable fact that all we are is the result of what we have thought. From intellection comes desire. From desire, will. From will, our deeds. And from deeds, our destiny. Self-control, therefore, is so essential for the spiritual life and a practical life well led that it is even favourably compared to martial conquest: 'He that is slow to anger is better than the mighty; and he that ruleth his spirit than he that taketh a city' (16:32) in a line strikingly similar to one equally famous that we find in the first-century BCE Buddhist *Dhammapada* ('Path of Virtue') – 'If one man conquer in battle a thousand times a thousand men, and if another conquers himself, he is the greatest of conquerors.'* In the world's religious traditions, eastern and western, the Way of understanding and wisdom begins by sumptuously feeding the spirit and starving the illusory sense of the ego into extinction ('Trust in the Lord with all thine heart; and lean not unto thine own understanding. In all thy ways acknowledge him, and he shall direct thy paths. Be not wise in thine own eyes:' (3:5–7)), and is realized through a worldly practice that gives priority to the experience of our elders (our global inheritance) over ephemerae in a life that embodies humility, service, and a culture's loftiest ideals, which in Pilgrim's case would be the Ten Commandments.

Wisdom in *Proverbs*, we might say, is thought winging its way home.

Naturally, many couplets in *Proverbs* inveigh against people who are *not* mindful, those who 'eat the bread of wickedness and drink the wine of violence', and break the Commandments. This book does not suffer fools gladly. At first glance, Pilgrim might see the less demanding, hedonistic path and its players as alluring

---

* *The Dhammapada*, trans. by Irving Babbitt (New Directions: New York, 1965), p.18.

and sweet – and fun! But the seeds of *Proverbs* (practical wisdom) cannot grow in that polluted soil (the 'froward'). Pilgrim is advised not to envy or even 'fret' over the fallen state of these caitiffs and poltroons, for the Lord shall 'render to every man according to his works'. In other words, just as there is inexorable causation in the physical realm, so too is there cause-and-effect in the moral universe. The kingdom of God, at bottom, is a meritocracy; its logic is that of *karma* ('as you sow so shall you reap'). The unmindful cause their own downfall – they 'eat of the fruit of their own way'. Time and again, *Proverbs* drives this point home, and nowhere more vividly than in its parable-like description of the industrious ant, or when the book cautions against lapses of vigilance in language so lovely the words almost pirouette and leap on the page: 'Yet a little sleep, a little slumber, a little folding of the hands to sleep: so shall thy poverty come as one that traveleth; and thy want as an armed man' (25:33–4).

However, it would be wrong to say that *Proverbs* is simply a map for avoiding life's pitfalls in order to bow one's knees to Baal. Throughout its chapters, Pilgrim is urged, 'Labor not to be rich' and he is reminded how 'riches certainly make themselves wings; they fly away as an eagle toward heaven', and 'Better is the poor that walketh in his uprightness, than he that is perverse in his ways, though he be rich'. Does this advice contradict the practicality that infuses *Proverbs*? Does it ask us to be poor? No, for a crucial distinction is drawn: 'Wealth gotten by vanity shall be diminished:

but he that gathereth by labor shall increase'. The book points our Pilgrim toward industry, not that he might be 'greedy of gain', but rather that he or she might become the sort of provider who 'leaveth an inheritance to his children's children', honors his mother and father (and, one might add, his teachers), and 'stretcheth out her hand to the poor'. In effect, Pilgrim's labor is for others. Always life's true wealth in *Proverbs* is found in God, in wisdom and love; and love is realized through work and indefatigable service to the things loved.

In *Proverbs*, the portrait – the character sketch – that emerges of a successful pilgrim is that of a man or woman who is a quiet embodiment of culture. Not perfect by any means because he knows all too well his flaws. But in his life of building, serving, creating, he mightily strives to be righteous. He is soft-spoken and hates lying. In him there is the continuity of generations, one of the requisites for civilization itself. He is the joy of his mother and father and his children as well, for by honoring the wisdom of his predecessors and transmitting that (along with the fruit of his industry) to his posterity, his past (parents) meets his present (children) and vouchsafes their future. His good name the pilgrim values highly, and he is not garrulous, knowing how to hold his tongue and keep his own counsel. He never acts rashly or 'answereth a matter before he heareth it'. Concerning the needy, he is socially conscious and never 'stoppeth his ears at the cry of the poor'. Though he experience failure and 'falleth seven times', the just man struggles to his feet again to do the Lord's work, ignoring his weariness. According to *Proverbs*, at night his sleep is 'sweet'. Such a person always heeds the helpful criticism of friends, but never wearies them with his presence or overstays his welcome. And, despite his hard-won victories and integrity, he never boasts, allowing instead 'another man [to] praise thee, and not thine own mouth'. Finally, the man of mindfulness is the very foundation of society – 'bold as a lion', the sort of citizen who, if he assumes a position of authority in the state, makes the 'people rejoice'.

Clearly, the path mapped out in *Proverbs* is exacting. Straight and narrow, 'like the edge of a sword', as Mahatma Gandhi once described the spiritual life. It is fitting, then, that *Proverbs* ends by letting our pilgrim know that he need not – indeed *can*not – travel to his goal alone. The righteous man needs a companion, a spouse equally mindful and just who will 'do him good and not evil all the days of her life'. A life-partner of such luminous morality that his heart 'doth safely trust in her, so that he shall have no need of spoil'. And so, in its remarkable finale – just before the curtain falls – this Old Testament book extolling wisdom and virtue closes by incarnating its heady idealism in an astonishing homage to the *concrete* beauty and goodness of God-fearing women (one surely influential for Chaucer's Wife of Bath), a breathtaking, unforgettable praise-song to this 'good thing', this 'favor of the Lord', this ravishing 'wife of thy youth':

Strength and honor are her clothing;
  and she shall rejoice in time to come.
She openeth her mouth with wisdom;
  and in her tongue is the law of kindness.
She looketh well to the ways of her household,
  and eateth not the bread of idleness.
Her children arise up and call her blessed;
  her husband also, and he praiseth her.

May we all be blessed with such radiant partners. And, as we travel through this life, may we recognize that *Proverbs*, in its fierce, uncompromising purity, is a work worthy of our trust.

THE SONG OF SOLOMON

Thy lips, O my spouse, drop as the honeycomb: honey and milk are under thy tongue; and the smell of thy garments is like the smell of Lebanon.

(4:11)

authorised King James version

A.S. Byatt

The Song of Songs is a cry of erotic longing and a description of erotic bliss. It is a lyrical drama whose speakers and episodes run into each other as in a dream or a vision. There is a female voice, which is both virginal and knowing, triumphant and lost. There is a male voice, impatient, exulting, wooing. There is a chorus of unseen commentators, and other groups, the women of Jerusalem, the watchmen, the threescore valiant men who stand around the bed of Solomon. The scene shifts from walled garden to walled city to green bedchamber to the mountains. The woman is black but comely; the man is white and ruddy, with a head like fine gold and with bushy locks, black as a raven. The ending is abrupt and the story is fragmentary. It is a canonical biblical text, and yet there is no mention of God or of religion. It haunts many cultures, eastern and western.

It was ascribed, along with *Ecclesiastes* and *Proverbs*, to King Solomon, son of David. Solomon, according to *The Book of Kings*, had 'seven hundred wives, princesses, and three hundred concubines'; he was famous both for his wisdom and his lechery. The *Song* was thought to refer to his marriage with the daughter of Pharoah, or to his fabled meeting with the Queen of Sheba, who tested him with riddles, the answers to which were to do with the bodies of women.* Jewish commentators saw the woman as Israel, black with her sins; the reading of the *Song* was prescribed during the festival of the Passover. The Fathers of the Christian church were perturbed by its erotic charge, its voluptuous incitation. They assumed that a sacred text must have a spiritual meaning. As Origen wrote in the third century, 'If these things are not to be understood spiritually, are they not simply fabulous tales? If they have no hidden mystery, are they not unworthy of God?' The *Song* became part of an intricate web of allegorical readings of Scripture. These readings constructed both the theology and the poetry of a religion centred on the historical incarnation of the eternal and spiritual. The *Song* became also an extraordinary paradox – a rich, fleshy metaphor for the divine longing that would cause the wise soul to reject the flesh and its desires. Origen's explication turned on the doubleness of the Latin word, *amor*, love, which was used to describe carnal desire and spiritual yearning. Origen himself went as far as self-castration in his search

---

* The queen said, 'Seven there are and nine that enter, two yield the draught and one drinks.' Said he to her: 'Seven are the days of a woman's defilement, and nine the months of pregnancy, two are the breasts that yield the draught and one the child that drinks it.' Whereupon she said to him, 'Thou art wise.' Louis Ginzberg, *Legends of the Bible*, pp. 560ff.

for pure spiritual love. He allegorised the Bride's withdrawal into the marriage chamber as the withdrawal of the pure soul from all extraneous earthly desires.

Origen identified the Bride with Ecclesia, the embattled, sinful Christian church, who had to learn to respond to the loving care and demands of her Divine Spouse, Christ. The *Song*'s imagery of the bridegroom knocking at a locked door, the bride waking too late, became assimilated to Christ's own parable of the sleepy, unwatchful bridesmaidens. In the twelfth century commentators interpreted the *Song* in terms of the Virgin Mary, the Mother-Bride, the sister-spouse, the mediator. The allegory had for them a literal historical meaning, to be teased out. The Bride also became the Hetaira, romantic heroine and childlike maiden, wooed by Christ the very perfect knight. Poems about Mary Magdalene, repentant beauty, spiritual sinner, who broke an alabaster vase of precious ointment over her Lord's feet, used the imagery of the *Song*. The spiritual interpreters, most strikingly St Bernard of Clairvaux, in his sermons on *The Song of Songs*, saw the individual human soul itself as the Beloved, drawn towards Christ initially through love of the created world. The Latin word for the soul is *anima*, which is a feminine word, and it is striking that the allegorical commentaries and interpretations of the *Song* written by celibate monks, take the passive, open, receptive female consciousness as the central consciousness of the drama. The human soul, male or female, in this erotic mysticism, is a woman waiting for her master, her lord, her bridegroom. The saint's rhetoric, like his vision of the *Song*, includes the erotic, lingers over it, only to dismiss it.

> You must not give an earth-bound meaning to this colouring of corruptible flesh, to this red liquid suffused beneath her pearly skin, to enhance her bodily beauty in the pink and white loveliness of her cheeks. For the substance of the soul is incorporeal and invisible . . .

Or

> Shall we imagine for ourselves a huge powerful man, gripped by love for an absent girl, rushing to her desired embraces, bounding over those mountains and hills which we see raised up so high over the plain that their summit seems to penetrate the clouds? It is certainly not proper to fabricate bodily fantasies in this way, and especially when treating of this spiritual Song . . .*

And St Bernard, preaching to the abbots of his order, on 'remembering the breasts' makes them into imagined women and mothers: 'Be gentle, avoid harshness, give up blows, show your breasts: let your bosoms be fat with milk, not swollen with wrath.'

---

* These passages are quoted, with some retranslation, from Anne W Astell, *The Song of Songs in the Middle Ages* (Cornell University Press, 1990). I am much indebted to this excellent book.

The fathers of the church were preaching an incarnate God to an incarnate congregation, creatures made up of flesh and spirit. They could rationalise their treatment of *The Song of Songs* – which is not a rational structure – by saying that its inspired author had used the language of the flesh to entice the incarnate souls to the love of the Incarnate Word, speaking through the flesh. Their ingenuity and resourceful reconstructions and deconstructions can seem both beautiful and absurd to an unbeliever seduced and baffled by the literal presence of the *Song* itself. Is it the nature of the text or the nature of the theology that brings about all the building of these airy places, such a reader may ask her or himself.

The Jungians, as we might expect, have an answer. They are drawn to the *Song* by the presence of the woman and the idea of a marriage. The female persona in the story, or stories, can be seen as the Jungian *anima*, the complementary female self who must be integrated into the psyche for wholeness. The four major feminine archetypes of Jungian psychoanalysis Virgin, Mother, Medial Woman and Hetaira – can all be found easily in the *Song*. A Jungian reading of the *Song* includes the alchemical Coniunctio, the mystical marriage of opposites. In alchemical terms the Shulamite's blackness signifies the 'feminine personification of the prima materia in the *nigredo* stato'. Jung quotes alchemical texts in which the Shulamite attributes her blackness to the original sin of Eve: 'O that the serpent roused up Eve! To which I must testify with the black colour that clings to me.'* 'She is the *anima mundi* or Gnostic Sophia, caught in the dark embraces of *physis*.' Here is a psycho-analytical and alchemical version of the interpretative anxiety about incarnation, spirit and matter. It leads to a consideration of the extraordinary proliferation of quotations, objects, metaphors from the *Song* throughout many centuries and literatures.

Ann Astell gives some beautiful examples of love lyrics, sacred and profane, from the Middle Ages. I myself found *The Song of Songs* everywhere in the thesis I never finished, which was about sensuous metaphors for the spiritual in the seventeenth century, and turned out to be about narratives of fleshly temptations in gardens, from Spenser's 'Bower of Bliss' to *Paradise Lost* and the temptation of Christ in *Paradise Regained*. The words of the *Song* sing enchantingly in English, for instance in Henry Vaughan's 'The Night'.

> God's silent searching flight
> When my Lord's head is filled with dew and all
> His locks are wet with the clear drops of night
> His still, soft call;
> His knocking time; the soul's dumb watch,
> When spirits her fair kinred catch.

Marvell's delightful conceits in 'The Nymph Com-plaining for the Death of her Fawn' combine classical pastoral with the *Song*'s imagery of innocence in a closed

---

* Jung, *Mysterium Coniunctionis*, Collected Works 14, para 591.

garden, lilies and roses, the beloved as a hart or a roe deer on the mountains. And Milton compares his Paradise garden to

> Those gardens feigned
> Or of revived Adonis, or renowned
> Alcinous, host of old Laertes' son,
> Or that, not mystic, where the sapient king
> Held dalliance with his fair Egyptian spouse.
> (*Paradise Lost,* IX, ll. 439–43)

Alastair Fowler, a great editor, points out that Milton is here drawing an analogy between Solomon and Adam, both wise, both uxorious, both lovers in gardens. He points out the ambiguity of the word 'sapient', meaning, in its Latin root, 'gaining knowledge by tasting'. This concept, like most commentary on the Song, finds the spirit in the flesh. Fowler goes on to point out that Milton's references to 'sapience' in *The Song of Songs* tend to associate Solomon with Satan, and with the latter's interest in Eve's beauty, and in the taste of the apples of the Tree of the knowledge of Good and Evil. In *Paradise Lost* (Book v, ll. 40–8), Eve recounts to Adam a dream in which Satan tempts her in a parody of the lover of the *Song*. It is interesting in this context that Solomon turned to the worship of Ashtaroth through the persuasion of his wives.

For it came to pass, when Solomon was old, that his wives turned away his heart after other gods:

and his heart was not perfect with the Lord his God, as was the heart of David his father.

For Solomon went after Ashtoreth the goddess of the Zidonians, and after Milcom, the abomination of the Ammonites . . . (1 Kings 11:4–5)

St Augustine, before Milton, compared the sins of Adam and Solomon, led into temptation by their love for their wives. Modern scholars see *The Song of Songs* as an echo of something more ancient, the marriage songs of the sacred marriages of the ancient Mesopotamian gods and goddesses, Inana and Dumuzi, Ishtar and Tammuz, gods whose worship entailed sacred prostitution, the making of gardens, the mourning of the vanished young god and the celebration of his return with the spring. These deities were, in some versions, brother and sister – 'my sister, my spouse'. The return and the rebirth of Adonis (who was the same god as Tammuz, since Adonis simply means 'Lord') coincided with the Spring, and the return of vegetation.

For, lo, the winter is past, the rain is over and gone;
The flowers appear on the earth;
the time of the singing of birds is come,
and the voice of the turtle is heard in òur land;
The fig tree putteth forth her green figs,
and the vines with the tender grape
give a good smell. Arise, my love, my fair one,
and come away.

Frazer, in *The Golden Bough*, compares the kings of the Bible to the priest-kings of the Syrian Lord Adonis, and quotes St Jerome, who 'tells us that Bethlehem, the traditional birthplace of the Lord, was shaded by a grove of that still older Syrian Lord Adonis, and that where the infant Jesus had wept, the lover of Venus was bewailed.' Jerome, Frazer says, appears to have believed that the grove was planted by heathens to defile the sacred spot. Frazer himself believes that the grove was older, and that in any case the Christian god who was the bread of life, born in Bethlehem, 'the House of Bread' was related to the older corn spirit.

Whatever the spiritual meanings and antecedents, the immediate experience of reading the *Song* is both sensuously exciting and baffling. As a narrative, it does not hold together. Moments of intense dramatic feeling – the Shulamite's description of her rejected blackness, the knocking and vanishing of the bridegroom, her wandering the streets of Jerusalem, the unidentified 'we' expressing concern for their little sister who has no breasts – all these are both entirely memorable and fleeting. The same, in a different way, can be said of the descriptions, concrete and metaphorical, of the bodies of the lovers. The woman is seen as a city with walls and turrets, as a garden enclosed and a fountain sealed, as an army with banners, as a flock of goats, as sheep, as corn and wine, as perfumes. She is both vividly solid and somehow diffused into city, army, riches and jewels, the landscape of pastoral herdsmen, and orchards with every kind of tree. I remember my first bewildered reading, as a western child with a compulsory Bible in her desk, of this dreamworld. What corresponded to that longing for love with which we are all born (or so I supposed) were powerful abstract phrases: 'For love is as strong as death; jealousy is cruel as the grave: the coals thereof are coals of fire, which hath a most vehement flame.'

There was something deliciously disturbing about all the liquids, the milk, wine and honey, something tantalising about the glimpses of bodies and doors. But many of the specific metaphors were disturbing differently – 'thy teeth are as a flock of sheep which go up from the washing, whereof every one beareth twins, and there is not one barren among them.' The analogy between teeth and sheep (whiteness, similarity) seems tenuous, and is made more tenuous by the overloading of the twins and the fertility – it is as though, I intuited even as a child, the speaker is a shepherd congratulating himself on the abundance of his possessions, flocks and women. There is something immediately powerful, in most cultures, I should think, about the virginal images: 'A garden enclosed is my sister, my spouse, a spring shut up, a fountain sealed.'

The image of woman as tree – 'this thy stature is like to a palm tree and thy breasts like clusters of grapes' – allows the imagination to make and combine both flesh and plant. But again and again this is simply not possible. There is an element of excess, of too much, too much fruit; too many riches, too much landscape, too much architecture, eyes like fishpools, nose like a tower of

Lebanon, breasts like twin roes, a creature who in one verse is fair as the moon, clear as the sun, and terrible as an army with banners. When the navel is compared to a round goblet, which wanteth not liquor and the belly is immediately afterwards compared to a heap of wheat set about with lilies, the effect is to make the wine and wheat richly present and the human body shadowy, vanishing, mysterious. Everything is present, the lovers are a whole world, rich and strange, metamorphosed by the poetic, or religious imagination, into both the natural world and the world of human artefacts and precious things. The winds blow from both north and south, the sun and the moon both shine, fountains, wells and streams are full of living water. And the more the metaphors are heaped up, the more they become interchangeable, the more the desire which sings in the *Song* becomes a polymorphous celebration of everything.

Or perhaps of itself, which is why I have always preferred to call it *The Song of Songs*, rather than *The Song of Solomon*. It is a poem about the making of poetry, the naming of the world, the construction of the world by the human imagination, powered by the erotic desire which both Freud and Darwin celebrated also. Later English poets learned from it a kind of eastern poetry which was diffused and exceeding, rather than precise and contained. The mythical erotic English gardens of Tennyson's *Maud* owe much to the *Song*. Tennyson combines his Isle of Wight cedars with the cedars of Lebanon, as he combines the lilies and roses of the *Song* with an English garden. Browning complained that

Tennyson had diffused the feeling that should have been applied to the woman into the landscape. But Tennyson knew what he was doing. He had been reading Persian poetry, and understanding the *Song* in his way.

The *Song* continues to haunt our imaginations, between the absurd and the sublime. Dorothy Sayers' *Busman's Honeymoon* quotes it absurdly. Harriet Vane, watching Lord Peter Wimsey in a blazer, reflects that she has 'married England'. But her lord, on waking after their wedding night, addresses her as 'my Shulamite'.

And in quite another world, the *Song* inhabits some of the greatest and most terrible poetry of our time, the poems in German of Paul Celan. The figure of Shulamith, whose name occurs only once in the Bible, appears in many forms in his work. His riddling poems about terror and loss, about the Holocaust and Israel, mourn both the Rose of Sharon, and, specifically, 'my sister, my spouse', the lost and destroyed. His biographer, John Felstiner, traces the tradition by which Shulamith, whose name is associated with *Shalom*[*] (peace), was seen by the mystical tradition as a figure both for the *Shechinah* (the divine light) and for the promised return to Zion. 'Return, return, O Shulamite; return, return, that we may look upon thee.'[**] She appears in *Todesfuge* (*Deathfugue*) in a repeated, chanted juxtaposition with the doomed Margaret of Goethe's *Faust.*

---

[*] Edward F. Edinger, *The Bible and the Psyche* (Inner City Books, 1986) p. 137.

[**] John Felstiner, *Paul Celan, Poet, Survivor, Jew* (Yale, 1995).

Dein goldenes Haar Margarete
Dein aschenes Haar Sulamith

(your golden hair, Margareta,
your ashen hair, Shulamith)

Here, Shulamith's burned blackness, her ashen hair, are irredeemable, made smoke, buried in the air. Her darkness cancels and darkens Margarete's innocent suffering. This new, dreadful figuration of Shulamith ends a poem as powerful and unforgettable as the *Song* itself. It adds a meaning and a figure that can never again be separated from the changing poetic world of the *Song*, whatever else may be added.

THE BOOK OF ISAIAH

And there shall be upon every high mountain, and upon every high hill, rivers and streams of waters in the day of the great slaughter, when the towers fall. Moreover the light of the moon shall be as the light of the sun, and the light of the sun shall be sevenfold, as the light of seven days, in the day that the Lord bindeth up the breach of his people, and healeth the stroke of their wound.

(30:25–26)

authorised King James version

Peter Ackroyd

We must approach this sacred text with great respect, doubting the ability of our mind to comprehend it and of our tongue to describe it. The book of *Isaiah* is not the work of one writer or one prophet but, like the Homeric epics, incorporates the voices of many authors in a tradition of oral poetry. Yet even though it comprises various sources its shape, like a river made out of many streams, is fluent and harmonious. Within its 66 chapters passages of lyrical melody are pressed up against words of prophetic force, moments of vision vouchsafed beside occasions for denunciation; the narrative combines stories, poems, descriptions, revelations and lamentations. It is, in little, representative of the Bible itself.

The origins of the various texts, original or interpolated, date variously from the eighth to the sixth century BCE. Yet in a book where history and poetry mingle, for devotional or ritual purposes, there is no need to attempt to locate a substratum of real or observable fact; just as the original documents have long since crumbled to dust, so we cannot sift the episodes concerning forgotten battles and distant kings.

The composition of the book itself is more certain – chapters 1 to 39 are the work of several authors, but all moving within a realm concerning prophecies of redemption as well as fierce polemic against pagan idolaters and the profligate among the Lord's own people. The 40th chapter marks the beginning of the work of the 'Deutero-Isaiah', perhaps the single most eloquent and inspiring of all the biblical writers who within 15 verses offers a vision of hope and of redemption for the people of Israel at the same time as, in a magnificent panegyric, he launches an attack upon Babylon and all the powers of this world. The third part, verses 55 to 66, acts as a coda to the first two sections, where interpolated hands have provided passages of prophecy and eschatology.

Harmony itself is achieved through the introduction of very clear formal preoccupations, together with an abiding and overriding concern for rhetorical elaboration and amplitude. Scholars of the Hebrew text, for example, have enumerated instances of alliteration and onomatopoeia designed expressly to lift a cadence or emphasise a phrase. The construction of the phrase itself is of the utmost significance, where simplicity and force work together in unison. That is why some of the lines from *Isaiah* have entered folk memory beyond the tribes of Israel –' and they shall beat their swords into plowshares (2:4) . . . For unto us a child is born, unto us a son is given (9:6) . . . The wolf also shall dwell with the lamb, and the leopard shall lie down with the kid (11:6) . . . How art thou fallen from heaven, O Lucifer, son of the morning! (14:12) . . . Let us eat and drink; for tomorrow we shall die (22:13) . . . All flesh is grass (40:6) . . . There is no peace, saith my God, to the wicked' (57:21) . . . No rest for the wicked. The provenance of some of these phrases is disputed as not springing from the lips of the 'historical' Isaiah, but their relevance and influence are not in dispute. These are words which have literally changed the consciousness of the world.

Yet they are important, too, in maintaining the urgency and relevance of a narrative which speaks to many nations concerning the central aspirations of humankind. That is also why the economy and brevity of *Isaiah* allow a single phrase to denote the passage of many years or the history of one city. The utter simplicity of the author's voice emerges in passages of perfect pitch and power – 'Then shalt thou call [upon the Lord] . . . , and he shall say, "Here I am."' (58:9). Here I am. It is as if the whole world resounded with God's voice, and we may recall here William Blake's visionary conversation with Isaiah – 'I saw no God nor heard any,' the prophet informed the poet, 'in a finite organical perception; but my senses discover'd the infinite in everything.'

This in fact is one of the glories of *Isaiah*, where the grandeur or ineffability of the 'infinite' is expressed in terms of a local landscape or a specific activity, so that 'the burden of the valley of vision' (22:1) can be carried by details of weaving or of threshing. Here the aspiration towards the infinite and the illimitable is combined with a very clear and articulate presentation of contemporary realities. Israel is 'a lodge in a garden of cucumbers' (1:8), and the Lord tells Isaiah to walk towards 'the end of the conduit of the upper pool in the highway of the fuller's field' (7:3). The Lord shall tread down Moab 'even as straw is trodden down for the dunghill' (25:10) and will put forth his hands 'as he that swimmeth spreadeth forth his hands to swim' (25:11). *Isaiah* celebrates a universe in which the particulars of the social and natural world are revealed as tokens of spiritual activity, where world and spirit do indeed become one, like the swimmer, in a living pulse of energy – 'for the earth shall be full of the knowledge of the Lord, as the waters cover the sea' (11:9).

The economy of effect, together with the use of repetition, renders these sacred verses not unlike the texts of Anglo-Saxon poetry – or, indeed, the expression of any bardic people. The recitation may even have been accompanied by music, so that the whole narrative becomes a kind of performance in which the aspirations of both orator and audience alike are embodied. No one can ignore, either, the dramatic aspects of *Isaiah* where, for example, the anonymous author proclaims the fate of one unhappy man – 'He is despised and rejected of men; a man of sorrows, and acquainted with grief' (53:3). This has often been characterised as a prophecy of Christ's passion, yet it is more appropriately and less anachronistically seen as a most dramatic and human revelation of the outcast. In that sense, like the rest of *Isaiah*, it becomes a story of universal significance rather than a sample of pre-Christian revelation.

There has been much discussion, in recent years, of the Bible as a literary rather than a sacred or historical text. Certainly the narrative devices are clear, with affiliations to western poetry and fiction. There is, for example, satire approaching an almost Swiftian vision of disgust at the flesh, in the description of the women of Zion 'with stretched forth necks and wanton eyes, walking and mincing as they go, and making a tinkling with their feet' (3:16), or in the depiction of the priests of Ephraim so drunk that 'all tables are full of vomit and filthiness' (28:8). But there are other forms of narrative in place here, as mysterious and as melodious as anything in epic poetry – 'And the posts of the door moved at the voice of him that cried, and the house was filled with smoke' (6:4). 'And his heart was moved, and the heart of his people, as the trees of the wood are moved with the wind' (7:2). 'For the heavens shall vanish away like smoke, and the earth shall wax old like a garment' (51:6).

Coleridge once remarked, of cadences like this, that the first chapter of *Isaiah* might be 'reduced to complete hexameters . . . so true is it that wherever passion was, the language became a sort of metre'. In truth the words of *Isaiah* are neither prose nor poetry but, rather, a series of incandescent utterances which effortlessly find their true form. That is why the question of whether this is a poetic rather than a sacred text is redundant – there is no necessary distinction between the two since the highest poetry is always a manifestation of the sacred, while the most sacred insights will necessarily take on the vesture of poetry.

As such the effect of *Isaiah* upon European literature has been extensive and profound; its plangent combination of prophetic passages, with visionary epiphanies and lyrical enchantments, have affected the understanding of epic and pastoral as well as the nature of poetry itself. It stands out like a great melody, informing the future and irradiating the past.

THE BOOKS OF JONAH, MICAH AND NAHUM

Then Jonah prayed unto the Lord his God out of the fish's belly, and said, 'I cried by reason of mine affliction unto the Lord, and he heard me; out of the belly of hell cried I, and thou heardest my voice. For thou hadst cast me into the deep, in the midst of the seas; and the floods compassed me about: all thy billows and thy waves passed over me.'

(2:1–3)

authorised King James version

Alasdair Gray

The thirty-nine books called The Old Testament in the King James Bible show the state of the Jews between 900 and 100 BC and preserve legends from more ancient times. They were edited into their present form by scholars defending their culture from an empire ruling the place where they lived: an empire of people equally clever and literate: Greeks whose books were as various as their gods. Jews were then unique in worshipping a single God: their folklore, laws, politics and poetry kept mentioning him. The editors arranged these books in the chronological order of the subject matter, producing a story of their people from prehistoric times and making their God the strongest character in world fiction. It began with a second-century BC poem telling how he made the universe and people like a poet, out of words, followed by a fifth-century BC tale of how he made man like a potter, out of clay. It then showed God adapting to his worshippers from prehistoric times to their own.

Adam, Cain and Noah find God punitive but soothed

by the smell of burnt flesh, mostly animal. He connives with the tricks of Abraham and Isaac, polygamous nomads who get cattle or revenge by prostituting a wife or cheating foreigners and relatives. When Moses leads Jewish tribes out of Egypt God commands them like a Pharaoh, promising unlimited protection for unlimited obedience. He is a war god when they invade Palestine, smiting them with plague when they do not kill every man, woman, child and animal in a captured city. Their leaders (called prophets because God tells them the future) are fathers of tribal families and military commanders until they get land and cities of their own where (as in other lands) wealth is managed by official landlords and priests who exploit the poor. New kinds of prophet then arise: poets inspired by moral rage who speak for the exploited. They say that if Jewish rulers don't obey God by being just and merciful he will use the might of foreigners to smash their new-made kingdoms. That happens. From 680 BC to 1948 Jews are ruled by foreign empires, first Assyrian and at last British. They outlive so many empires that Norwegian Ibsen calls them the aristocrats of world history, for they can survive without a land and government.

That was not wholly true. They were governed by the words of their prophets, especially those in the last Old Testament books who said the Jewish God is also God of all people, even people who oppress them; that God has created Jews to keep his words alive until the whole world learns justice and mercy by obeying him; that before then Jews should welcome suffering as punishment for sin or tests of faith. After the first destruction of Jerusalem in 586 BC this must have sounded a new policy to those who wanted to repossess a national territory gained (as all nations have gained territory) by killing folk. No wonder many Jews assimilated with foreigners and the faithful sometimes sang psalms begging God to leave them alone.

The book of *Jonah* is a prose comedy about a Jew who wants God to leave him alone and cannot grasp that God's policy is now for those of every nation.

Jonah is an unwilling prophet. His Jewish conscience orders him to denounce the wicked Assyrian empire in its capital city so he at once sails towards a different city where he hopes foreign gods will prevail over his own. This breaks the first of the ten commandments: *You shall have no other God than me* (*Deuteronomy* 5): hence the tempest. The international crew see it is aimed at someone aboard. Many verses describe their reluctance to fling Jonah out, even when he tells them it is the one way to save themselves. The book is insisting that mercy is not just a Jewish virtue; but out Jonah goes and God saves him in the belly of a fish. Here the prophet chants a psalm saying God can save those who cry unto him from the belly of hell. This hell is not the eternal torture chamber later adopted by official Christianity. For Jews hell is the worst that living people can suffer and Jonah IS suffering it, unless the fish intestines are a cosy place. But now he knows that God is always with him and he need not fear death.

Then comes a parody of *Exodus*, Chapter 11, perhaps

the cruellest book in the Old Testament. In it the God of Moses sends Pharaoh a message then hardens Pharaoh's heart to reject it, giving Moses an excuse to condemn all Egyptian first-born children and cattle to death by plague. But God uses Jonah to send the Assyrians a message that softens their king's heart. The king leads his people into abandoning their evil ways, so *God repented of the evil that he had said that he would do unto them; and he did it not* (*Jonah* 3:10). This contradicts the Mosaic code, which says evil MUST be rewarded with evil.

So Jonah learns he is not a scourge in the hand of God, like Moses, Joshua and Samson, but a reformer, and like many reformers he now looks stupid. It is obvious that the enemy king who thought his people might be persuaded to deserve mercy knew more about God than God's Hebrew prophet. Jonah's short but influential career ends not with a bang but with his dismal whimper: *I knew that thou art a gracious God, and merciful, . . . Therefore now, O Lord, take, I beseech thee, my life from me, for it is better for me to die than to live* (*Jonah* 4:2–3). God cuts this self-pitying cackle with a short question: *Doest thou well to be angry?* (*Jonah* 4:4) Jonah is too cowardly or childish to admit anger and squats outside the city determined to die by sunstroke if the promise of destruction is not fulfilled. Not even the mercy of miraculous shade cast over him softens this determination. The shade is withdrawn. In a fever Jonah hears God repeat something like his last question. He now answers truthfully and is favoured by words framed like another question. They suggest reasons for both God's action and his inaction: most evil is caused by folly; widespread slaughter is not the best cure if a warning of disaster helps folk to change their ways. We are not told if Jonah learns these lessons because they are meant for *us*.

Believers and unbelievers have argued pointlessly about the truth of Jonah's book because they did not know great truths can be told in fantasies. It was known by editors who put *Jonah* before *Micah* and *Nahum*, realistic books about the destruction of Jerusalem and Nineveh.

Micah starts a prophetic sermon in verse by denouncing the Jews who live in Samaria: God has let Assyria enslave them for disobeying him; soon the princes and priests of Jerusalem will be conquered too, for they seek wealth and luxury instead of justice and mercy, oppressing the poor of their own nation while thinking God's forgiveness can be bought by animal sacrifices. Micah foretells a disastrous but not hopeless future: after much warfare the whole world will find peace by accepting the one true God, for a Jewish ruler from the little town of Bethlehem will become lord of every nation. This prophecy must have inspired hope and dread in every imaginative child born afterwards in Bethlehem.

Nahum came eighty years later. He was probably an Assyrian slave when all Jewish territory had been conquered as Micah foretold. Nahum saw the destruction of Nineveh by the combined armies of Babylon and Persia: these killed and enslaved the people and washed the city away by channelling the River Tigris into it. The only grand truth in Nahum's triumphant song is that nations who keep living by armaments will perish by them. Most governments, including the British, think this only true of foreign nations. I quote from Tom Leonard's *On the Mass Bombing of Iraq and Kuwait, Commonly Known as 'The Gulf War' with Leonard's Shorter Catechism.* AK Press published it in 1991.

Q. What did Britain take part in on Tuesday, February 19, 1991?

A. It took part in what was at that point 'one of the most ferocious attacks on the centre of Baghdad', using bombers and Cruise missiles fired from ships.

Q. What did John Major say about the bombing the next day?

A. He said: 'One is bound to ask about attacks such as these: what sort of people is it that can carry them out? They certainly are consumed with hate. They are certainly sick of mind, and they can be certain of one thing – they will be hunted and hunted until they are found.'

(He was talking about 5 lb of explosive left in a litter basket at Victoria Station in London. This killed one person and critically injured three.)

Major's government contained people privately enriched by weapon sales to both Britain's army and the army of the dictator we fought. We fought him again before Christmas 1998 when our most highly respected newspapers said that, though wicked and undemocratic, this dictator had better stay in power to stop Iraq falling apart and increasing the cost of our petrol. Meanwhile, since our troops in 1991 fired bullets tipped with uranium, babies are now being born in Iraq with distorted bodies and heads, others without heads.

When a child, Ernest Levy lost faith in a purely national god by living through Auschwitz and Belsen. He became a cantor in a Glasgow synagogue and now believes God is the innocent, creative, spiritual part of everyone. This sounds like the merciful God of *Jonah* but can any God be merciful to a nation that does not repent of the evil it does? That makes, sells and uses what kills, cripples and warps even the unborn? Jesus learned from *Jonah*, *Micah* and *Nahum* what governments of Britain and the USA refuse to learn from Jesus. They act like Moses and Elijah, deliberately killing and diseasing thousands of civilians who cannot harm them. They do it without the old Hebrew excuse of being slaves wanting freedom or wanderers needing a homeland, without the Crusaders' excuse of defending a True Faith, without the Liberal excuse of spreading democracy. The one idea behind such war is that any number of foreigners can be killed to keep up global company profits, though politicians give nicer-sounding reasons. The inevitable victory of big arms-selling nations over small arms-buying ones has provoked counter-attacks. Just now these have killed very few, but enough to prove that this world ruled by greed is hatching one ruled by revenge. Old and New Testaments should teach us to reform our ways for our children's sake.

I belong to a small nation that for centuries has exported more soldiers and weapons than the defence of it ever needed. It now contains more destructive nuclear missiles and launching machines than any nation outside the USA. England has the good sense to contain hardly any. I hope the reform of Britain starts in Scotland.

THE WISDOM OF SOLOMON

For wisdom is more moving than any motion; she passeth and goeth through all things by reason of her pureness. For she is the breath of the power of God, and a pure influence flowing from the glory of the Almighty.

(7:24–25)
authorised King James version

Piers Paul Read

As a child I was greatly impressed by the story in the Bible of how King Solomon came to acquire great 'riches, and wealth, and honour' and innumerable concubines and wives. God appeared to him in a dream and promised to give him anything he asked for. Solomon chose wisdom which so pleased God that he gave him everything else besides. Here was the formula, surely, for the God-fearing hedonist to have his cake and eat it.

Despite Solomon's example, however, I suspect that few of us, if given the same opportunity, would make the same choice today. Wisdom has gone out of fashion. The very word is one of a number in the English language that we find frequently in works of literature but seldom in everyday life. In the half-century that has passed since I reached the age of reason, I can scarcely remember ever having heard a philosopher, statesman or indeed anyone else described as wise. Our most common terms of approbation tend to be 'intelligent', 'clever', 'astute', 'shrewd' or 'high-powered'. The skills of our rulers lie in reading the runes of focus groups and opinion polls, and the image they want to project is of someone vigorous, forceful, youthful, dynamic – not wise. In the academic world, professors are appointed for their specialist knowledge, not their overall sagacity, and university chancellors are chosen more for their abilities as administrators and fundraisers than as the elders of their people.

Even philosophers who, from the etymology of the word that denotes their calling (love of wisdom), might be expected to give it some meaning, are no longer wise. Continental philosophers spew out incoherent gibberish while British linguistic philosophers have narrowed their focus to the point of irrelevance. The Professor who taught me at Cambridge was actually called John Wisdom but he restricted speculation in our seminars to how we could know whether or not our desks existed. Bertrand Russell and A J Ayer were undoubtedly highly intelligent men but, to judge from their private lives, could not be called wise.

What do we learn about wisdom from *The Wisdom of Solomon?* Had I read it as a child, I would have been disappointed to discover that it is not a handbook on how to have your cake and eat it. Nor was it in fact written by Solomon: his putative authorship was as a commonly used literary convention. Modern scholarship suggests that it was composed by a Jewish sage living in Alexandria [in Egypt] in the first century before Christ. Alexandria at the time had a largely Greek population and an essentially Greek culture: *The Wisdom of*

Solomon was written in Greek and quotes from the Greek version of Scripture but it is addressed to Jews – reminding them of their special destiny and warning them against the spiritual and intellectual temptations that surround them – mysterious cults, pagan rituals, sophisticated philosophical systems. It has none of the anguish of the Book of *Job* or the pithiness of *Proverbs*, but it is fascinating first as a text that was familiar to the first Christians and then as a critique of the kind of sceptical, hedonistic society that we find in the developed world today.

The influence of *The Wisdom of Solomon* on St Paul and the Christian Evangelists, particularly St John, make it a link between the Old and New Testaments. The description of Wisdom could be that of the Holy Spirit: 'For she is the breath of the power of God, and a pure influence flowing from the glory of the Almighty: therefore can no defiled thing fall into her. For she is the brightness of everlasting light, the unspotted mirror of the power of god, and the image of his goodness . . . and remaining in herself, she maketh all things new: and in all ages, entering into holy souls, she maketh them friends of God, and prophets'. (7:25–27).

There is also the author's esteem for virginity: 'Better to have no children and to have virtue . . .' (4:1). 'Wherefore blessed is the barren that is undefiled, which hath not known the sinful bed: she shall have fruit in the visitation of souls. And blessed is the eunuch, which his hands hath wrought no iniquity, nor imagined wicked things against God' (3:13–14). This was a radical departure from the accepted notion in Judaism that fertility was a sign of God's blessing and sterility a sign of his disapprobation; and it echoes the passage in St Matthew's Gospel (19:12) where Christ blesses those who make themselves eunuchs for the sake of the Kingdom of God – the text that justifies celibacy as a Christian ideal.

The Wisdom of Solomon's critique of the permissive society of Alexandria in the first century BC goes some way to explain why, in an agnostic age, wisdom has gone out of fashion. To the author, God is the source of wisdom and it is vain to believe that we can reach a true understanding of our condition through the use of our own intellectual resources. 'For what man is he that can know the counsel of God? Or who can think what the will of the Lord is? For the thoughts of mortal men are miserable, and our devices are but uncertain. For the corruptible body presseth down the soul, and the earthy tabernacle weigheth down the mind that museth upon many things' (9:13–15).

Thus, to be wise, a man must be virtuous because sin blocks the conduit from God to man. A virtuous king will be a wise king and therefore a good king, benefitting the community he serves. 'But the multitude of the wise is the welfare of the world: and a wise king is the upholding of his people' (6:24). The benefits of wisdom accrue also to the individual and those around him while the sinners' families share their fate – their 'wives are reckless, their children depraved, their descendants accursed'.

However, the source of the happiness that comes with

wisdom is not necessarily the riches, honour and triumph of a Solomon: wisdom will ensure that even if a man does not prosper in this life, he will find his reward in the next. Here we see how the Platonic distinction between body and soul solves the riddle posed by the earlier book of *Job*, and by our observation of the suffering of innocent people. In contrast to the prevailing Jewish view that prosperity and longevity are marks of divine approbation, the author warns the reader not to search for happiness in precisely those things that came to Solomon with his gift of wisdom – honour, riches, concubines and wives. The first twenty verses of the second chapter are in fact a satirical apologia of those who believe that we should eat, drink and be merry for tomorrow we die. 'Our life is short and tedious . . . the breath in our nostrils is as smoke . . . Come on, therefore, let us enjoy the good things that are present: and let us speedily use the creatures like as in youth. Let us fill ourselves with costly wine and ointments: and let no flower in the spring pass by us' (2:1–2, 6–7).

To the modern ear, there is something bleak and perhaps a little crabby about the teaching of this Jewish sage. Was he, one wonders, jilted in his youth or passed over for promotion? The nearest equivalent in the present day might be a disgruntled old Catholic priest in San Francisco or New York who feels that society has gone to the dogs – everywhere; 'manslaughter, theft, and dissimulation, corruption, unfaithfulness, tumults, perjury, disquieting of good men, forgetfulness of good turns, defiling souls, changing of kind, disorder in marriages, adultery, and shameless uncleanness' (14:25–6). He seems to relish the fate that awaits sinners: and is delighted that God vents his wrath on their children too, but he is not as vindictive as he at first seems. He wants to persuade his readers that they will benefit from Wisdom because it fosters temperance and prudence, justice and fortitude 'which are such things, as men can have nothing more profitable in their life' (8:7). In other words, wisdom, like virtue, is its own reward.

Although Wisdom is not given an existence distinct from that of God in *The Wisdom of Solomon*, it is personified in the female gender and there are passages, as in *Solomon's Song*, where the author uses the language of a male lover. 'I preferred her before sceptres and thrones, and esteemed riches nothing in comparison of her. Neither compared I unto her any precious stone, because all gold in respect of her is as a little sand, and silver shall be counted as clay before her. I loved her above health and beauty, and chose to have her instead of light; for the light that cometh from her never goeth out' (7:8–10).

In an age when enquiry is perceived as something aggressive that attacks the pit face of the unknown with the pick-axe of the intellect, or seeks to dissect the mysterious with the scalpel of an analytical intelligence, it is surprising to find knowledge presented as feminine – intuitive, passive, receptive. However, this conforms to the perception of one of the few thinkers in modern times who I *would* call wise – the psychoanalyst C G Jung.

Jung was a revered figure in my childhood: my father, Herbert Read, greatly admired him and published his collected works. But he balked at Jung's answer, when asked if he believed in God: *I do not believe, I know.* Like many in his generation, my father was a professed agnostic but, as G K Chesterton once wrote, when we cease to believe in God, we do not believe in nothing, we believe in anything – and the god worshipped by my father was art.

How is this relevant to *The Wisdom of Solomon?* In its final section, which describes the role of Wisdom in the deliverance of the Jews led by Moses from the Egyptians, there is a contemptuous digression on idolatry which, according to the author, brings all kinds of evils in its wake – fornication, adultery, orgies and infanticide. At first sight, it seems difficult to point to any modern equivalent to the worship of graven images: perhaps the closest, in a major world religion, is the Hindu's veneration of his different gods.

But if the author of *The Wisdom of Solomon* was to be miraculously transported into one of the great metropolises of the modern world, what would he think? In Wall Street or the City, would he not see a multitude worshipping a golden calf? And if he were to visit our great art galleries, with their august spaces and imposing portals, might he not mistake them for temples? Looking at the solemn, reverential expression of those studying the modern works of art, would he not suppose that here was the worship of idols – images a man 'hath carved . . . diligently, when he had nothing else to do, and formed . . . by the skill of his understanding, and fashioned . . . to the image of a man' (13:13–14). Would he not conclude, with some justice, that at the end of the twentieth century art has largely replaced religion as the object of popular devotion? Are not the great galleries our temples? And do not pilgrims stream to the shrines of culture – the Guggenheim Museum in Bilbao, the Museum of Modern Art in New York? Can we really say that idolatry is a thing of the past?

I ask this with some regret because my father devoted much of his life to the cause of contemporary art – and indeed came to be known in Britain as the apostle of modernism. But his was a god that failed. Towards the end of his life he wrote that he had always found less sustenance in the works of those who deny the reality of a living God – he cited Marx, Nietzsche, Freud, Shaw and Russell – than in those of writers such as George Herbert, Pascal, Spinoza, Kierkegaard, Gerard Manley Hopkins and Simone Weil who affirmed God's existence. He had come to realise, like the Jewish sage in Alexandria twenty-one centuries earlier, that wisdom is not a human accomplishment but a gift from God.

THE NEW TESTAMENT

THE GOSPEL ACCORDING
TO MATTHEW

And seeing the multitudes, he went up into a mountain: and when he was set, his disciples came unto him. And he opened his mouth, and taught them, saying, 'Blessed are the poor in spirit: for theirs is the kingdom of heaven. Blessed are the meek: for they shall inherit the earth.'

(5:1–5)

authorised King James version

Francisco Goldman

Spina proposed various goals. One was to form gather ings for reading the Bible. Another – which must have seemed quite strange – was to practice Christianity.
– Jorge Luis Borges,
'German Literature in the Age of Bach'

In Gabriel García Márquez's *Love in the Time of Cholera,* Dr Juvenal Urbino teaches his insolent parrot 'selected passages from the *Gospel according to Saint Matthew.*' Climbing into the upper branches of a mango tree to rescue the parrot, the elderly doctor plunges to his death. So the parrot is a harbinger of chaos and death, but the doctor's demise also sets in motion the novel's extraordinary love story. The metaphorical choice of putting the *Gospel of Saint Matthew* in the mouth of a Caribbean parrot is apt in more ways than one.

Without a doubt, the greatest event of the millennium now ending was the discovery and conquest of the New World. The Spanish historian Francisco López de Gomara called it 'the most major thing since the creation of the world, only excepting the incarnation and death of He who created it.' The story of the Bible among us in the Americas – and I speak as an American, the son of immigrants to the United States, a Russian-Jewish father and a Guatemalan-Catholic mother – is of course completely different from its story in the Old World. The Old and New Testaments evolved over millennia there alongside the civilizations that wrote them and formed themselves according to their teachings, but in the Americas, the Bible arrived all at once, a completed text, undoubtedly spreading chaos and death, but also beauty and love and mystery.

The classic narrative of the first prolonged encounter between Europeans and *los naturales*, the Indians, is *The True History of the Conquest of New Spain*, written by Bernal Díaz del Castillo, who marched with Hernán Cortés through Mexico. As the relatively small army of conquistadores marched from village to village on their fateful way to the bloody denouement in the capital of the Aztec Empire, they encountered a civilization clearly in the grip of Satan, one that worshiped horrific 'dragon-like' stone idols through bloody human sacrifice and practiced cannibalism – practiced it with gluttonous enthusiasm. The native priests were smeared in blood and reeked of human carrion, wore their hair down to their waists, and liked to sodomize each other in their sacred pyramid sanctums, while Indian caciques offered their aristocratic virgin young daughters up to Cortés and his captains in submissive (and sometimes treacherous) gestures of brotherhood. In village after village, when violence could be avoided, Cortés responded in the same way: speaking through Doña Marina, 'La Malintzín,' his Indian translator and lover, he introduced the Indians to Christianity. Indeed, strikingly in the manner of the Jesus of the *Gospel according to Saint Matthew*, Cortés wandered in the wilderness and from village to village, teaching, 'Stop your sacrifices and do not eat the meat of your fellow man, nor commit sodomy, nor the other ugly things you tend to do, because that is the command of Our Lord God, who we adore and believe, and gives us life and death, and leads us to heaven.' And Cortés would tell the caciques that not until their virgin daughters had been baptized would the Spanish consent to receive and 'know them as women.' The Spanish friars accompanying Cortés would attempt to teach about the Virgin Mary, who conceived without sin, and the Divine Infant, who was the Son of God, and the meaning of the crucifixion. Sometimes, if they found themselves in a position of uncontested strength, the Spaniards would smash the Indian idols; usually, they built an altar and attempted to conduct a mass and, before marching on, raise a cross, and sometimes cleaned up one of the Indian priests, dressed him in white robes, and instructed him in how to keep the altar neat. Once one of the friars protested that it was too early to be leaving a cross 'in the power of such a pueblo, because they are shameless and without fear,' and this might well have been when one of the most well known of the many instantly recognizable proverbs from *Matthew* was first spoken in the New World: 'Give not that which is holy unto the dogs, neither cast ye your pearls before swine, lest they trample them under their feet, and turn again and rend you.'

It probably would have been this book, *Matthew*, that the Spanish friars would have preached and read from. Jorge Luis Borges called Jesus Christ 'the greatest of oral teachers' and reminded us that, except for a few words drawn on the ground, Jesus left no writings. It fell to his disciples and followers to write up his life and teachings. Out of the many Gospels subsequently written, only four were canonized in the New Testament, and the rest were eventually designated as 'apocryphal.' Matthew's Gospel is the most fundamental, the one that is perhaps most like a manifesto of the new religion. (The apocryphal Gospels include one attributed to the 'pseudo Matthew' and another, attributed to Thomas, which amusingly describes the growing pains and antics of an impudent child Jesus.) Composed sometime toward the end of the first century after Jesus' death, Matthew's Gospel displays a sense of limited continuity with Judaism while enunciating the manifold terms of a sharp split. A. N. Wilson has described *Matthew* as 'by paradox an intensely Jewish, and an intensely anti-Jewish work – it is indeed the great Ur-text of anti-Semitism.' In Matthew, which is constructed as 'a miniature Torah,' Jesus, like Moses, 'goes up to a mountain and delivers a New Law to his followers.' And that law is like a step-by-step primer, delivered mainly in parables, on how to live one's life in preparation for the Final Judgment. *Matthew* defines and explains the will of God, and where to look for God, and what the comportment of a Christian should be. Eternal salvation is set forth as the fruit of a life of discipline and faith and work, rather than as the result of a long-awaited messianic apocalypse.

Of course, there are many ways of reading, hearing, experiencing *Matthew* – for example, through the heavenly music of Bach's *Saint Matthew's Passion*. Or through the fire-and-brimstone castigations of a fundamentalist pastor, locked into *Matthew*'s graphic images of the eternal suffering awaiting all sinners, which, if this implacably exacting book is the only authority (this is the Gospel that announces that not only adultery but merely looking with lust in your heart is a sin) condemns nearly every last one of us. A contemporary reader might peruse the Gospel with no other object than to deduce which passages Dr Urbino might have chosen to teach his parrot. But I am not a partisan of simply literary readings of the Bible. I admire the attitude of the Catholic Flannery O'Connor, who, when Mary McCarthy said that she thought of the Host as a symbol, responded, 'Well, if it's a symbol, to hell with it.' I do not practice a religion, but I try to read the Bible with respect for its intentions, as the Holy Book to which all of us who live in the West are, one way or another, inextricably bound. It was to worship this book as they pleased that the Protestant English and Dutch settled North America, the heathen-devils they found already living there be damned – or exterminated. In Spanish America, this book was imposed as essential to the faith of the Catholic empire, in whose dominion everyone had to either profess belief or be enslaved and killed, often slowly and horribly.

That newly washed and shorn Indian priest, in his new white linen smock. Did he keep the altar clean? Did he spread the new teachings? Did he compose an apocryphal Aztec Gospel of his own that has since been lost to time? What most impressed him in the teachings of the Spanish fathers?

Was he impressed when they read from the *Gospel according to Saint Matthew*, 'The Kingdom of heaven is at hand.' and 'Heal the sick, cleanse the lepers, raise the dead, cast out devils: freely have ye received, freely give. Provide neither gold, nor silver, nor brass in your purses.' How did this sound, coming from the gold-obsessed, smallpox-plague-spreading Spanish conquistadores and their friars?

Or: 'Behold, I send you forth as sheep in the midst of wolves: be ye therefore as wise as serpents, and harmless as doves. But beware of men: for they will deliver you up to the councils, and they will scourge you in their synagogues.' This certainly must have sounded like good advice: the enemy warning against himself.

Did he respond to the thrillingly strange images, the poetry of angels, the bewitching mysteries of parable and metaphor: 'and, behold, the whole herd of swine ran violently down a steep place into the sea, and perished in the waters'; 'But the very hairs of your head are all numbered.' And: 'The son of man shall send forth his angels, and they shall gather out of his kingdom all things that offend, and them which do iniquity, and shall cast them into a furnace of fire: there shall be wailing and gnashing of teeth.'

Did he weep during the eternally moving scene of the crucifixion, with pity for the Jesus who cries, 'My God, my God, why hast thou forsaken me?' and with offended pity for the Jews, an entire people condemned unto eternity in this Gospel as those responsible for the revilement, suffering, and death of Jesus? (Perhaps, as we enter a new millennium, it is time for a Third Testament, one that will preserve the beautiful and give us many new and as yet unimagined teachings, and not set religion against religion – to be dictated and written by both Jesus and 'J' the redactor, returned to earth.)

In *Matthew*, Jesus defines the greatest commandant as 'Thou shalt love the Lord thy God with all thy heart, and with all thy soul, and with all thy mind.' The second greatest, he says, 'is like unto it, Thou shalt love thy neighbor as thyself.'

For all of its beautiful teachings, indeed because of them, it is impossible, in our American, in our worldly, context not to read and regard the *Gospel according to Saint Matthew* as its own negation as well – as inevitably evocative of all the horrors, injustice, and racist and hypocritical acts committed in its name. Thus the exemplary response of Hatuy, the cacique of the Indians being exterminated in Cuba, who said that if Heaven was where the Spaniards went, then he wanted to go to Hell.

Then why is Latin America so devoutly and often inspiringly and movingly Christian? At least one answer

(I don't deny that there are many) is to be found at the heart of the teachings in the *Gospel according to Saint Matthew.* A Catholic priest in Guatemala once told me that this teaching was, for him, the heart of Catholicism, that you could throw out all the rest and, keeping just that one parable, justify faith.

Guatemala certainly feels biblical. Sheep, swine, donkeys, serpents – these are everywhere, as are centurions, all manner of wandering false prophets, pharisees, lepers, and whores. The poor, rural, mainly Mayan landscape has an aura of the miraculous; as a setting it is the perfect backdrop for religious parables about fields both barren and fertile, fruits and harvests, hunger and plenty.

For thirty-six years a civil war spread death over the country as if in a biblical plague. An evangelical Protestant pastor who became military dictator of the country directed one of the most horrifying campaigns of violence, invoking the name of God to justify waging a campaign of genocide (as the United Nations has defined it) against the rural Mayan population. It is a country so astoundingly gripped by greed and corruption that a mere 2 percent of the population owns some 98 percent of the wealth. Children routinely die of diseases that were probably curable even in the time of Jesus. I have a relative in Guatemala who once tried to establish a barefoot doctor program so that rudimentarily trained people could at least give out such basics as dysentery medicine; his first seventeen barefoot doctors were almost immediately murdered or chased into exile;

he was derided as a 'communist' and, in grief and guilt, suffered a massive stroke. I remember how, only a few years ago, sitting in his upscale clinic's office, I asked him what he thought Guatemala most needed and he said, 'For Jesus Christ to come back to earth and teach people how to act better.' That wasn't a very scientific answer; the doctor smiled back at what must have been my openly skeptical expression. 'Isn't this the devil's reign?' he asked. 'Is that any more unbelievable?'

During those years, I began to realize that it was religious faith – whether essentially Catholic or Protestant or Catholic-Mayan or even Jewish (I am thinking of certain fellow Jews in that country's human-rights community, of the Jewish sense of justice and the twentieth-century commitment to fight Nazism in all its strains) – that sustained so many, with dignity and even courage, through so much harrowing and unrelenting hardship. And only the Catholic Church, for all its internal contradictions, stood up with any effectiveness and consistency on behalf of the poor. Of course, because of this many priests and nuns and religious activists were murdered. I'll never forget the defiance on display on the walls of the ancient church in Santiago Atitlán, where in 1979 Father Stan Rother had been murdered by soldiers in the rectory, a martyr to the same violence still engulfing the town a decade and a half later. With little pastel pieces of paper, each piece of paper bearing someone's hand-printed name, two large paper crosses had been put up on the wall, one commemorating all those from the town known to have been murdered in the violence, and the other all those who had been 'disappeared.' Those paper crosses seemed the work of angels, the naming of unnameable names.

'Whoever shall lose his life for my sake shall find it,' says Jesus in the *Gospel according to Saint Matthew*, and from Father Rother to the great human rights activist Bishop Juan Gerardi, murdered in Guatemala City a year ago, Guatemalan clergy have shown their readiness to live by that word. But what did Jesus mean, by 'for my sake'?

Of course, one of the most controversial teachings of Jesus in *Matthew* is the remarkably strong stance taken against the rich, and on behalf of the poor. This is the Gospel wherein it is said, 'It is easier for a camel to go through the eye of a needle, than for a rich man to enter the kingdom of God.' (And even the disciples, as if exasperated, respond, 'Who then can be saved?') But is Jesus' hostility to the rich, and his insistence on the superiority of the poor, enough to inspire martyrs, or enough even to solely comfort the poor?

The great metaphor at the heart of the *Gospel according to Saint Matthew* is that those who suffer and those who show love for those who suffer are joined through suffering and grace to Jesus Christ. That is the lesson of the great parable the priest told me was enough to justify his faith. Jesus announces, 'Come, ye blessed of my Father, inherit the kingdom prepared for you from the foundation of the world: For I was an hungered, and ye gave me meat: I was thirsty, and ye

gave me drink: I was a stranger, and ye took me in . . .
I was in prison, and ye came unto me.' And the righteous people Jesus is addressing answer, 'Lord, when saw
we thee an hungered, and fed thee?' They don't recall
helping or feeding Jesus, or finding him in prison,
because they saw only poor, hungry, imprisoned people.
And Jesus answers, 'Verily I say unto you, Inasmuch as
ye have done it unto one of the least of these my
brethren, ye have done it unto me.'

Pier Paolo Pasolini

A Spark of Life

It's rather distressing to discuss a two-thousand-year-old book. It makes me feel like a hermetic poet, or a poetess, or a professor with a television programme. Discussing a two-thousand-year-old book as if it were the latest thing always confers a certain legitimacy to the speaker – one of 'the greats' – or at very least, a participant in greatness. Whereas for me, this was all an accident. Over these last few weeks, I've been rereading *The Gospel according to Matthew*[1] for the fifth or sixth time for work reasons. The truth is that I have to start transposing the text – not into a screenplay though, for it should stay just as it is, without mediation, as if it were already a screenplay. I have to create a text that is literally unaltered, but technical. For example:

(1) FULL FRAME: Mary, about to give birth
(2) CLOSE-UP or EXTREME CLOSE-UP: Mary looking wounded, humbled, ashamed

---

[1] Pasolini intentionally discards the 'Saint' before 'Matthew'. (All footnotes are by the translator.)

(3) CLOSE-UP or EXTREME CLOSE-UP: Joseph returning her wounded look, but with more severity. He's rigid

(4) FULL FRAME: Joseph walking away, CAMERA STAYS on him as he leaves the room

(5) FULL FRAME: CAMERA MOVES with Joseph as he walks through the garden (or little arbour, or vineyard) and lies down under a tree

(6) CLOSE-UP: Joseph, exhausted, painfully closes his eyes and sleeps.

(7) FULL FRAME: The angel appears to Joseph and says: Joseph, thou son of David, fear not to take unto thee Mary thy wife . . .

This is the best possible way to read a text. Formalists could never have engineered this kind of analysis – a way to study the function of each fragment, the power of visualisation to provide even those connective elements, which, according to Spitzer's[2] method, serve to 'accelerate' and 'slow down' the pace of the text. (*Saint Matthew* is full of these kinds of stylistic rhythms – the ellipses and disproportions that characterise his Romantic-Barbarism.) Etc., etc.

It's easy to imagine a much longer discussion about why I might have undertaken such work. I'll only say one thing on the matter (another technical fact – and he that hath ears to hear, let him hear). The moment

---

[2] Leo Spitzer (1887–1960) Austrian literary critic, proponent of Stylistic Criticism.

that I finished reading the *Gospel according to Matthew* (it was one day this past October in Assisi – all around me were the moribund, alien, and deeply hostile festivities celebrating the Pope's arrival) I felt the immediate need to 'do something'. It was a terrible urge, to do something almost physical – something manual. This is the 'rising vitality' that Berenson[3] has spoken of – a notion that has become so dear to my own 'circle' – Soldati, Bassani, Bertolucci, Moravia[4] . . . Rising vitality generally becomes concrete through the labours of critical analysis, the exegesis that really *illustrates* the text, carries it beyond that first pre-grammatical impulse, the enthusiasm, empathy, logic or historical import. But what could I do for *Saint Matthew?* I had to do something; I couldn't possibly remain inert, unproductive, after having experienced such an emotion, such an aesthetically profound emotion the likes of which I've seldom been touched by in my life. I'll use this phrase 'aesthetic emotion'. That is honestly the form it took: an overwhelming, visionary, rising vitality. The way this sacred text brings together mythic violence ('Hebraic', in the almost racist, provincial sense of the word) and the culture of daily life – the culture that literate Matthew

---

[3] Bernard Berenson (1865–1959) American art critic. Author of *The Italian Painters of the Renaissance.*

[4] Mario Soldati (1906–99) writer and director. Giorgio Bassani (1916–2000) writer, best known for *The Garden of Finzi-Contini.* Attilio Bertolucci (1911–2000) poet. Alberto Moravia (1907–1990) writer.

can no longer operate within. This triggered a parallel series of symbolic worlds in my imagination, parallel but often connected. There is the brutally alive, physiological one, the biblical period as I saw it travelling through India or along the northern coast of Africa, and the period as it was reconstructed in the iconography of the Italian Renaissance, from Massaccio to the black mannerists. Think of the first frame, 'Close-up on Mary about to give birth.' Is there any way to escape the image of Piero della Francesca's Madonna at San Sepolcro? That baby girl with her blonde, maybe slightly reddish hair, almost bald of eyelashes, the heavy eyelids, and protruding belly, which in profile has the same chasteness as an Apennine hillside. Behind her, the garden or arbour where Joseph is curled up, asleep, doesn't look at all like one of those dusty desert clearings with red goats that I saw in the Egyptian villages around Aswân or at the feet of the violet volcanoes of Aden.[5] Does it?

But, I should repeat, this was the external aspect, the stupendously visual effect of rising vitality. Beneath it, there was something even more forceful rattling me.

It was the figure of Christ as seen by Matthew. Here is where my aesthetic-journalistic vocabulary dictates that I should stop talking. Although I'd only want to add that nothing seems more at odds with the modern world than this Christ – gentle of heart, but *never* gentle of mind, never shrinking a moment from his own terrible freedom, whether it's the will to constantly assert

---

[5] Now Yemen

his religion, or to be constantly disgusted by the hypocrisy and scandal around him. Parse out Matthew's 'stylistic accelerations': the Barbaric/functional modes of his story, the abolition of chronology, the elliptical leaps that encompass schematic disproportions and stasis (the stupendous and endless Sermon on the Mount). In the end, the figure of Christ has to posses the violence of resistance – something that radically challenges life as modern man is configuring it – challenges the grey orgy of cynicism, irony, daily brutality, compromise, conformity, the glorification of the self through the classification of the masses, the hatred of all diversity, the theological bitterness in the absence of religion.

From Il Giorno *6 March 1963*

Six Letters

From Pier Paolo Pasolini to Lucio S. Caruso of the Pro Civitate Christiana of Assisi

February 1963

Dear Caruso,

I think I can explain better in writing what I was confusedly trying to express to you in person.

When I first stayed with you in Assisi, I found the Gospels lying next to my pillow – your splendid/diabolical master plan! Which in fact worked perfectly. I re-read, after some twenty years (it was 1940 or '41 when I read it as a child for the first time – which gave birth to 'The Nightingale of the Catholic Church'[6] – then I'd read a passage from it now and again for salutary reasons, the way one does . . .)

But that day at your establishment I read it from start to finish like a novel. And caught up in the exaltation of reading – you know, it's the most exalting read there is! – among other things, the idea of making a film came to me. At first this idea struck me as utopian, sterile, in

---

[6] Pasolini's 1958 book of poetry, *L'Usignolo dell Chiesa Cattolica.*

itself *exalted*. But no. As days, and then weeks passed, the idea became more powerful and singular; it cast into the shadows all the other projects that were in my head, debilitating them, stripping them of life. This idea was the only one that stayed with me, alive and luxuriant inside.

Only after two or three months, once I'd explored the idea and it had become utterly familiar to me, did I confide in my producer. And he agreed to do this difficult, and risky for both of us, film.

Now I need help – Don Giovanni's[7] help, your help, the help of your colleagues. I need technical support, philological assistance, as well as moral support. And so I come to you (and through you, to whom I feel closest, to the Pro Civitate Christiana) asking for help in the preparation of the film, and then farther along, assisting me with the directing of the film.

My idea is to follow line for line the *Gospel According to Saint Matthew* without writing any sort of treatment or screenplay. I want to translate the story faithfully into images, without making any sort of additions or cuts. The dialogue should be Saint Matthew's – without even a sentence of explanation or exposition – because there isn't an image or word that we could add which would match the poetic heights of the original.

That poetic height is what so fervently inspires me. It's a work of poetry that I want to make. It's not a religious work in the proper sense of the term, nor is it in any way ideological.

---

[7] Fr. Giovanni Russo, founder of the Pro Civitate Christiana of Assisi.

In simple, meagre words, I don't believe Christ is the son of God, because I am not a believer – as least not to my knowledge. I do believe that Christ is divine. I believe that his humanity is so great, so rigorous, and so ideal as to extend beyond the common meaning of 'humanity'. That's why I say 'poetry' – an irrational instrument to express my irrational feelings about Christ. But I want my film to be shown during Easter week in all the parishes of Italy and the world. And that's why I need your help and support. I don't want my creative expression, my poetic inspiration, to contradict the feelings of believers. Because if it did, I will have failed in my ambition to present this life as a model – albeit an unattainable model – for everyone.

I hope you have faith in me.

With warmest regards,

Yours,

Pier Paolo Pasolini

From P. Grasso S.J. to Pier Paolo Pasolini

Rome – 5 April, 1963

Dear *Dottore*,[8]

I would also like to express in writing my pleasure at

---

[8]*Dottore* is a common term of address for someone with a university degree. In this case it's both a term of respect and an acknowledgement of achievement, and there is no precise English equivalent – 'Sir' is an inappropriate substitution.

having made your acquaintance – for which I must thank Caruso. The impression that I had formed of you from reading about you and hearing about you didn't correspond to reality. It's always a joy to rediscover and to affirm the great Gospel truth not to judge others. It is always risky to violate the mystery that surrounds every man. I see a good man in you, one in search of values that are capable of giving sense to life. This is the only genuine vice that is common to all men and makes *accattoni* – or bums – of all of us. We all go forward, searching for the next image of God – so difficult to see – yet that in itself constitutes the one thing that makes Him worthy of our respect and love. You may not share this point of view, but it is frankly, and without a doubt, present in your books and the film you showed me yesterday – so much more than you may think.

And then there is the figure of Christ between us. I believe that he truly is the Son of God, because that is the only hypothesis that could explain his character. You still don't dare to say as much. That's not important. The person of Christ is so great as to merit the utmost respect – if only in his human aspects. I can assure you that your knowledge of Jesus will keep growing deeper until you are able to understand his mystery in its entirety. The Gospels give us the best path to knowing and loving our neighbours, especially the poor and disinherited, because no one understood it more profoundly than Jesus Christ.

As for your film,[9] I can only repeat what I said to

---

[9] 'La Ricotta' one section of the omnibus *Ro.Go.PaG* (1963)

you in person. It made quite an impression on me and made me reflect. The purity of your intentions leaves me without doubts. I am also sincerely convinced that one cannot conclude that it demonstrates contempt for religion. Your own explanations and in particular the contact we've had has forced me to exclude outright such a position.

My hope is that our encounter was only the first of more to come. It will always be a pleasure for me to discuss with you these issues that concern all men.

I pray you'll accept my fervid blessings for your work and my most sincere esteem.

Yours,

D. Grasso S.J.

From Pier Paolo Pasolini to Don Giovanni Rossi of the Pro Civitate Christiana of Assisi

May, 1963

Dearest Don Giovanni,
I haven't left my house for three or four days, I've been so caught up in the fire and torment of my work. I've done what I can – hardly more than some rushed notes. I hope that you and your associates can see through this arid, technical language to what lies beneath, the design of which I've only just sketched here.

I will keep working in the meantime and on Friday I will bring the rest of the screenplay with me to Assisi.

I send you an affectionate embrace (I keep seeing you before me standing by the garden gate calling after me and waving – it's an image that's been with me as I've worked over these last days). I also send my warmest greetings to all of your friends at the Cittadella.

With my devotion,

Pier Paolo Pasolini

From Lucio S. Caruso of the Pro Civitate Christiana to producer Alfredo Bini

12 May, 1963

Dear Dottor Bini,

I read the script of 'The Gospel According to St Matthew'[10] in one sitting. It's gorgeous! My immediate impression is amazement. How can this possibly be the same author, Pasolini, about whom so many journals speak so poorly? Not only does the script adhere most closely to the Sacred Text, and is completely both ethically and doctrinally orthodox, but it also demonstrates extraordinary exegetical acuity.

Over the next few days I will hear Don Giovanni Rossi's opinion along with that of eminent theologians Father Favaro, Professor Grasso and Professor Angelo Penna.

Will you at this point allow me to venture a thought

---

[10] It should be noted that the Italian title of Pasolini's film does not include the 'St' before Matthew – it was added to the accepted translation of the English title.

that I will elaborate upon more precisely in person: My feeling is that this film must be made, or at least attempted. Everything now depends of Pasolini and his faith. Is he capable of nourishing the great flame of Faith in himself? Making a film about Jesus requires above all believing in Jesus – otherwise the result will be cold and academic. What we have received so far from Pasolini, in terms of his assurances and a first-rate script, are all most promising to me.

I look forward to our next meeting. Please accept, dear Bini, my most cordial greetings.

Yours,

Lucio S. Caruso

From Don Giovanni Rossi of the Pro Civitate Christiana to producer Alfredo Bini

15 May, 1963

Illustrious Dottor Bini

I, along with volunteers and qualified persons from Rome and Milan, have examined the script for 'The Gospel According to St Matthew' and found it to be good and without errors of faith or morals.

Several small corrections remain to be made, but I believe the director has already seen to them.

We are pleased to have received your and Pasolini's request that a priest from the Pro Civitate Christiana act as guide on a location-scouting in the Holy Land. It seems like quite a useful idea to me. Don Andrea Carraro will probably be able to come.

Obviously I cannot judge a film before it has even been filmed, but I have ardent faith based on the preparations up to this point and the reassurances we've received that everything will move forward in the best possible way.

Accept my cordial greeting,

Don Giovanni Rossi

Pier Paolo Pasolini to Alfredo Bini

June 1963

Dear Alfredo,
You asked me to summarise in writing for your use the criteria that will govern my realisation of 'The Gospel According to St Matthew'.

From a religious perspective – what I've always attempted to reveal in my own secularism is its religious character, and in that respect there are two ingeniously ontological factors at play: the humanity of Christ is driven by an immensely interior force, by an irreducible longing for knowledge and will to assert that knowledge without any fear of scandal or challenge – so great is this drive that the metaphor *divine* comes up against the limits of the metaphorical; it is ideally a reality. Beyond that, beauty for me is always 'moral beauty', but such beauty always comes to us mediated – through poetry, philosophy, or practice. The only instance that I've ever experienced of unmediated and immediately pure 'moral beauty' came to me through the Gospel.

As for my 'artistic' relationship to the Gospel – it's rather curious. You perhaps know that as a writer born from the ideas of the Resistance and Marxism and so forth that throughout the 1950s my work tended towards rationalism and was polemical about the irrationality of decadent literature (which I studied and loved). The idea of making a film about the Gospels and its technical intuitionism is instead, I confess, the fruit of a frenzied irrational urge. I want to make a work of pure poetry, tempting perhaps, some aesthetic dangers (musical commentary by Bach and a little Mozart; Piero della Francesca and some Duccio are figurative inspiration; while the realism of the background and setting is based in the pre-historical and exotic Arab world). All of this puts my entire writing career dangerously back into question. I know. But it would be wonderful if, loving Matthew's Christ as I do, my fear were of throwing something back out for questioning.

Yours,

Pier Paolo Pasolini

A.N. Wilson

You are holding in your hands a tiny book which has changed more human lives than *The Communist Manifesto* or Freud's *Interpretation of Dreams*: a book which has shaped whole civilizations: a book which, for many people, has been not a gospel but The Gospel.

And you are bound to ask, because you are born out of time in a post-Christian age, into a world of newspapers and investigative reporting and science – 'Is it true?'

Did a Virgin really conceive (1:23) and give birth to a boy-child in Bethlehem (2:1)? Did wise men, guided by a star, come to worship him (2:2)? Did he grow up to be able to walk on water (14:26), to perform miracles, to found the Church (16:26), to rise from the dead?

Stop, stop. Don't ask. They are all questions which seem reasonable enough, but they will lead you into the most pointless, arid negativism. Your educated, scientific, modern mind will decide that no one ever walked on water; no Virgin ever conceived; that corpses do not come to life. And by rejecting this Gospel, you will reject one of the most disturbing and extraordinary books ever written; not, as you might think, on intelligent grounds, but because you (and I, alas) are too hemmed in by our imaginative limitations to see the sort of things this book is doing.

Before you apply to it the supposedly rational tests which you would apply to a newspaper report or a television documentary, imagine the chapters which describe the trial and Crucifixion of Christ set to music in Bach's *Saint Matthew Passion*. Consider the millions of people who, for the last 1900 years have recited the prayer (6:9–13) which begins 'Our Father'. Think of the old women in Stalin's Russia, when the men were too cowardly to profess their loyalty to the Church, who stubbornly continued to chant the opening verses of the Sermon on the Mount in defiance of the KGB. 'Blessed are they that mourn for they shall be comforted' (5:4).

This is a book, not of easily-dismissed fairy tales but of power and passion; more arresting, disturbing and truthful than most reading-matter which you could buy for the price of a magazine on a station bookstall or in the paperback store. This is the Gospel of Christ, in all its terribleness, its wonder, its awe-inspiring truth and its self-contradictions.

Nor should you think that the contradictory emotions which assail and trouble you as you read it – as trouble you they must – are all storms and tempest inside *you*. For this book itself was born out of conflict and struggle and contradiction.

Matthew's Gospel reflects the tension which saw the new religion – what we call Christianity – being fashioned from the old – Judaism. It is by paradox an intensely Jewish, and an intensely anti-Jewish work – indeed it is the great Ur-text of anti-semitism. The historical Jesus is not to be found in this book, nor in any book. He eludes our search. Matthew's Jesus is seen through the prism of a particular faith, of a particular group, somewhere in the Mediterranean world. Rome? 85–100 AD?

By the time the book reached something like its present form (50 years after Jesus had left the scene?) Christianity was emerging as something which, if not distinct from Judaism, was at least repellent to most Jews. Paul's Letter to the Galatians (of *circa* 50 AD) describes a rift between the first Christians of Asia Minor, converts of Paul, and the followers of Peter and James in Jerusalem who had known the earthly Jesus. It seems like an angry and irreconcilable quarrel. Paul, though, or because, a Jew, had decided that those who followed the Jewish Law (*Torah*), the Law given by God on Mount Sinai to his people, were living in bonds from which Christ came to set them free. For Peter and his friends, the dietary laws of Judaism, the requirement of circumcision, and so forth, were 'not bonds but wings'; they were symbols of lives dedicated to God.

No compromise, surely, was possible, between these two ways? Either you circumcise your son or you don't. Either it is sinful to eat pork, or it isn't.

But to another generation, Matthew's, the problems were different. The irreconcilables, rather than being fudged, are held together in self-contradiction. Peter and

Paul, who in earlier New Testament texts were the leaders of opposing Ways, emerge in this text as co-partners (though, of course, Paul's ideas, rather than his name, are what we find here).

It is Jesus himself, in this legendary reconstruction, who speaks lines which, in an earlier generation of Christianity, had been assigned to protagonists in the quarrel. On the one hand, with the followers of Paul, he wants to leave the synagogue. See chapter 12, a key moment, when the Pharisees accuse Jesus of breaking the Law by healing a man on the Sabbath. His reaction is to lead his people away from the mainstream of Jewry, but he does so, as Paul had done, by quoting the Jewish Scriptures. 'I will put my spirit upon him, and he shall shew judgment to the Gentiles' (12:18). On the other hand, Matthew's Jesus is not simply a libertarian like Paul. He wishes to reassure the Jewish conservatives: 'Think not that I am come to destroy the law, or the prophets: I am not come to destroy, but to fulfil' (5:17).

How is the miracle accomplished? It is done by seeing the new congregation or synagogue, or gathering-together of the Elect as the New Israel: the Church.

So Matthew constructs his book as a miniature *Torah*. Like Moses, Matthew's Jesus goes up to a mountain (5:1) and delivers a New Law to his followers. At the end of the tale, in a gesture which could never have taken place in history but which is heavy with religious paradox, a pagan, Roman Governor performs a Jewish purification ritual – he washes his hands – to demonstrate his innocence of Christ's murder. It is the Jewish mob who cry out, 'His blood be on us, and on our children' (27:25). A terrible text which would have profound consequences in Europe during the centuries that it penetrated the collective consciousness. It was not just a few Jews in this Gospel who are responsible for the torture and death of Jesus. It is 'all the people' (27:25).

Matthew's Gospel is not just the product of the embryo-Church. It is, really, a book about the Church, and it shapes what the Church, both in East and West, was destined to become.

The Church is a house founded upon a rock; and that rock is, primarily, the teaching of Christ. 'Therefore, whosoever heareth these sayings of mine, and doeth them, I will liken him unto a wise man, which built his house upon a rock: and the rain descended, and the floods came, and the winds blew, and beat upon that house; and it fell not: for it was founded upon a rock' (7:24–5).

The teachings, of course, are the exact reverse of worldly-wise notions of security. Our obsessions with security – financial, military, domestic – are blown sky high by Jesus's teaching: not to lay up treasure, not to resist evil with violence. Yet a detachment from what we would call security seems like a prerequisite here for church membership. And the Church, for Matthew, is the ante-chamber of the Kingdom of God.

And notice the extraordinary emphasis on the superiority of the poor over the rich. When John the Baptist asks (chapter 11) whether Jesus is the One who is to come, the message comes back, 'Go and shew John again those things which ye do hear and see'. A list follows, reaching a rhetorical *crescendo*. 'The blind receive their sight, and the lame walk, the lepers are cleansed, and the deaf hear, the dead are raised up' . . . Each thing is more remarkable than the last. But what is more remarkable even than the resurrection of the dead? The final item in the list: 'The poor have the gospel preached to them' (11:4–5).

That is not because Jesus was a sentimentalist or a socialist. It is because only the detached and the dispossessed, that is the poor, can hear his gospel. When a rich young man tried to follow Jesus, he 'went away sorrowful' (19:22) because the message was too simple, and too stern. Only those who live as though there is no tomorrow, and who do not store up treasure, can enter the kingdom.

This is the rock on which the Church is founded. It is founded on a rock in another sense: it is founded on Simon whose title or nickname, given to him by Jesus in one of the most dramatic scenes in the Gospel, is Peter. There is no name 'Peter' in the ancient world. You find it on no ossuary or tomb. It is a word meaning 'Rock'. It is a Gospel word. In chapter 16, Jesus asks his friends who do men say that he is? And they tell him – some say he is a prophet, or Elijah come back to earth. But you? Who do you say that he is?

The fisherman from Galilee blurts out, '"Thou art the Christ, the Son of the Living God.' And Jesus answered and said unto him, 'Blessed art thou, Simon Bar-Jona: for flesh and blood hath not revealed it unto thee, but my Father which is in heaven. And I say unto thee, that thou art Peter, and upon this rock I will build my church;' (16:16–18).

This is the Simon who, only a little while earlier (14:27–31) has attempted to walk with Jesus on the water of the stormy lake of Galilee and who has sunk because he had no faith. This is the Simon Peter who, as Jesus had predicted, has no courage at the last. As Jesus had predicted, when his Master had been arrested, Peter denies even knowing him; and, when he confronts his own cowardice and weakness, 'he went out and wept bitterly' (26:75).

Here we see how the Christian community which shaped the Gospel has reconciled the early conflicts between Paul – for whom the Gospel was the acceptance of Grace – and Peter for whom it had been an observance of Law. For the Rock on which the Church is founded is not a rock of success, or moral strength, but of doubt, weakness, failure. The boat (another metaphor for the Church throughout this book) runs into storms and its crew panics. Only Jesus, apparently asleep, can calm the storms. 'And he hath said unto me, "My grace is sufficient for thee, for my strength is made perfect in weakness".' (2 *Corinthians* 12:9).

The attempt to follow the new *Torah*; the Sermon on the Mount, will not lead to a new legalism. Nor will anyone be able to follow Jesus's command to be perfect, even as God is perfect (5:48). Instead, it will lead to an understanding that, though we might abstain from murder, we shall still be angry; though we might avoid adultery, that is nothing to be proud of: for we shall still feel lust. It is Matthew the sinner and tax gatherer who is accepted in the Beloved. Christ the physician comes to heal sinners, not the righteous.

The author of this book did not attempt to write a realistic narrative of the kind we might expect from a post-enlightenment historian. For instance, judging from the earliest Christian writings and the *Letters of Paul*, it seems fairly likely that the Church began in Jerusalem. But *Matthew* has it beginning on a hillside in Galilee. *Mark*, the Gospel on which this book relies so heavily, says nothing about a miraculous conception, or a birth in Bethlehem. But the tale of a Virgin-birth and the recognition of the child by the wise men from the east perfectly illustrates the double-sided purpose of this book. On the one hand, the child is born to fulfil the Messianic prophecies of Judaism. On the other hand, he is recognised, not by the king of the Jews, but by wise Gentiles. Just so, at the end, he tells his followers to go into the ends of the earth, baptizing and teaching all people.

The sceptical mind will find these 28 chapters to be a catalogue of improbabilities. To any student of ethics, who has studied Aristotle or John Stuart Mill, or Dewey or Rawls, here is no morality at all but what Chesterton called 'The Ethics of Elfland'.

At the centre-stage is Jesus, calling the rich to discard their wealth and offering the kingdom to the poor. He offers not peace but a sword (10:34). Yet he says (11:28), 'Come unto me, all ye that labour and are heavy laden, and I will give you rest.'

Perhaps the most distinctive and haunting of all Matthew's stories – perhaps the most haunting passage in the entire New Testament – is that parable in the final discourse (25:31–46) when Jesus predicts that the King will welcome the chosen into his kingdom. They are those who have seen him, not in his glory, but as poor, naked, hungry, in prison and in need. Neither the blessed, nor the damned, in this tale, understand during their lifetimes, that in so far as they responded to the depths of human need in others, they had responded to God. It is in the context of this story that we begin to understand the sense in which this book is true. By the stern test of that parable and of this Gospel, most of us will feel like that rich young man. We will go away sorrowful, deeply conscious of our inability either to understand the Gospel, or to live up to its precepts or to have the humility to accept Divine Grace. Yet, though we are sorrowful, and though we go away, we shall never read this text without being, in some small degree, changed.

THE GOSPEL ACCORDING
TO MARK

And he arose, and rebuked the wind, and said unto the sea, 'Peace, be still.' And the wind ceased, and there was a great calm. And he said unto them, 'Why are ye so fearful? How is that ye have no faith?' And they feared exceedingly, and said one to another, 'What manner of man is this, that even the wind and sea obey him?'

(4:39–41)

authorised King James version

Nick Cave

When I bought my first copy of the Bible, the King James version, it was to the Old Testament that I was drawn, with its maniacal, punitive God, that dealt out to His long-suffering humanity punishments that had me drop-jawed in disbelief at the very depth of their vengefulness. I had a burgeoning interest in violent literature coupled with an unnamed sense of the divinity in things and, in my early twenties, the Old Testament spoke to that part of me that railed and hissed and spat at the world. I believed in God, but I also believed that God was malign and if the Old Testament was testament to anything, it was testament to that. Evil seemed to live so close to the surface of existence within it, you could smell its mad breath, see the yellow smoke curl from its many pages, hear the blood-curdling moans of despair. It was a wonderful, terrible book and it was sacred scripture.

But you grow up. You do. You mellow out. Buds of compassion push through the cracks in the black and bitter soil. Your rage ceases to need a name. You no longer find comfort watching a whacked-out God tormenting a wretched humanity as you learn to forgive yourself and the world. That God of Old begins to transmute in your heart, base metals become silver and gold, and you warm to the world.

Then, one day, I met an Anglican vicar and he suggested that I give the Old Testament a rest and to read *Mark* instead. I hadn't read the New Testament at that stage because the New Testament was about Jesus Christ and the Christ I remembered from my choir-boy days was that wet, all-loving, etiolated individual that the church proselytised. I spent my pre-teen years singing in the Wangarafta Cathedral Choir and even at that age I recall thinking what a wishy-washy affair the whole thing was. The Anglican Church: it was the decaf of worship and Jesus was their Lord.

'Why *Mark*?' I asked.

'Because it's short,' he replied.

Well, at that time I was willing to give anything a go so I took the vicar's advice and read it, and *The Gospel According to Mark* just swept me up.

Here, I am reminded of that picture of Christ, painted by Holman Hunt, where He appears, robed and handsome, a lantern in His hand, knocking on a door. The door to our hearts, presumably. The light is dim and buttery in the engulfing darkness. Christ came to me in this way, *lumen Christi*, with a dim light, a sad light, but light enough. Out of all the New Testament writings – from the four Gospels, through the *Acts*, and the complex, driven *Letters of Paul*, to the chilling, sickening *Revelation* – it is Mark's Gospel that has truly *held* me.

Scholars generally agree that Mark's was the first of the four Gospels to be written. Mark took from the mouths of teachers and prophets the jumble of events that comprised Christ's life and fixed these events into some kind of biographical form. He did this with such breathless insistence, such compulsive narrative intensity, that one is reminded of a child recounting some amazing tale, piling fact upon fact, as if the whole world depended upon it, which of course, to Mark, it did. 'Straightway' and 'immediately' link one event to another, everyone 'runs', 'shouts', is 'amazed', inflaming Christ's mission with a dazzling urgency. Mark's Gospel is a clatter of bones, so raw, nervy and lean on information that the narrative aches with the melancholy of absence. Scenes of deep tragedy are treated with such a matter-of-factness and raw economy they become almost palpable in their unprotected sorrowfulness. Mark's narrative begins with the Baptism and 'immediately' we are confronted with the solitary figure of Christ, who is baptised in the River Jordan and driven into the wilderness. 'And he was there in the wilderness forty days, tempted of Satan; and was with the wild beasts; and the angels ministered unto him' (1:13). This is all Mark says of the Temptation, but the verse is typically potent owing to its mysterious simplicity and spareness.

Christ's forty days and forty nights in the wilderness also say something about His aloneness, for when Christ takes on His ministry around Galilee and in Jerusalem, He enters a wilderness of the soul, where all the outpourings of His brilliant, jewel-like imagination are in turns misunderstood, rebuffed, ignored, mocked and vilified and would eventually be the death of Him. Even His disciples, who we would hope would absorb some of Christ's brilliance, seem to be in a perpetual fog of misunderstanding, following Christ from scene to scene, with little or no comprehension of what is going on around them. So much of the frustration and anger that seems at times to almost consume Christ is directed at His disciples and it is against their persistent ignorance that Christ's isolation seems at its most complete. It is Christ's divine inspiration versus the dull rationalism of those around Him that gives Mark's narrative its tension, its drive. The gulf of misunderstanding is so vast that His friends 'lay hold of Him' thinking, 'He is beside himself' (3:21). The scribes and Pharisees, with their monotonous insistence on the Law, provide the perfect springboard for Christ's luminous words. Even those Christ heals betray Him, as they run to the towns to report the doings of the miraculous healer, after Christ has insisted that they tell no one. Christ disowns His own mother for her lack of understanding. Throughout *Mark*, Christ is in deep conflict with the world He is trying to save, and the sense of aloneness that surrounds Him is at times unbearably intense. Christ's last howl from the cross is to a God He believes has forsaken Him, 'Eloi, Eloi, lama sabachthani.'

The rite of Baptism – the dying of one's old self to be born anew – like so many of the events in Christ's life, is already flavoured metaphorically by Christ's death and it is His death on the cross that is such a powerful and haunting force, especially in *Mark*. His preoccupation with it is all the more obvious if only because of the brevity with which *Mark* deals with the events of His life. It seems that virtually everything that Christ does in Mark's narrative is in some way a preparation for His death – His frustration with His disciples and His fear that they have not comprehended the full significance of His actions, the constant taunting of the church officials, the stirring up of the crowds, His miracle-making so that witnesses will remember the extent of His divine power. Clearly *Mark* is concerned primarily with the death of Christ, to such an extent that Christ appears completely consumed by His imminent demise, thoroughly shaped by His death.

The Christ that emerges from *Mark*, tramping through the haphazard events of His life, had a ringing intensity about Him that I could not resist. Christ spoke to me through His isolation, through the burden of His death, through His rage at the mundane, through His sorrow. Christ, it seemed to me, was the victim of humanity's lack of imagination, was hammered to the cross with the nails of creative vapidity.

The Gospel According to Mark has continued to inform my life as the root source of my spirituality, my religiousness. The Christ that the Church offers us, the bloodless, placid 'Saviour' – the man smiling benignly at a group of children, or calmly, serenely hanging from the cross – denies Christ His potent, creative sorrow or His boiling anger that confronts us so forcefully in *Mark*. Thus the Church denies Christ His humanity, offering up a figure that we can perhaps 'praise', but never relate to. The essential humanness of *Mark*'s Christ provides us with a blueprint for our own lives, so that we have something that we can aspire to, rather than revere, that can lift us free of the mundanity of our existences, rather than affirming the notion that we are lowly and unworthy. Merely to praise Christ in His Perfectness, keeps us on our knees, with our heads pitifully bent. Clearly, this is not what Christ had in mind. Christ came as a liberator. Christ understood that we as humans were for ever held to the ground by the pull of gravity – our ordinariness, our mediocrity – and it was through His example that He gave our imaginations the freedom to rise and to fly. In short, to be Christ-like.

Barry Hannah

Mark, leanest of the Gospels, composed around 70 A.D., when the Jewish War saw the destruction of the temple by the army of Titus, was written in a climate of misery and apocalypse. Mark invented the form of the gospel, which means 'good news.' Yet much of his work countenances despair, doubt, treachery, and death.

These are the same conditions that attend the Turkish earthquake as I write now in the final months of the millennium. Whole cities have collapsed, forty-five thousand body bags have been requested by the government, the rebuilding cost surpasses the state resources, and signs of hope seem far away, even alien.

Mark may have addressed persecuted and refugee Christians of a community in the Roman province of Syria. They looked for an imminent Parousia (second coming) upon the destruction of the temple, and were disappointed when the end had not come, as the scholar Wilfrid Harrington explains.[*]

---

[*] In *Mark,* Collegeville, Minn.: Liturgical Press, 1991.

This gospel is neglected, and the least quoted. Thomas Jefferson hardly includes material from *Mark* at all in the Jefferson Bible, wherein he intended to concretize, from the Gospels, 'the most sublime and benevolent code of morals which has ever been offered to man.' *Mark* may have seemed obscure or elliptical to him. Harrington accounts for the neglect of *Mark*: 'The gospel is uncompromisingly uncomfortable . . . suffering Messiahship and suffering discipleship . . . between the times of resurrection and consummation.'

Scholars seem to agree that the most reliable manuscripts of Mark's Gospel end at 16:8, not at 16:20, as supplied by many versions. It is helpful to look at the final verses for a tone of the whole gospel:

And when the sabbath was past, Mary Magdalene, and Mary the mother of James, and Salome, had brought sweet spices, that they might come and anoint him. And very early in the morning the first day of the week, they came into the sepulchre at the rising of the sun. And they said among themselves, 'Who shall roll us away the stone at the door of the sepulchre?' And when they looked, they saw the stone was rolled away; for it was very great. And entering the sepulchre, they saw a young man sitting on the right side, clothed in a long white garment; and they were affrighted. And he saith unto them, 'Be not affrighted; ye seek Jesus of Nazareth, which was crucified. He is risen; he is not here; behold the place where they laid him. But go your way, tell his disciples and Peter that he goeth before you into Galilee: there shall ye see him, as he said unto you.' And they went out quickly, and fled from the sepulchre; for they trembled and were amazed; neither said they any thing to any man; for they were afraid.

There is plainly more fear than hope here, even from the women who have remained faithful throughout the crucifixion while the disciples fled for reasons of personal safety – the very men who dropped their nets to follow Jesus, who saw the healing and the miracles and the walk on water; four of whom heard God speak to Christ from a bright cloud, and one of whom, Peter, the famous denier of Christ three times before the cock crew twice, would be the rock on which Christianity was built. These men could not honor the last hours of Christ by staying awake while he pled with his Father to commute his sentence of death on the cross.

Fear and fatigue, the atheism of evident biology, wherein no man returns from death – these beset the *best* men Christ was able to assemble and appoint as apostles, that is, missionaries of the good news. Judas Iscariot, the crassest and most cowardly of all, has already betrayed Christ to the officials for thirty pieces of silver and then hanged himself in a late attack of conscience. We should remember, however, that Judas *was* a disciple. He was no stranger.

Mark is a book of utter realism, very uncomfortable. It is the vase, basic, without the amplified blooms given to it by the later gospellers Matthew, Luke, and John. The vase, in its abiding economy, has great beauty and holds promise of eternal life, but its theme is heavy on bafflement, misunderstanding, and grief. Even Jesus seems to misunderstand the capabilities of his chosen twelve. He constantly upbraids them and is surprised by their obtuseness. Simply, he has found the men too human – skeptical, cowardly, unimaginative, power seeking, weak. They have quit their professions to follow him, but they never intended to follow him into the precincts of death.

They behave like the deists who had much to do with founding America. God has created the world but then forgotten it. They behave like present bad Christians, like many of us, in fact. The disciples may even be worse than modern believers. They have had hard evidence to believe – visual, aural, physical. We have manuscripts two thousand years old and the testimonies, quite often, of those we dislike and distrust, many who seem a plague of new Pharisees, the screaming Law.

Here is a curious example of the complaint of a modern man against apostles of Christ: Englishman H. E. Arnhold, leading businessman and former chairman of the Shanghai Municipal Council, protests the behavior of a large number of up-country American missionaries in a Japanese internment camp at Chapei (China) during World War II. The missionaries would not comply with camp rules, neglected cleanliness in the lavatories, occupied more floor space than they were entitled to, interfered with the distribution of eggs, and, most annoying of all, propagated the species.

Considering the overcrowded and undernourished condition of the camp one would have thought that self-restraint would have been exercised, so that the camp would not have been deprived of most necessary food (eggs and milk) to provide for this increase in population, apart from the indecency of sexual intercourse in overcrowded dormitories and the embarrassment, annoyance, and disturbance caused to other inmates. . . . One person went through the nightly performance of quoting the Bible to an unwilling spouse until she submitted to his importunities.[*]

I have never heard Christians accused of being too sexy in public.

Such reportings of the worldly have trailed Christians ever since I have been alive, and there is hardly need to list the more lethal depredations of the Crusades, the Inquisition, the Conquistadors, the Witch Trials, and the collusion of the Vatican with anticommunist fascists, even Hitler; or the late squalor and greed of Jim and Tammy Bakker and Jimmy Swaggart, or other hypocrites and wolves unto the sheep, in order to fill the cyclorama of misdeeds that we are invited to by secular

---

[*] Bernard Wasserstein, *Secret War in Shanghai*, Boston: Houghton Mifflin, 1998, pp. 139–140.

humanists, liberal atheists, and common gleeful wags. We breathe the very air of disbelief and doubt and are currently led by an ostentatious Baptist Bibletoter who delighted in fellatio in the Oval Office just minutes after the funeral of his supposed pal Ron Brown. We did not need to know this, but apparently we adored it when we did. Because we are assured that nobody is better than we are, and this gives comfort to our nasty republican hearts.

But remember that the disciples, constantly upbraided, cowardly, treacherous, obtuse, much weaker than their women, became the apostles of light and went on to their own heroic sufferings, persecutions, jails, and crucifixions.

They were good enough.

Christ appeared living to them in Galilee and sent them out. They were not only forgiven but adored. They were promised constant friendship and direction by the Savior. This at a time when by all outer appearances the day was doomed, men were confused and abandoned, women huddled in slavish existences, their Savior mocked and destroyed in the humiliating scandal of the cross.

The message of *Mark* is heartening to bad Christians such as myself, who doubt daily, in our comfort, and even doubt the earthly thing that has brought them the most joy – the writing of stories, in my case. But what serious writer has not doubted the efficacy of words themselves, or their relative courage and truth? We might all be set aside under the leisure section, in the club of idlers and dabblers, of the Great Newspaper in the Sky. Sunday newspaper hell. Such doubts have led to total renunciation of earlier works by born-again converts like Tolstoy, or just rational despair, as with Beckett, who, when bragged upon by some last visitor to his deathbed, said, 'But it's just words. Only words. Nothing.'

Every day, honest men and women awake to misery, restlessness, doubt, even torture, *if* they awake, and we forget that things were always so, and much worse. We are not in Turkey, dead, or bereft of loved ones overnight. We are in the great nation founded on Christian inclusiveness and forgiveness and tolerance, are we not? That it is an inconceivably wasteful ant colony of Darwinian fascism, the crassest, most materialistic monster the world has ever witnessed, does not occur to us that often, as it does to foreigners, many of whom clamor to enter and drain their brains therein. An exponential amplitude of old Rome, inflicting itself internationally almost with the perfection of flood water.

But it is hopeful to know that not only forgiveness but the power of the Savior's friendship remain available to each unworthy one. And that through the layers of comfort we can reach a decision that will make us happier and the world much better, although Christ has warned that this is the most unlikely decision of all, more difficult than the decision of the early disciples. They were merely fishermen and had only to drop their nets.

Now I offer a poem inspired by Mark's gospel, a brutal and exquisite work, in paravoice of the Savior as I have perceived it.

Do not think so much.
Surrender. Believe.
Unprepared, move out to the world and testify.
The words will come. Serve.
From now on service is kingly.
There are no more kings.
Serve. Help. Love. Others as thyself.
This is impossible but do it.
You have seen enough. You have seen it all,
The miracles, the walk on water, Father speaking
    from a bright cloud.
You were not there but the centurion was,
Through the last hour.
The women, faithful, down the hill, waiting and
    watching.
'Truly this was the Son of God,' told the centurion.
To all near the cross. Not you, craven.
The temple did not fall but its veil was rent
Top to bottom. Enough. You do not need the whole
    catastrophe,
For it has already taken place.
God is not in the temple anymore.
You cowards, keep running, but now you are mine,
My brothers and sisters.
Tell them. Help. Love. Service.
My good cowards, weaklings, doubters,
How I love you,
Whom I serve, and will see in Galilee.

I am not aroused to poetry very often but Mark has done it, with his mysterious compact power. I hope the poem will be forgiven its deficiencies, as I do not those of my students, in the spirit of *Mark* and a recent movie by Robert Duvall, *The Apostle*. The movie is exceptional in modern circumstances because of its favorable testimony to a Christian apostle (a murderer) and the power of his tiny church.

The apostle invited everyone to bring their instruments to the first service. An old black man has brought a trumpet and blurts on it horribly in praise of the Lord. The apostle chuckles – one of Duvall's best faces ever – and exclaims something like 'Beautiful!' It put me in mind of Christ himself, in His love for our spirits despite all outward proof.

THE GOSPEL ACCORDING TO LUKE

And Jesus answering said, 'A certain man went down from Jerusalem to Jericho, and fell among thieves, which stripped him of his raiment, and wounded him, and departed, leaving him half dead.'

(10:30)

authorised King James version

Thomas Cahill

Within the covers of the New Testament we find four Gospels (or accounts of the life and teachings of Jesus), written in Greek by four evangelists (or Gospel writers) whose names ancient tradition has given us as Matthew, Mark, Luke, and John. Though three of these men were what publishers today would call 'one-book authors,' one of them, Luke, wrote a second book, the *Acts of the Apostles*. This second book continues the story of Jesus into the period *after* his earthly life in order to show us how Jesus remained present to his followers even when he was no longer with them physically. The four Gospels, together with the *Acts of the Apostles*, make up the first five books of the New Testament, and correspond in position and importance to the Five Books of Moses, which the Jews placed at the head of their Sacred Scriptures, usually called by Christians the Old Testament.

Among the four evangelists, Luke stands out for several reasons, especially because he is the best writer of the bunch. As far as we can tell, he was not a Jew (probably the only non-Jew to author a book of the

Bible) but a Greek-speaking Syrian of the first century who knew Paul (Paul described him as 'the beloved physician') and other figures prominent in the early Christian Church but who did not know the earthly Jesus – because he had come to the Christian 'Way' only after Jesus' departure. His Gospel shares many things with the other Gospels, particularly those of Matthew and Mark, but whereas the other evangelists write like Aramaic-speaking, Hebrew-reading Jews who had picked up Greek somewhere along the line, Luke writes with the high style of someone who absorbed Greek with his mother's milk and understands how to use it with elegant balance and refinement. He is a beautiful writer. His Gospel, indeed, was called by Ernest Renan '*le plus beau livre qu'il y ait*,' the most beautiful book ever written. (Its sequel, the *Acts of the Apostles*, bids fair to be considered the most beautiful sequel ever written.)

I hope someday to write a passage-by-passage appreciation of Luke's writing. Mine will not be the appreciation of a theologian or Scripture scholar but of a writer who can only admire Luke's magisterial construct. I shall, as needed, take into account Luke's influence on theology and Christian history and shall tap the best resources of Scripture scholarship to keep me on track, but the goal of the hunt will be to catch not Luke the theologian or Luke the ecclesiastical controversialist or Luke the linguist but Luke the writer. It is the essence of his art that I would hope to bag. Here I can sound only the first notes of such an appreciation – by offering an analysis of Luke's first twenty-seven verses.

Luke 1:1–4

Luke's very first sentence alerts us to his facility. A long, perfectly sustained periodic sentence, it exhibits all the modest indirection of true classical writing while at the same time reassuring the reader that Luke has done his job diligently: he has consulted eyewitnesses and other accounts, and he will deal with all this material with completeness, accuracy, and thoroughness – and, perhaps most important to a Greek reader, the account will be systematic, that is, presented according to the classical rules of Order, the great virtue of Greco-Roman civilization.

Even in his first sentence, Luke strikes the first notes of a theme that will be repeated throughout his account: 'the events that have come to fulfillment among us' (a more accurate translation than the King James's 'those things which are most surely believed among us'). So this will be a story, not a thesis, packed with 'events' that are not just happenings but *fruitions*: the effects will be intended, not haphazard. Intended by whom? Luke does not say as yet, but we must already suspect that he is not talking about the effects a writer can produce by his craft. No, Luke means to bring on the stage a force much more powerful than himself. So the ultimate assurance that the reader has is not Luke's diligence or intelligence but the assurance of someone quite other and much larger than the author. In the Greek, the last word of the sentence, *asphaleia*, 'assurance' ('certainty' in the King James Version), creates an effect that is virtually impossible to render in English. For the last word of a

Greek periodic sentence must bear all the accumulated weight of the sentence's meaning. So the promise Luke is making to Theophilus is a bold one, indeed; he is promising a great deal.

We have no idea who Theophilus was or why he is addressed as 'Your Excellency,' but the name means Lover of God, so we may assume that Luke is addressing a person of some importance whose name suggests that he has already taken his first steps in exploring the new 'Way' of the Christians. Given this, there is no reason to doubt that Luke also meant to address each one of us, you and me. For, in Luke's view, the events have come to fulfillment *among us* – and he means to include even us. To know that this ancient writer, who wrote in a language few of us can understand, really intended to address even *us* across all the centuries alerts us to the fact that what we are about to read is, at the least, an unusual story.

Luke 1:5–25
By invoking the name of King Herod, Luke anchors his narrative in a historical time familiar to his initial readers and no more distant from them than, say, Woodrow Wilson is from us – in other words, in a time their parents or grandparents could remember. But Greek (not unlike Hebrew before it) had two words for time: *chronos,* meaning the measure of time, as in 'What time is it now?' and *kairos,* meaning the *right* time, as in 'Now is the time!' Luke repeatedly uses *kairos* when he means the right time, the time of fulfillment, God's time. 'God's

time' is not the easiest idea to get hold of, for we human beings have no way of measuring it. Only God knows when is the right time for something to happen. But more than this, Luke sees the whole of human history – the whole human story – as God's time, in which he brings to fruition those things that he has ordained, according to his own promises to human beings whom he has chosen for his own utterly mysterious reasons. Right now, in the wicked reign of Herod, God has decided: this is the right time for his promised fulfill ment to begin to come to fruition.

The passage about Zacharias's encounter with Gabriel is full of notes of fulfillment, words that speak to us subliminally or forthrightly of fruition: *descendant, children, barren, bear you a son, he will be great, the children of Israel, parents turning to their children, old, well on in years, the day these things will take place, my words which will find fulfillment in their own time, sometime later, Elizabeth became pregnant, how the Lord has dealt with me at the time he saw fit!* These are a great many chords of fulfillment for a few short paragraphs – so much so that we can say that it is as if Luke wants us to think of the cosmos itself as pregnant with God's meaning, of the whole of the created universe as groaning in labor, heavy with the fruit it is about to drop.

The purpose of human history itself is about to be revealed, and Luke's text invokes, for a reader who knows the Old Testament, some of the greatest figures of Jewish history: Abraham and Sarah, whose old age also brought forth a son, despite their initial skepticism, so like Zacharias's; the spirit and power of the prophet Elijah, who left such an impression on Jewish imagination, because he never died but was taken up into the heavens in a chariot of fire; the prophet Malachi, who first spoke the ringing phrase that promised an age in which 'the hearts of parents' would be turned 'to their children.' All these figures Luke, as it were, summons as witnesses to a momentous revelation.

And what will this revelation, this fulfillment, be exactly? Whatever it will be it will involve reconciliation, love, and justice –' to make ready a people fit for the Lord.' For the other set of notes that these paragraphs contain are the great qualities repeatedly emphasized throughout the Jewish Scriptures, the qualities by which man becomes like God: *blameless* and *upright,* the qualities that bring *joy* and *delight.* This passage, then, is a kind of fugue in which two themes are intertwined and finally fused together, as the upright Zacharias and the blameless Elizabeth, both ancient representatives of those who understand, the upright of Israel, conceive out of their ancientness a child of joy and delight, a boy of greatness, filled from his birth with a holy Spirit.

Even in this early passage we may take note that the mysterious fulfillment to come, though obviously communal – that is, meant for the whole nation – is also to be individual, for it involves these two very human characters, Zacharias, the understandably skeptical old priest, and Elizabeth, who ground her teeth over 'the disgrace that [she] endured among people.' It involves too the child to come, the mysteriously great John; and soon it will involve an even larger cast of quite distinct personalities.

Is Zacharias made mute as a punishment for his skepticism, which is no greater than Abraham's or Sarah's, nor greater than (as we shall soon see) Mary's? To me, at least, this muteness is simply an instance of the great truth that God treats individuals individually. Apparently, Abraham, Sarah, and Mary, though all quite as skeptical as Zacharias, were able to grasp the revelation they had received without God having to resort to making them mute. Zacharias – we don't know why – was not. His personality, for reasons we are not told directly, required this remedy. He was, after all, a priest, someone used to being listened to, in all likelihood not someone used to listening. But in the coming nine months of enforced silence, God will succeed in getting through to him in a spectacular manner – which will blossom forth in his thrilling song (*Luke* 1:68–79).

Most of us are somewhat like Zacharias, unable to believe that God has chosen us for his purpose. We too need a time of quiet in which we obey not our own interminable voice but the voice of the Other, who has been trying to speak to us for so long. We need to pray the insightful prayer of Cardinal Newman:

God has created me to do him some definite service: he has committed some work to me which he has not committed to another. I have my mission – I never may know it in this life, but I shall be told in the next. Somehow I am necessary for His purposes. . . . I have a part in this great work; I am a link in a chain, a bond of connection between persons. He has not created me for nought.

Like Zacharias, most of us need a time of withdrawal, of retreat from our ordinary tasks and daily busyness, of mute silence, if God is ever to get through to us and impress on us what it is that he means us to do. It is unlikely that what God has in mind for us involves great matters of state – that we are meant to advise prime ministers or presidents or popes. But whatever it is, God surely expects of us that we will do our part to 'make ready a people fit for' him, that we will play our role, however humble, to enable the coming of *kairos*, the acceptable time.

Luke 1:26–27
When Elizabeth is six months pregnant, Gabriel, the busy angelic messenger, appears in Galilee to a virgin whose name is Mary. Much ink has been spilled over this virgin, most recently in an attempt to prove that she was no virgin – just another pregnant teenager in need of a cover story. But there is no reason to think that Luke has any doubts on this score or that he doesn't really mean 'virgin,' only 'young girl.' Matthew, in his account of Mary's pregnancy, makes direct reference to Isaiah's prophecy 'A virgin shall conceive . . .' and while it is true that Matthew is quoting the traditional Greek translation of this prophecy, which uses *parthenos*, the Greek word for 'virgin,' it is also true that the original Hebrew uses a word that means 'young girl.' So while

it is possible (though pretty unlikely) that Matthew thinks that Mary was no virgin, there can scarcely be any doubt about Luke's meaning: 'But how can this be,' Mary will ask skeptically in verse 34, 'since I have no relations with a man?' Luke's meaning is clear as crystal: Mary, betrothed, probably in childhood (after the tradition of Palestinian Jews), long before actual congress with her husband, has not yet come to live with him.

What we see here is a great instance of parallelism, the chief device ancient Hebrew writers used to achieve emphasis. Parallelism courses through the Psalms, to such an extent that it may be found in couplets and triplets everywhere. It is the simple but extremely effective device of repeating an idea in new words:

Sweeter than honey,
than honey dripping from the honeycomb.

For you will not abandon me to Hell,
Nor can you allow your faithful servant to see the
    Abyss.

In Luke's account the parallelism is on a grander scale and occurs between the events leading up to (and including) the birth of John the Baptist and the events leading up to (and including) the birth of Jesus. One set of events is a repetition in different words of the other – but with a difference: the birth of Jesus is accorded more importance and requires even greater intervention on God's part. This is called step parallelism.

Mary's name (Miryam, in all likelihood, in her original Aramaic, though the name Maria was not unknown among Palestinian Jews) means something like summit, pinnacle, apogee: she is, therefore, the culmination of all this fruitfulness. And, once again, Luke's writing is full of fruit and offspring, wombs and promises of miraculous births. We are about to experience a cosmic explosion of fecundity. Fulfillment is at hand, so reality itself is pregnant.

Luke's allusions remind me of a Flemish painting of the Annunciation (as this scene is called) that hangs among the paintings of the northern Renaissance in the Metropolitan Museum of Art in New York. It depicts a modest, almost tentative Mary, her eyes downcast in the presence of the angelic apparition who is very nearly her mirror image – but slightly more ruddy and vigorous, coming as he does from Heaven. The artist (the painting has most recently been attributed to Memling, but who knows?) has surrounded the scene with symbolic reminders of fertility: an upended vase, a blooming lily, a riotous summer garden beyond the open window, pillows and bedroom draperies arranged to mimic the protrusion of pregnancy, even (I think) the 'buzz' between the two principals.

And, as in the scene with Zacharias, the long procession of Old Testament figures is once again invoked. Elizabeth is the descendant of Aaron, the brother of Moses. Mary's husband is a descendant of David, the great king, and his name calls up our memory of the Joseph of *Genesis*, the son of Jacob, who was also called

Israel. All the many passages of the Old Testament in which one generation begat another is now come to its culmination. All that vigorous begetting is about to have its final issue. We have considered only the first twenty-seven verses of Luke's Gospel, one-fifth of his prologue (which is his first two chapters). Now – in Mary's encounter with the angel – the story commences in earnest. As you read on, allow Luke to continue to speak to you in his exquisitely thoughtful way. Take time to appreciate Luke's unique material, the stories only he tells us. One wonders how Christianity would have managed without the episodes found only in his Gospel. Besides this prologue of pregnancies and births, there are Luke's other unique stories: the Good Samaritan (*Luke* 10:29–37), Martha and Mary (10:38–42), the Rich Fool (12:16–21), the Prodigal Son (15:11–32), Dives and Lazarus (16:19–31), the Pharisee and the Publican (18:10–14), Zaccheus (19:1–10), the Lament over Jerusalem (19:41–44), and the Good Thief (23:39–43), as well as Luke's delicious coda of the Disciples on the Road to Emmaus (24:13–35). Do not fail to note Luke's juxtapositions, which are always full of significance. (Consider, for instance, the unified trilogy of anecdotes that stretches from 10:29 to 11:4, in which Jesus teaches us that kindness to others is primary but only possible if we are willing to take time out from our daily preoccupations and pray to the Father.) From the Good Samaritan to the Good Thief, Luke, whose zephyr-like prose caresses his readers, is telling us always of the mercy of God. This mercy is

Luke's profoundest theme, the one to which all his other themes are subservient. With good reason Dante called him '*il scriba della gentilezza di Cristo,*' the scribe of the kindness of Christ.

Richard Holloway

There is a lot to be said for attaching a health warning to religion. It can be a hazardous business, because it is often based on a seductive deceit. In its most dangerous form it claims to have found words that exactly express one of the great mysteries that obsess the imagination, the possibility of God. So words *about* God are treated as though they were equivalent to God, and religious authorities demand our assent to them. Our fidelity or infidelity is tested by our relationship to the official vocabulary that is supposed to express the divine mystery. Since there is no final way of either verifying or falsifying such claims, the opportunity religious language offers us for violence and discord is endless. This is why many of the sanest minds in history have been wary of religion and its explosive, but unsustainable claims.

Apart from the danger religion may pose to our physical health, it can also endanger us spiritually, because it can trap us in language *about* mysteries rather than open us to the mysteries themselves. One of our problems as humans is that our greatest gift, language, is also our greatest danger. We destroy ourselves by our words. The difficulty is that things are not what we say they are. The word 'water' is not itself drinkable. Words point to things, but they can never be the things they point to. This may seem too obvious to waste time on, but it is a truth that is often ignored in religious circles. All theology is a doomed but necessary attempt to express the inexpressible. God is the elusive mystery we try to capture and convey in language, but how can that ever be done? If the word 'water' is not itself drinkable, how can the words we use to express the mystery of God be themselves absolute? They are metaphors, analogies, figures of speech, yet religious people have slaughtered and condemned each other over these experimental uncertainties. Our glory and agony is that we long to find words that will no longer be words, mere signifiers, but the very experience they are trying to signify; and our tragedy is that we can never succeed. This is the anguish that lies at the heart of all religion, because, though our words can describe our thirst for the absolute, they can never satisfy it.

But there is something that comes close. There is a human experience that sometimes captures the mystery that haunts us. Music is usually held to be the experience that does this best. In music there is an almost perfect equivalence of form and content. Music evidences itself, is itself the experience we experience, and is not just a sign or symbol for something else. All great art does this. It breaks through the frustration of language and unites us with that which words only usually signify. I say, 'only usually', because there is a language that, like music and art, is also capable of this same perfect tautology, this mysterious equivalence between the longing and the thing longed for. I am, of course, talking about poetry. Art, particularly music and poetry, unites us with the thing beyond, places us in its midst, rather than talks unceasingly and ineffectively about it, which is what religion usually does.

One test of great art is the shiver factor, the prickle at the back of the neck, the involuntary twitch of muscle that shows that a connection has been made between us and the matter to which we are paying attention. By this standard, Luke's gospel is a work of great art. In place after place it achieves that mysterious equivalence between the word spoken and the word felt, the situation described and the situation experienced. This is why it has influenced other artists who have translated Luke's words into painting of equivalent power. One of these paintings hangs in the Royal Scottish Gallery in Edinburgh. It was painted by Giovanni Francesco Barbieri for Cardinal Rocci in 1639 and it is called *Peter the Penitent*. It shows Peter crying bitterly, tormented by anguish and guilt, just after his third denial of Jesus. All the gospels recount the prediction of Jesus that Peter would deny him, and they all go on to describe Peter's betrayal. Only in *Luke*, however, do we get the detail that makes dramatic sense of Peter's desolation. After the third denial the cock crows, and Luke tells us: 'And the Lord turned, and looked upon Peter. And

Peter remembered the word of the Lord, how he had said unto him, "Before the cock crow, thou shalt deny me thrice." And Peter went out, and wept bitterly' (22:61–2). The words are few and simple, yet they have carried that look of grieving love through history. And they connect us to our own denials. Peter's tragedy is not that he was a bad or cynical man, but that he was an ordinary man who could not live up to his own ideals. Luke does not use abstract language about human remorse and the nature of guilt, yet in a few brush-strokes he brings us right into the experience and we confront ourselves. Unlike much conventional religious teaching that alienates us by its hectoring abstractions, Luke connects with us again and again by the immediacy of his art.

But that way of putting it is misleading, because it suggests the self-conscious presence of a writer working away to put a perfect polish on the text. We do not know who Luke was, and it does not matter, because it is the very anonymity of this text that confirms its power. All great art is essentially anonymous in its impact. We do not need to know anything about its provenance for it to affect us. We do not really know who wrote *Genesis* or many of the other ancient writings and we need not care, because these great texts communicate truth to us at a level that goes beyond the artistry of any particular individual. They create archetypes that express the general condition of humanity, and its sorrow and loss, heroism and betrayal. This is also why the gospels go on touching us long after we have abandoned the ortho-doxies that have been built on them. We do not know who wrote them or when, but they still have power to connect with our lives today, so that, reading them, we sometimes have to put them down and look into the distance as their words strike ancient chords within us.

If we fed the four gospels into a computer programmed to do literary detective work, we would make some interesting discoveries. The first thing we would notice is that *John*, the fourth gospel, is unlike the other three in voice and perspective. There are differences among the first three gospels as well, of course, but not only do they have a similar feel, they actually share a lot of material. For instance, it is quite obvious that *Matthew* and *Luke* simply repeat large chunks of *Mark*; they each quote another source, not found in *Mark*; and there is a certain amount of material peculiar to each of them. And all these layers of text had their own history. The gospels were not written down the way a biographer would work today. The process would be more like that of a musical historian who goes round the highlands and islands of Scotland to record folk tales, poetry and songs that are in the memories of people, but have never been written down in hard form. Most of our ancient literature comes from a long-standing oral tradition before it was committed to ink on parchment. The gospel writers would have been engaged in a similar exercise. They would collect stories about Jesus, remembrances that were handed down and sermons or meditations that were the result of long contemplation on the meaning of his story. In time, these would be woven into a whole garment, but only whole in the sense that a patchwork quilt is whole, stitched together out of many pieces.

Some of the most attractive and colourful of the patches are found only in *Luke*. It is Luke who tells us that at his birth Jesus was laid in a manger, 'because there was no room for them in the inn'. Luke brings more women, and more details about them, into his narrative than any of the other gospel writers. We have already noted the little thread of narrative that frames Peter's grief at his denials of Jesus; even more vivid are the parables that have gone into the memory and vocabulary of the western world, such as the Good Samaritan and the Prodigal Son. The message of Jesus, the good news, or gospel, as it was called, was expressed most memorably in the immediacy of stories rather than in religious abstractions. This is why the parables in *Luke* continue to connect with us today. They are about our experience of guilt, and our need for forgiveness; they are about the dangers of tribe and religion, and the way they insulate us against the needs of our neighbours. This is the point of the parable of the Good Samaritan in chapter 10. It is not about religious hypocrisy, and the way religion often says one thing and does another. The reason why the priest and the Levite passed by on the other side, leaving the man lying by the roadside, is that their code would not allow them to come to the aid of a stranger who might be a source of religious pollution to them. Interestingly, the Samaritan also followed a code that was just as defensive towards strangers, but it was simply blown away by the force of the pity he felt for the man who had fallen among thieves. Jesus is warning us that the codes that define our religious and national identities can shut our hearts against one another. Compassion should overrule code.

The story of the Prodigal Son in chapter 15 is even more profound. It is about the ways we hurt one another, and withhold the forgiveness that alone can heal the wounds we have inflicted. The most difficult of the predicaments that face us is what to do about the evil we do to one another. Our pain at being injured, as well as our sense of justice, require confession and repentance from the offender. Being the offender is even more imprisoning. The complexity of guilty self-knowledge often leads to a blustering defensiveness, rather like Peter's denials of Jesus, that prevents us from asking for the forgiveness we desperately want. In this way a dynamic of mutual recrimination is created that traps us in anger and despair. In the parable of the Prodigal the father rushes to forgive the son before he can say a word: 'When he was yet a great way off, his father saw him, and had compassion, and ran, and fell on his neck, and kissed him'. And it is this act of compassionate forgiveness that frees the son from the burden of his own guilt and gives him the strength to confess it: 'Father, I have sinned against heaven, and in thy sight, and am no more worthy to be called thy son'. Jesus is not discussing the ethics of forgiveness, how we can earn it and under what circumstances we can offer it. He simply shows us that without it we are all in prison, so we should try to get our forgiveness in first. If we refuse to forgive, we tear down the very bridge we ourselves will one day have to cross.

The Gospel of Luke is an old book and there is much in it that will seem strange to someone picking it up for the first time today. Nevertheless, it is impossible to read it without being challenged by the mysterious presence of Jesus. As well as a sense of enormous compassion for the human condition, we find in him a burning anger against all systems, religious or political, that come between God and the poor of the earth. In the furious pity of Jesus we catch a glimpse of God's dream for a transformed humanity. But the long narrative of the crucifixion at the end of the gospel reminds us that dreamers are usually disposed of with cruel efficiency by the people who have put themselves in charge of the world. Yet Jesus keeps breaking out of the tombs into which we have consigned him, so the dream lives on.

Ray Loriga

Every Man for Himself

THE LAST DAY OF THE INNOCENT

Jesus was first a tenant.

I had barely learnt to cycle in a straight line when I was forced to take on board the dark weight of guilt.

Is it possible that Jesus should die nailed to the cross to save me, simply to show a genuine concern for my soul?

I just wanted to receive First Communion so they would buy me the battery-driven submarine I had been longing for in my bathtub. What a huge impact it made when they told me that I would carry within me, from now on and until the very end of my days, the body of Christ. What a tiny dwelling-place for such a great guest. I had just turned six.

I got my submarine, of course, a perfect machine, capable of moving silently beneath the waters of my bath and even the ocean of the Olympic-size swimming pool of the Jiménez Swimming Club, a breeding place of champions to which I brought no glory.

However, already at that stage, I feared the whole business had just started. From then on Jesus was my tenant, the inconvenient guest who would accompany me on every step I took, the shadow of my shadow, the strangest part of my soul.

Long after, in a hotel on the outskirts of Phoenix, Arizona, I read the Bible for the first time. Arizona is a very large state that makes you feel very small. The Gospels are very small texts that have determined the direction of the world. They lack the magnificent brutality of the Old Testament, but in their concise exactness, they manage to cast a certain amount of light upon the wounded hearts of all men. I have re-read the Bible many times and I have always lost more than I thought I had found. But, after all, isn't this the ultimate end of all important literature?

JESUS CHRIST IS NOT A MAGICIAN

The power of a miracle is in the faith that sustains it and not in the challenge that it presents man's limited understanding of the sciences. The power of a miracle goes way beyond its real impact upon our affairs. More or fewer loaves or more or fewer fishes have not altered the course of history. A miracle is not a trick. A miracle is a myth. One can question the truth of a miracle scientifically, but that does not affect the power of the myth.

Junger says that it's high time for the gods to show themselves again, but perhaps it's the sublimation of science that prevents the voice of the gods from being heard in our days, and which reduces to zero the possibility of new miracles. In that case, are miracles mere inventions of faith? The very question is irrelevant and the answer to it would also be irrelevant. An apparition, however questionable it may be, is necessarily more important than, let's say, a Volkswagen, however real this may be. It seems certain, and must be acknowledged, that there's no worse blind man than one who doesn't want to see. The way things are, in a world of men without cars, it's not easy for good songs to be heard.

Are we getting closer, then, or are we moving further away? Have we burnt the old bridges without knowing how to build new ones? And once these ones are built, will they be bridges that can be crossed? Will they be built to suit the slow pace of men?

The answers are not written. The reading of these texts in the changing light of the centuries only increases in an alarming way the number of questions. 'Do you think that I have come to give peace on earth? No, I tell you, but rather division.' (*Luke* 12:51)

MAN AGAINST MAN

Is faith often, as Nietzsche said, a 'suicide of reason'? More questions stolen from Nietzsche: 'How is the suppression of the will possible? How is the saint possible?'

'If any man would come after me, let him deny himself and take up his cross daily and follow me.' (*Luke* 9:23)

The saint represents the ultimate victory over one's own will and, consequently, the ultimate defeat of oneself. The ultimate defeat of the individual. The image of the son of God on the cross remains the most terrifying paradox. Victory through annihilation.

More Nietzsche. His scorn for the New Testament is surprising. He considers it unworthy of forming a single body with the splendid book of divine justice that is the Old Testament. And yet, the formula 'God on the Cross', as he himself terms it, belongs to the Gospels and is, without doubt, the guiding image in all this labyrinthine business of faith.

It may be that for a guy as hard as Nietzsche, the New Testament fits better with the simplicity (i.e. weakness) of our mediocre hearts. As far as my own 'small soul' is concerned, I have to say that the texts of Saint Luke frequently strike me as perfect heirs of the cruelty and fear that emanate from the Old Testament. To put forward Jesus as the impossible model for man already seems to me sufficient cruelty in itself. 'For whoever would save his life for my sake, he will lose it; and whoever loses his life for my sake, he will save it.' (*Luke* 19:24)

THE LAST AND THE FIRST

Since I was a child I have found it hard to accept that one should kneel so much during mass and that one should deny one's own dignity in order to be accepted into a higher order. Nothing good can be achieved kneeling (leaving sex to one side), I used to say to myself, and I have to recognise that, in this aspect at least, I've hardly changed.

Jesus says: 'For everyone who exalts himself will be

humbled, and he who humbles himself will be exalted.'
(*Luke* 14:11)

This raises a doubt in me. He who lowers himself knowing that by doing this he will be raised up, isn't he raising himself up by this? He who raises himself up not knowing that he will have to be put down, isn't he putting himself down more than he knows or is able to?

ROSES WITHOUT THORNS

For those who thought that God demanded too much of poor Abraham when He asked him for the life of his own son as the ultimate sign of his absolute love, the Almighty shows that His love for men has no limits, and for that reason gives us the sacrifice of his son Jesus, who in his turn also gives us what's dearest to him: his life. That's why Jesus does not rush to follow the way of the cross, the way of his own death, full of suicidal pleasure but full of pain and anguish. Because one can only sacrifice what one loves, if not it's not a sacrifice. Because there are no roses, glory, without thorns, pain.

'If anyone comes to me and does not hate his own father and mother and wife and children and brothers and sisters, yes, and even his own life, he cannot be my disciple.

Whoever does not bear his own cross and come after me, cannot be my disciple.' (*Luke* 14: 26–27)

What kind of love is this, made of such great cruelty?

Absolute love towards God that carries with it absolute duty towards him.

And all for a submarine.

AN UNGAINLY SOLDIER OF FAITH

Faced with this prospect, it's not strange that I should have abandoned the path of religion at the age of fourteen and that, for a long time, I should have prided myself on being a perfect agnostic. I now feel like a leper who claims to be free of leprosy, without realising that the illness, once it has become contagious, is beyond the control of the patient's will. While I scoffed at my faith, my faith scoffed at me. While I thought I was free, without even realising it, I was still dragging around my cross.

'To what shall I compare the kingdom of God? It is like leaven which a woman took and hid in three measures of flour, till it was all leavened.' (*Luke* 13:20–21)

GOD'S LAW

J. Stuart Mill, one of the greatest defenders of individual freedom, cast doubt upon the way in which most believers accepted doctrines, capable in principle of producing the most energetic impression upon the spirit, without being subjected to the imagination, the feelings or the intelligence, turning them therefore into dead beliefs. Christian ethics, which after all rule over our world and our time and proceed in large measure from the New Testament, have to be considered in their original form, and not merely taken for granted in the tide of acquired gestures and vices that they have generated. Mills considered it a mistake to regard Christian doctrine as a complete code of conduct, something that he considered a 'serious practical ill that takes value away from moral instruction'. Be that as it may, believers and non-believers should approach the Gospels with their guard up and their hearts awake. You can only accept or reject what is known, and knowing implies taking a truth or a real proposition down to its foundations and reconstructing it in the light of one's own judgement.

God's law, which is when all's said and done our own, appears in Saint Luke's Gospel, sailing over some teaching pre-established by the Old Testament and, on rare but crucial occasions, colliding head-on with some of its precepts. Forgiveness and mercy are, probably, the most noteworthy inclusions, in opposition to an avenging, angry and even capricious God. What is it exactly that poor Job has done to deserve so much punishment? What game is God playing with the devil at the expense of his followers?

The Gospels, despite their obscurity, seem ready to offer us something more than coherence; perhaps for that very reason they are less impressive in literary terms. It could be said that the son of God is less dazzling but also less arbitrary than his father. The ultimate and also the first aim of the Evangelists is to transmit knowledge of a model experience. Men cannot and should not be like God, but they certainly can and should be like Jesus. Christ's journey is the journey of all men.

The Gospels can be read like the road map to salvation, but they can also be read like the plans of a prison. In them is specified the thickness of the walls but also, for the person who has the ability to interpret them, the only possible escape route. Here a new paradox unfolds. It may be that reading the Gospels is the only way of finally fleeing from Christian morality. Saint Luke's Gospel is at one and the same time a trap and a splendid escape map. A free man is not the one who doesn't know the prison, but the one who manages to escape from it. Going back to leprosy, ignoring the disease is not the same as healing oneself.

EVERY MAN FOR HIMSELF

Returning to the matter of Christian morality, it is disappointing to realise that it is composed of more negatives than positives. It's more about what you will not do, than about what you will do. Original sin and guilt submit the Christian to a negative process, one in which the individual uses his meagre strength to deduct interest from the debt before the final payment is due. This very payment casts doubt upon the whole process, turning Christian morality into a fundamentally selfish morality; everything is done for one's own salvation, not because goodness is an end in itself. Knowing beforehand what awaits you at the end detracts from the effort that you put into the journey. One other doubt: Is faith a means or an end? Goodness that expects to be rewarded is a way of paying for paradise and has, clearly, less value than goodness without aspirations, which has its origin and its end in itself. This goodness without reward seems the only proper way of formulating a real manual of ethics.

Are the saints the only pirates who know the way to the treasure and how it will affect the purity of their hearts?

'Sell your possessions, and give alms; provide yourselves with purses that do not grow old, with a treasure in the heavens that does not fail, where no thief approaches and no moth destroys. For where your treasure is, there will your heart be also.' (*Luke* 12:33–34)

A WORLD WITHOUT GOD

And what if Stephen Hawking and the crazy quantum theorists who accompany him are right and the universe is no more than a giant self-defining bubble, without beginning or end, without the need of or the place for a god, any god at all?

In that case who is that poor man who invents unfathomable parables as he goes along, who walks over the mists that cover the shore making us believe that he's walking on water, that he's surrendering himself in the end to a meaningless sacrifice? Who is this madman who faithfully follows the designs of a non-existent father, who clings onto a telephone which has nobody at the other end of the line? What cross is it that he drags around and what cross is it that all of us drag around after him?

Perhaps all the submarines, digital watches, bicycles and paint boxes that we received in those hectic First Communion parties were not, after all, poisoned gifts.

The children of science should, in any case,

approach the knowledge of God. Because if in the end it's He who's right. What seems certain is that God will know everything about science and about everyone and about each one of the children of science. We had better be prepared. We can ignore God, but it does not seem likely that God can ignore us.

THE PROBLEM IS THE PRICE

The Gospel of Saint Luke may be the hardest one to accept, the one that does the least to hide the price, the one that moves the prize furthest away. It may be that these texts do the greatest harm to faith, to possible faith that is, precisely because of the existence of this doubt, the impossible faith. The problem always lies with the size of the doubt, because any doubt, however tiny it may be, is by definition too big. Only the eradication of doubt leads to faith. There are no percentages of faith, there is only absolute faith.

Faith is total or not at all. The Gospel according to Saint Luke is a Gospel for resolute Christians. It's not a promise, but an obligation. Of course, it would be easier for all of us if the text were slightly sweetened, if the promise were lowered, even by a couple of millimetres, down to the reach of men; but, however cruel the way might seem, the greatness of the prize demands the impossible harness of the rules of the competition. In short we are talking about the absolute salvation of the soul and life eternal.

There are easier games, but there are no better prizes.

THE GOSPEL ACCORDING TO JOHN

In the beginning was the Word, and the Word was with God, and the Word was God. The same was in the beginning with God. All things were made by him; and without him was not any thing made that was made. In him was life: and the life was the light of men. And the light shineth in darkness; and the darkness comprehended it not.'

(1:1–5)
authorised King James version

Blake Morrison

From the age of eight to fifteen, I spent every Sunday morning in the choirstalls of an English village church. To be in the choir didn't require singing talent. You just turned up each week and stood there, like something out of Thomas Hardy, raising a song in praise of God, to the accompaniment of a wheezing organ. Our predecessors in the graveyard had done the same. The dusty black cassocks and white surplices waiting for us on pegs in the vestry – they had worn them, too. The choir was small, just six or eight, all children, most of them present under parental duress. With me, it was different: my father was an atheist, my mother an Irish Catholic, and I'd had to fight to join up. It was not that I had a sense of calling. It was simply a way of getting to see my friends on Sunday. We weren't always well-behaved. Gum was surreptitiously chewed during prayers, then deposited in sticky balls and left to harden. Cruel names were invented for those in the paltry congregation. Whispering and giggling were routine. Still, until confirmation (which for me confirmed doubts, not faith) we kept coming.

And though I'm no church-goer now, those Sundays will always be part of me. The touch of cold stone flags on a bended knee; the lovely sound of 'daily bread' and 'trespasses'; the melting nothingness (neither flesh nor manna) of a communion wafer; the head-swoon from a sip of wine; the rotting-body smell from water that stood too long in flower-vases; the whitewash walls, the spread-winged golden-eagle lectern stand, the pale-lemon morning light, the wood of the nave so dark it might have been burned – the hours of boredom have long faded, but the sensuousness has stayed.

The Gospels have stayed, too, the miracles and sayings and Passion. To begin with, I preferred the Old Testament, which read like a boy's adventure story spanning several generations: Noah's flood, David's slingstone, Daniel in the lion's den, Moses in his basket, the parting of the Red Sea. Jesus had adventures, too, but you'd not have known it from the face in the stained-glass windows. He looked wan, frozen and passive, too pious for his own good – someone who'd change wine to water, not the other way about. The only impressive thing about him was that it had taken four men to tell his tale. Matthew, Mark, Luke and John: the names sounded familiar, reassuring, trustworthy, and it didn't seem surprising that their stories should vary – when my friends and I related the same events, didn't our versions vary, too? As years passed in the choir-stalls, I became more interested in the Apostles, and tried to put faces to their names. John was the hardest to visualise. He was said to be the son of Zebedee, 'the beloved disciple', but this didn't help much. All I did dimly perceive was that he was the odd one out.

At fifteen, I swapped the Apostles for another Fab Four, the Beatles, whose John was likewise the outsider. Soon enough, the phrase 'gospel truth' had a hollow ring for me – I was discovering stranger, more various truths through drink, drugs, girls, music, the mystic east. The only lingering affection I felt for the c of e came from thinking of Jesus's story as myth or legend – literary fiction, not monotheistic truth. The idea that the Apostles were contemporaries of Christ, writing factual first-hand reports, seemed ridiculous. But once I thought of them as storytellers, drawing on oral tradition, their gospels became more interesting. They were pedagogues, trying to convince others to follow their faith. But they were also, at least in the Authorised Version, hauntingly imaginative writers, John above all.

The literary status of the gospels, the identity of their authors, the degree of historical truth they impart – these are matters scholars debate to this day. Agreement is rare, but one can glimpse a consensus of sorts on several points.

– A man called Jesus did live and preach in Palestine shortly after the time of King Herod's death; a radical thinker and militant leader, he ran into trouble with the authorities and was put to death.

– Matthew, Mark, Luke and John wrote their gospels late in the first century, perhaps drawing on eye-witness accounts that had been passed down: their names were assigned to the Gospels only around 180 AD, and they probably worked closely with other Christian opinion-formers, in effect as editorial teams.

– Each gospel went through several versions, perhaps as many as five, building up from sayings and sermons through 'pericopes' (teaching or episodic units) to full-blown narratives.

– Their purpose was to proclaim the 'good news' of Jesus's life, through accounts of his story and teachings: 'these are written, that ye might believe that Jesus is the Christ, the Son of God; and that believing ye might have life through his name' (*John* 20:31).

– *Mark* was the first gospel to be composed and *John* is probably the last.

The apparently late composition of John's gospel is one of several reasons why it's often treated as marginal and inferior. Its resemblance to *Mark* (and *Luke*) suggests that, if not directly dependent on them, it drew on the same sources for episodes such as the walk on the lake, the feeding of the 5,000 and the miraculous draught of fishes. The chronology of the first three ('synoptic') gospels coincides to a very large degree, whereas *John* ('the fourth gospel') differs in suggesting that Jesus's ministry lasted over three Passovers, not one, and in putting the scourging of the Temple episode early on. The synoptic gospels are also fairly consistent about the teachings of Jesus, whereas what he preaches in *John* shows the influence of later schools of thought, including the Hellenistic and the Hermetic. Many commentators find the structure of *John* dislocated and suggest an alternative arrangement of the chapters. All in all, as E P Sanders puts it in his study *The Historical Figure of Jesus*, 'The synoptic gospels are to be preferred as our basic source of information about Jesus.'

What claims can be made for *John*, then? First, it is the most *poetic* of the gospels. Compare the various openings. *Matthew* begins with a dull, Old Testament-like genealogical table: 'Abraham begat Isaac; and Isaac begat Jacob; and Jacob begat Judas', etc. *Mark* goes in for skittish anecdotes and dress-notes about John the Baptist: 'John was clothed with camel's hair, and with a girdle of skin'. *Luke* writes in drab bureaucratese to Theophilus, the recipient of his missive: 'Forasmuch as many have taken in hand to set forth in order a declaration of those things which are most surely believed among us . . .' By contrast, *John* opens with one of the greatest passages of poetic prose in the language, philosophically dense, metaphorically rich and rhythmically lucid at the same time:

> In the beginning was the Word, and the Word was with God, and the Word was God. The same was in the beginning with God. All things were made by him; and without him was not any thing made that was made. In him was life; and the life was the light of men. And the light shineth in darkness; and the darkness comprehended it not . . . And the Word was made flesh, and dwelt among us (and we beheld his glory, the glory as of the only begotten of the Father), full of grace and truth. (1:1–5, 14)

John is thick with symbols and incantations: light, darkness, bread, water, flesh, word. It's also full of lines that have gone into the language: 'God so loved the world, that he gave his only begotten son . . .'; 'Rise, take up thy bed, and walk'; 'He that is without sin among you, let him first cast a stone at her'; 'I am the good shepherd'; 'I am the resurrection, and the life'; 'The poor always ye have with you'; 'In my father's house are many mansions'; 'Greater love hath no man than this, that a man lay down his life for his friends'; 'Put up thy sword into thy sheath'; 'What I have written I have written'. Part of what makes *John* special is that *it uses metaphors where the other Gospels use similes*. 'Destroy this temple,' Jesus tells the Jews, speaking not of their temple but his body, 'and I will raise it up' (2:19). 'Whosoever drinketh of this water shalt thirst again,' he tells the woman of Samaria by her well, 'but whosoever drinketh of the water that I shall give him shall never thirst' (3:13–14). 'I have meat to eat that ye know not of,' he tells his disciples, '. . . my meat is to do the will of him that sent me' (4:32–4). Or again to his disciples: 'I am the bread of life: he that cometh to me shall never hunger . . .' (6:35). Or again: 'I am the light of the world' (8:12). Or: 'I am the true vine, and my Father is the husbandman' (15:1).

Metaphors aren't always easy to understand. They trouble the literal-minded. Jesus causes this trouble. One of the themes of John's gospel is *the difficulty people have in communicating with one another*. Jesus's protracted metaphor about entering into a sheepfold leaves his listeners baffled: 'they understood not what things they were which he spake unto them' (10:6). Talk of the impossibility of their following him also causes confusion: 'Then said the Jews, "Will he kill himself?" Because he saith, "Whither I go, ye cannot come."' Nicodemus is perplexed by the promise of rebirth: how *can* a man be reborn, he asks, stirring Jesus into new poetry: 'Marvel not that I said unto thee, "Ye must be born again." The wind bloweth where it listeth, and thou hearest the sound thereof, but canst not tell whence it cometh, and whither it goeth: so is everyone that is born of the Spirit.' *John*'s Jesus is more seer-like than the Jesus of the other gospels: a prophet, an enigma, a stranger from heaven. He is in touch with truths that defy easy comprehension. But he's also self-aware enough to realise his listeners sometimes find him hard-going: 'I have yet many things to say unto you, but ye cannot bear them now.' He doesn't bear listening to in part because he's gnomic. Or if not gnomic, Gnostic. He speaks an alien language, the poetry of God.

John's *characterisation of Jesus* is another reason why this Gospel stands out. Far from being meek and mild, Jesus here is self-assured, pushy, and somewhat dislikeable. It may not have been the author's intention, but we see why he caused such anger and resentment, and understand his enemies' wish to have him dead and out of the way. When he's not speaking in riddles, he's argumentative. He hectors. He harangues. He throws out insults and reproaches. He pulls rank, advertising his credentials as Son of God, Son of Man, Messiah, more divine than human, just passing through: 'Ye are from beneath; I am from above: ye are of this world; I am not of this world (8:23). There is a ferocious existentialist 'I am' about him. Desperate to defeat the doubters, he is not averse to using signs to establish his authority ('Except ye see signs and wonders, ye will not believe'), which the Jesus of Mark's gospel refuses to do, implying it would be a stunt, a piece of cheap magic ('Verily I say unto you, there shall no sign be given unto this generation'). One of the greatest commentators on the fourth gospel, Rudolf Bultmann, has said that 'Jesus as the Revealer of God reveals nothing but that he is the Revealer.' If this makes him sound like some latter-day cultist, prone to mystification and Me-ism, it should also be said that he's robust and resourceful, a cartoon character who keeps getting out of impossible scrapes: 'They took up stones to cast at him: but Jesus hid himself, and went out of the temple, going through the midst of them, and so passed by' (8:59). 'They sought again to take him: but he escaped out of their hand, and went away again beyond Jordan . . .' (10:39–40). These escapes continue even after the crucifixion, first when Pilate's soldiers fail to carry out an order to break his legs, then when he disappears from the sepulchre in death as well as life, he constantly outwits his enemies.

The Jesus of John's Apostle is often described as mystic. But *he is worldly as well as otherworldly.* When he scourges the temple moneychangers, it's his physical strength that John emphasises: 'and when he had made a scourge of small cords, he drove them all out of the temple, and the sheep, and the oxen; and poured out the changers' money, and overthrew the tables'. There's more physical immediacy when Jesus spits on the ground, 'and made clay of the spittle', to heal a blind man. And there's Martha's pungent reaction when Jesus proposes to raise her brother Lazarus: 'Lord, by this time he stinketh: for he hath been dead four days.' However high-flown some of the passages in *John*, we never lose sight of fleshly realities. Nor is there any skimping on political realities. Because the ruling powers in Palestine enjoy only limited independence from Rome, they see Jesus as a dangerous rebel, a threat to the status quo: if a popular uprising is sparked by his teaching, 'the Romans shall come and take away both our place and nation' (11:48).

John is also arguably *the most economical of the gospels: Mark* is shorter, with 16 chapters to *John*'s 21. But the fourth gospel includes and develops a number of episodes not to be found in the synoptic gospels: for example, the wedding feast at Cana, the raising of Lazarus, and the conversations with Nicodemus and the Woman of Samaria. As a result, its first half, up to Passover, seems to move with extraordinary speed. There is tension from the outset, with the threat to Jesus established as early as chapter 5 ('And therefore did the Jews persecute Jesus and sought to slay him') and the fact that Judas Iscariot will eventually betray him revealed in chapter 6. There's also a feeling of awful inevitability, as in Shakespearian tragedy: beauty and truth are going to pass from the earth because men love darkness rather than light.

Despite the prayer and teaching threaded through it, the narrative never slackens in pace. With the crucifixion and resurrection especially, small details do the work of whole paragraphs: the sponge of vinegar put in Christ's mouth, for example, or the empty linen cloths found in his tomb. At the very end, John acknowledges the conciseness of his method: 'And there are also many other things which Jesus did, the which, if they should be written every one, I suppose that even the world itself could not contain the books that should be written.'

This is the kind of sign-off often found in fairytales and fables, gesturing at riches left out. Heresy though it is to say so, the *Gospel of John* has the quality of a fairytale. It has theological and philosophical aspirations too, of course: as one commentator, John Ashton, has put it, 'It is like finding Hans Christian Andersen hand in hand with Soren Kierkegaard.' But in a secular age, when many people will be left cold by its more didactic passages, the narrative power of the fourth gospel is what redeems it. In Robert Browning's poem 'A Death in the Desert', a dying John foresees a day when readers will ask: 'Was John at all, and did he say he saw?' But whether John was or wasn't, his gospel is not yet redundant. Some will take it as literal truth, and others embrace its imaginative truth. But there's also what Jesus calls 'the truth [that] shall make you free' (8:32). For John, this is what matters most: the possibility that by reading his gospel we will in some way – emotionally, aesthetically, intellectually, spiritually – be liberated.

Liberation wasn't the sensation I got from it as a

rustic choirboy. But re-reading it again lately, I felt a story I'd half-forgotten open up again and carry me back to the place where I first heard it. The rhythms of John's gospel can be inspiring and sensuous in that way. He is an enigmatic guide, the odd one out among the Apostles. But he's also a poet through and through.

Darcey Steinke

A stranger once showed up at my father's church during a Sunday potluck supper. The parishioners had just filled their plates with lumps of tuna-fish casserole and Jell-O salad when a man with a white beard came to the back door, stood in the foyer, and ceremoniously unfolded a piece of paper. With a heavy German accent he read his birth date, his parents' names, and the name of the town where he'd been born seventy-seven years earlier, just outside Berlin.

My father jumped up from where we sat at the head table. He was about thirty then, blond, and lean in his black clerical suit. I was six years old and had never seen anyone so jittery and upset. Over and over, the old German repeated his birth date and asked if my father had known his mother, the lovely Berta from Frankfurt. He seemed unsure of his own existence and wanted my father to keep the birth certificate as proof that he was alive. The overhead fluorescent lights slickened the white cement-block walls and made the old German look even more exotic in the confines of the church basement.

The man refused to stay and eat, though as he left he seemed calmed by the fact my father had taken down the directions to his house and promised to drive out to visit him the following day.

I waited on the front steps of the parsonage for my father to return from visiting the old German. The cement steps were lined with wrought-iron railings, and as I watched my father through the black latticework get out of the station wagon and walk toward me, I could tell he was discombobulated. His black trench coat swung down from his narrow shoulders, and the way he let his arms dangle at his sides suggested that he was slightly unhinged.

'Is the man lonely?' I asked, grasping at his cold fingers and standing up.

'Yes,' my father replied, 'the man is very lonely.'

I could tell my father was withholding information, so I followed him inside the house. But he was preoccupied and headed immediately downstairs to talk to my mother, who was loading clothes into the washing machine. I pretended to walk upstairs to my room, but then tiptoed back and stood with my ear inside the cracked basement door and listened as my father told my mother that the German's house had been filthy and teaming with cats, that he'd referred to magazine clippings of children as his daughters and to the naked department store mannequin sitting at his kitchen table as his wife.

I'd never heard such a thing! The German was like a character in a fairy tale, a wizard setting up his magic trick, or Cinderella's fairy godmother turning a pumpkin into a carriage and white mice into thoroughbreds. I was young enough to believe that miracles were possible and I understood the need for a lot of cats, but what was wrong with pretending your doll was your wife if you were feeling lonely and just wanted a friend? The old German was sort of like Jesus, a loner, an essentially sad character, never satisfied with reality, always trying to break into the spiritual world. Dark skinned and hairless, Jesus' thin body hung half dead on the cross in our kitchen like a changeling, someone who could take you to a better place. And like the German, Jesus was also freaky and out of control. I could always tell my mother disapproved of Jesus' behavior; she'd stiffen up as my father read about him changing water into wine and helping prostitutes.

I wanted to see where the old man lived and, though he insisted I wait in the car during the visit, my father let me ride along with him the following week. I was hoping for a derelict gingerbread house, a mailbox shaped like a swan, or kittens that could say the alphabet, some sign that the German did indeed have magical powers, so I was disappointed by the tilted front porch and the cat with sick eyes curled up on the broken-down recliner. The glass panes of the front window were splintered, so that the curtains inside showed brown patches of water damage.

My father left the car running, heat blew up from under the dashboard, and I played with the radio dial, hoping to find the latest Beatles single, 'I Want to Hold

Your Hand.' After knocking on the front door, my father motioned to me that he was going to walk around the back of the house. I watched him disappear around the corner of the building, carrying his traveling communion kit, with velvet nooks for the silver goblet and the tin of dove-stamped wafers. I had just learned in grade school that the planets revolved around the sun, and this fact filled me with admiration for God. What a concept! Gigantic brilliantly colored balls flying around a fireball for all eternity! So I sat there for some time, trying to imagine the earth spinning through space. After a while, when I couldn't convince myself any longer that the car was moving like a rocket ship, I thought about how hard it was going to be to find that one person meant just for me, and then I thought about God's son, Jesus; how if God hadn't sent him down to the earth and if Jesus hadn't told his disciples to love one another, I wouldn't even be sitting here in this car with hot air blowing on my knees waiting for a Beatles song to come on the radio.

I was so preoccupied that I hadn't seen my father walking back to the car, and as he yanked opened the door, I pulled my legs from where I had them sprawled out dreamily over his seat. I could tell by his countenance, shoulders raised, his face drained of all color, that he was angry at me.

'What happened, Daddy?' I asked him.

'It's not you, sweetie,' he said, 'it's Mr Kleinburg.' I could see him ordering his words. 'He's dead.'

'Maybe Mr Kleinburg is just sleeping,' I suggested.

My father gripped the steering wheel, his knuckles whitened, and he jerked his head forward, opened his mouth, and gagged. This surprised me so much I decided to stay quiet and thought about Mr Kleinburg reading from his birth certificate, how he'd been right to worry over his own existence.

Once back on the highway, we stopped at a gas station to call the police. My father dropped me off at home, then drove back to Mr Kleinburg's house. Late that night, when my father finally got home, I stood outside my parents' bedroom and listened to him detail the suicide scene: blood and tissue splattered up over the magazine pictures of his daughters, the chair flung backward, his body curled sideways on the ground, a shotgun between his legs. His chin was gone. This fact seemed to upset my father the most. His voice thickened up as it did when he read from the passion on Good Friday. I was so stunned I can still remember the texture of the latex paint on the bedroom door and the sound of branches scraping against the side of the house as I listened to my father's story. The elements of Mr Kleinburg's suicide – the shotgun, the blood-splattered magazine pictures, the tipped chair – were as vivid to me as Jesus' crown of thorns, his fake king's robe, the vinegar-soaked sponge.

The cadence of my father's first-person account – still quaking from a brush with fanaticism and death – reminds me of John's eyewitness Gospel account of Jesus, and listening to my father's story about the

German puts me in the same configuration as someone reading John's version of the life of Christ. *John* is unique among the Gospels because of the narrator's claim that he witnessed Jesus' life and death. This immediacy and intimacy of detail configures Jesus as a charismatic young radical. Teasing his friend Nathanael about being too enthusiastic about his divinity, Jesus says, 'Just because I said unto thee I saw you under the fig tree, believist thou? Thou shall see greater things than these.' Jesus' first miracle in chapter 2 is an aesthetic and rather groovy one; he changes water into wine. Later in that same chapter he commits an act of social anarchy worthy of any '60s revolutionary: making a scourge out of small cords, Jesus drives the money changers out of the temple. But unlike Che Guevara, whose demeanor and public agenda seem close to Jesus', the hero of the Gospels has a trump card to play: supernatural power.

This effusion of magic makes the atmosphere of *John* hallucinatory: it's the Gospel in which Jesus appears most like the brother from another planet. Structured like an *X-Files* episode, Jesus, a magnetic thirty-three-year-old, claims to be from his father's house in the sky. He performs a variety of trippy miracles – raising Lazarus from the dead, making a few loaves of bread and a couple of fish feed five thousand, and reattaching a severed ear – all the while speaking in cryptic parables about the urgency of the spiritual realm. When attacked by dark governmental forces, he gives up his corporeal envelope and makes a last ghostly appearance before ascending up to the mother ship.

Even the language in *John* can be as bizarre and distended as a channeled message. 'On the next day much people that were come to the feast . . .' and '. . . where was a garden, into the which he entered and his disciples.' The staccato rhythm and off-key cadence of these lines signify language operating under intense duress. These words pushed to the edge of comprehension remind me of the time my sister-in-law called to tell us about her husband's death. My own husband's eyes widened as he pulled his mouth away from the phone receiver and said, 'Steve gunned himself in the head and then died.' Reality was punctured and words were wrestled into configurations to bind together the incision. Shocked syntax straining toward understanding is the stylistic signature of John's prose. Above all the other Gospel writers, John values language. In the beginning he claims, *before everything else*, was the Word, and for him the Word and God are synonymous.

As a little girl listening through my parents' door while my father told the story of the German's demise, I craved *words*. All humans do, especially at that high level of narrative intensity. There is a great power in the authenticity of an eyewitness account, and as humans we also need witnesses – the German wanted my father to witness his lonely death. But even as we listen to the concrete details on the nightly news of the Oklahoma City bombing or the atrocities in Bosnia, or more personal stories of a friend's grandmother's final hour, or the birth of our brother's baby son, even as our emotions attach to the participant's pain or joy, nothing is really cleared up. Instead, mystery takes root inside of us.

Mystery in *John* is evoked on two levels: the fact that Jesus may actually be a messenger sent by the creator and, more mundanely but no less fascinating, the mysteries intrinsic in the intricacies of Jesus' own character. The evocation of the latter is the real strength of *John.* John's voice is intimate and urgent. He tells us the story of his crazy fanatical friend, but unlike my father's bleak suicide narrative, unlike any of the sacred human narratives that relay details of pain, death, and violence, John's story claims to contain particles of divinity. That's the message which vaults his account over all other biographies; Jesus was a fenestral opening, a direct communiqué from God. John's narrative affects us viscerally because Jesus' effect on him was so devastating and sublime that all these centuries later, through his unshored and hyperbolic prose, we can still get a contact high.

THE ACTS OF THE APOSTLES

And it came to pass, that, as I made my journey, and was come nigh unto Damascus about noon, suddenly there shone from heaven a great light round about me. And I fell unto the ground, and heard a voice saying unto me, 'Saul, Saul, why persecutest thou me?' And I answered, 'Who art thou, Lord?' And he said unto me, 'I am Jesus of Nazareth, whom thou persecutest.'

(22:6–8)

authorised King James version

P.D. James

No book of the New Testament has a plainer and less ambiguous title than has the fifth, *The Acts of the Apostles*, but it is hardly an accurate description of this complex, fascinating and occasionally puzzling testimony in which the majority of the Apostles are only briefly named. To read *Acts* is to be drawn into a world of dramatic incident thronged with characters from all walks of life, a world of many nations and tongues; Parthians and Medes, Elamites, Cretes and Arabians, some of whom briefly appear and then as mysteriously disappear. This personal account of the formative years of the Christian Church is dominated by two very different characters, both of immense stature and importance: Peter, the rock on which Christ said He would build His Church, and Paul of Tarsus, the religious genius who, following his dramatic conversion, carried the new faith to the Gentile world and formulated its theology.

The story opens with the command of Jesus that His disciples should wait in Jerusalem for the promised baptism with the Holy Ghost, after which they would be empowered to be witnesses to Him, 'both in Jerusalem and in all Judaea, and in Samaria, and unto the uttermost part of the earth' (1:8). By the end of the book we have seen this promise fulfilled. By the power of the Holy Spirit the faith has spread like sparks from a fire, leaping from community to community through the Mediterranean world until it reaches the gates of Rome itself.

From the end of the second century the tradition of the Church has ascribed authorship of *Acts* to Luke, who wrote the first gospel. Both works are dedicated to Theophilus. The style and vocabulary of both are consistent with the same authorship and it would seem that the two books were intended to be read as one narrative. Luke is mentioned only three times in the New Testament, all in the letters of Paul. In *Colossians* 4:14 he writes: 'Luke, the beloved physician, and Demas, greet you'. When writing to Philemon he refers to Luke as one of his fellow workers, and in the fourth chapter of the second letter to Timothy, he writes: 'Only Luke is with me' (4:11). It does seem likely that Luke accompanied Paul on some of his journeys, particularly since sections in the second half of the book changed from the third-person to the first-person narrative, and are obviously a personal account. But it is extraordinary that we know so little of the man who, through his writing, was so influential in the life of the Church.

We know even less of the dedicatee Theophilus. Luke, in his gospel, gave him the title 'Excellency'. Was he a provincial governor or other powerful man drawn to the new religion but waiting to be convinced of its truth before accepting baptism? Was he even a real person? But he certainly stands for the very many people whom Luke was addressing and seeking to convince and convert by this extraordinary, richly-populated and complex mixture of religious apologia, adventure story and travelogue. *Acts* was probably written about 60 AD, although some authorities date it twenty years later. If 60 AD is roughly correct, then Luke may well have spoken to witnesses who actually met Jesus during His ministry.

The most dramatic and arguably the most important episode in *Acts*, apart from Christ's ascension and the coming of the Holy Spirit, is the conversion of Paul, then called Saul. He was an indefatigable persecutor of the Way and had been present at the stoning to death of Stephen, the first martyr. Now 'breathing out threatenings and slaughter against the disciples of the Lord' (9:1), he obtained from the high priest letters to the synagogue at Damascus authorising him to bring in men or women followers of the Way bound for Jerusalem.

While he was on the road and coming close to Damascus, there was a sudden light from Heaven shining around him. He fell to the ground and heard a voice saying: 'Saul, Saul, why persecutest thou me?' Trembling and astonished he asked, 'Lord, what wilt thou have me to do?(9:6)' He was told to rise and go into the city and there wait to be told what would happen next. The men who were journeying with him stood speechless with amazement, hearing a voice but seeing no-one. When Saul got up from the earth he was blind and his companions had to lead him by the hand and take him into Damascus. There, after three days without sight and without food or drink, the disciple named Ananias came to him, restored his sight, confirmed to him that the Lord had indeed appeared to him on the way, and baptised him. In that extraordinary moment of revelation on the Damascus road Paul's life was irrevocably changed and the history of the Western world was set on a different course.

It would not, of course, be accurate to think of Paul's conversion in our present sense of the word; he did not abjure his old religion. He and the disciples remained Jews and, when they worshipped, did so in the synagogue. And when they preached the message of Christ crucified and risen, they could not possibly have envisioned that this new religion would spread to lands then undiscovered, or that Jesus of Nazareth would still be worshipped two thousand years after their deaths. They must, indeed, have been in expectation of Christ's early Second Coming.

No organisation with which human beings are concerned, even one divinely ordained or inspired, is ever free from controversy. The main problem facing the new Church was whether Christ's revelation was to the Jews alone or whether Gentiles could also receive the gift of the Spirit and be baptised. The decision, like many others, was preceded by a divine revelation following prayer. Peter, who was at Joppa, went up on the roof to pray. He was hungry and, while food was being prepared, he fell into a trance. He saw Heaven opening and a great sheet, knotted by its four corners, descend and ascend three times, containing all manner of 'four-footed beasts of the earth, and wild beasts, and creeping things, and fowls of the air' (10:12). Peter heard a voice saying: 'Rise, Peter; kill and eat', but he replied, 'Not so, Lord, for I have never eaten any thing that is common or unclean.' Then the voice spoke to him again: 'What God has cleansed, that call not thou common' (10:13–15). Peter perceived that God is no respector of persons; the new dispensation of love was to be taken to the whole world.

Inevitably this decision gave rise to further dissension; was it necessary for converts who were not Jews to be circumcised before they were received into the Church? It was decided that the Gentiles must be required to keep the Jewish dietary rules and abstain from fornication, but that they need not be circumcised. The decision was certainly not unanimous and was probably more controversial than Luke admits. It was, however, one more vital step on the journey of Christianity towards world acceptance.

Another decision which caused difficulty arose from the practice of the Church that possessions should be held in common and that distribution should be made according to need. A certain man named Ananias (the second of that name in *Acts*), with Sapphira his wife, sold their possessions, as they were required to do, but kept back part of the price. When Ananias laid the remainder at the apostles' feet, Peter asked Ananias: 'Why has Satan filled thine heart to lie to the Holy Ghost and to keep back part of the price of the land?(5:3)' On hearing Peter's words, Ananias fell down dead.

About three hours later, his wife, not knowing what had happened, came in and received the same question from Peter. She too fell down dead at his feet and was carried out. 'And great fear came upon all the church, and upon as many as heard these things' (5:11). I have always found this a disturbing story and can't help feeling some sympathy for Ananias and his wife. They probably felt it was prudent and not unreasonable, having sold all their possessions, to retain at least part of the proceeds; their punishment – since that is how it is presented in *Acts* – seems more typical of a vengeful Jehovah than of the God of love and forgiveness.

Acts is a restless book, full of comings and going, of dramatic incidents and violent events. We accompany Paul on his three great perilous journeys, but he is not the only traveller; almost all the characters are on the road, healing, raising the dead, preaching, defending themselves before the councils of the great, both in state and synagogue. Luke observes the dramatic events with the eye of a physician and describes them with the discriminating skill of a novelist, providing the human details which add verisimilitude and reinforce the story's humanity and universality.

An example is the release of Paul and Silas from prison in chapter 16, when a great earthquake at midnight shook the prison foundations and opened all the doors. The keeper of the prison, assuming that all his prisoners had fled, drew out his sword to commit suicide, but Paul cried with a loud voice, saying: 'Do thyself no harm for we are all here' (16:28). Then the keeper called for a light and, falling down before Paul and Silas, asked what he must do to be saved. They said: 'Believe on the Lord Jesus Christ, and thou shalt be saved, and thy house' (16:31). That same night he took them home, washed their weals from the flogging and he and all his family were baptised. The next morning the magistrates sent the serjeants to free Paul and Silas. Paul, however, insisted that the magistrates come in person to do the job, saying that he and Silas had been beaten and imprisoned without having been condemned, despite the fact that they were Roman citizens. Small wonder that, hearing the prisoners were Romans, the magistrates came themselves and exhorted them to leave the city.

The final chapter of *Acts*, chapter 28, ends so suddenly that one wonders whether Luke intended to continue writing. We are left uncertain of Paul's future; the last two sentences merely say that he dwelt for two whole years at Rome in his hired house and received 'all that came in unto him. Preaching the kingdom of God, and teaching those things which concern the Lord Jesus Christ, with all confidence, no man forbidding him' (28:31). The Holy Spirit which had descended upon the disciples in Jerusalem had led the Church to the heart of the Roman Empire. Although Luke's account of Paul's life and ministry ends so abruptly, tradition has it that he was executed in Rome in AD 64–5, under Nero's persecution. The path on which he had set out after that dramatic encounter on the Damascus road, and which he had followed so faithfully, led him at last to a martyr's crown.

THE EPISTLE OF PAUL THE APOSTLE TO THE ROMANS

For I am persuaded, that neither death, nor life, nor angels, nor principalities, nor powers, nor things present, nor things to come, nor height, nor depth, nor any other creature, shall be able to separate us from the love of God, which is in Christ Jesus our Lord.

(8:38–39) (22:6–8)

authorised King James version

Ruth Rendell

The Road to Damascus is a phrase which has entered our language and our literature, becoming a metaphor for the sort of life-changing experience which strikes with suddenness and leaves its object transformed. It first happened to Paul the Apostle whose course of life, beliefs and objectives were all overturned by what happened to him on that actual road to that actual city.

He is believed to have been born in Tarsus, now part of Turkey, and was a Roman Citizen, a useful status which conferred certain judicial privileges, including that of *appellatio*, appeal to Caesar himself. He spoke Greek as his mother tongue, but in his letters he refers to his Jewishness – he had been a rabbinical student. Yet by profession he was a tentmaker, a trade somewhat frowned upon by strict Judaic orthodoxy. It will be seen that there were inconsistencies in his early life which modern scholars cannot account for and mysteries they cannot solve.

What is beyond doubt is that he was initially at the forefront of those who persecuted the Christians of

Jerusalem. He might have been a temple guard and may possibly have been present at the arrest and crucifixion of Jesus. Certain it is that he played a significant part in the stoning of Stephen, a devout and active Christian. Stephen died and Paul 'made havoc of the [Christian] church, and entering every house and haling men and women, committed them to prison' (*Acts* 8:3). He asked the high priest for letters to the synagogues of Damascus, there to root out trouble-makers and bring them back as prisoners to Jerusalem. It was on this journey that the event took place which so immediately and entirely converted him.

Here, at one moment, we have a rabid oppressor and man of violence, 'breathing out threatenings and slaughter against the disciples of the Lord' (*Acts* 9:1), at the next the most obedient and devout of those disciples and an undoubted founder of the Christian religion. It is rather as if a camp guard suddenly became merciful to the inmates of Auschwitz and survived to become a great philosopher.

What happened to Paul on his Road to Damascus? Was he an epileptic, as some say, and this his first seizure? Had he been overworking and become, as we might put it today, 'stressed-out'? Or did he really hear the bidding of God? *Acts* says and he says himself that he saw a bright light and fell down, heard a voice call him by name and ask him, 'Why persecutest thou me?' (*Acts* 9:4) Paul inquired who this was and the voice replied he was Jesus and said, 'It is hard for thee to kick against the pricks.' The metaphor, of course, is that of the ass or ox kicking against the stings of the goad and the meaning that the speaker understood Saul's difficulties and the promptings of his conscience. From that moment, Saul now called Paul, saw himself as appointed to bear Christ's name 'before the Gentiles, and kings, and the children of Israel' (*Acts* 8:3).

He was somewhere between twenty and thirty years old, a small hook-nosed, bandy-legged man, humble and proud, brave and meek, the prisoner, as he joyfully (and sometimes with anguish) called himself, of Jesus Christ. Although he would have preferred everyone to be as he was, celibate and unencumbered by a family, he advocated marriage as 'honourable to all'. After his conversion he became a missionary and he wrote his epistles, thus becoming one of the greatest letter-writers the world has ever known and propounding principles and precepts of a startling originality. Of these the letter he wrote to the Romans, meaning to the Christians or 'church' of Rome, is generally thought the finest and perhaps the only one of whose sole and consistent authorship we can be certain.

Paul wrote this letter while staying in Corinth, capital of the Greek province of Achaia, during the cold months of the year, very probably a winter in the late fifties AD. When it was finished he appointed a woman called Phebe to carry it to Rome. In the final chapter, he asks its recipients to receive Phebe in a way becoming to them and to give her whatever assistance she may ask for, thus somewhat weakening the arguments of those critics who down the ages have called him a misogynist and despiser of women. Phebe must have travelled to Rome by sea, bringing to the beleaguered servants of the Roman church a foundation document of the faith.

Only by reading *Romans* in the knowledge of the kind of world Paul lived in can his letter be more fully understood. The Roman dominance of the known world was one of the most oppressive tyrannies nations have ever lived under. A huge proportion of the population was enslaved and few Romans, if any, thought of slavery as wrong. Punishment for any offences in the area of sedition was draconian. The Emperor Claudius had expelled the Jews from Rome and in a few years' time Titus was to sack Jerusalem, destroy the Temple and scatter the people of Israel. It was a superstitious world where sorcerers abounded, where signs and portents were part of everyday life, where cults of all kinds flourished, and where great religious ceremonies centred on blood sacrifice.

Today to believers, agnostics and atheists alike, crucifixion is a word both awesome and commonplace and one that brings to mind a single event: the execution of Jesus Christ. The sign of the cross is indicative of Christianity, and the idea of the cross is ineluctably bound up with Christ's death. But if we think about that death at all, even the most indifferent to the faith it gave rise to, think of it as honourable, a unique martyrdom. Anyone who travelled the Roman Empire at that time would have seen crosses on which the dead or dying hung, comparable perhaps to roadside gallows bearing their decaying corpses in mediaeval Britain. And to everyone, including Paul himself, crucifixion was a disgraceful manner of death, so that it is all the more extraordinary that he could write as he does in his letter to the Galatians, 'God forbid that I should glory save in the cross of our Lord Jesus Christ' (*Galatians* 6:14).

But perhaps the most important fact readers of this letter should know before they begin it, is how early it appears in the scheme of writings which form the New Testament. Most assume, and understandably, that the Gospels come first, then the *Acts of the Apostles* and after that the *Epistles of Paul*. Thus, Paul would have been writing with the Gospels as his source material. But none of those books existed when he set down his knowledge and beliefs. The earliest of the Gospels, that of *Mark*, cannot have been composed much before 70 AD, and by that time Paul's literary output was over and he was most probably dead. If readers today find a number of his precepts familiar, this is because they have come across them before, in church, in Sunday school, in literature and enshrined in Christian philosophy, as owing their provenance to the Gospels. But Paul came first.

Authorities have been commenting on *Romans* for nearly two thousand years. Every word Paul wrote in his letter has been minutely examined, both in translation and in the original, with commentators probing Greek prepositions and classical usage, in an effort to shed light on unfathomable obscurities. We shall approach it more humbly, remembering always that when Paul wrote it Jesus Christ had been crucified only about twenty-five years before.

He begins in the classical Greek fashion of starting a letter, with his name and his vocation: 'Paul, a servant of Jesus Christ, called to be an apostle,' then sets down the tenets of his faith. Kind and comforting messages for his letter's recipients follow; he mentions them always in his prayers and says how he longs to see them. Paul has never been to Rome but he intends to go, hoping for a safe journey in order to preach in person while there. He tells them he is not ashamed of the Gospel (in its sense of the good news). A tradition of shame prevails towards Christianity because Christ came not in majesty but in a way likely to be looked on as abjection and foolishness. Paul knows that this apparently weak message is in fact the supreme power of God himself directed towards man's salvation.

Faith can arise only through human beings' close contact with the Gospel. Paul explains the disastrous progress of evil in society as the natural process of cause and effect, not as the direct act of God. His first chapter ends with an exposure of certain kinds of 'unrighteousness' and here we come upon our first major difficulty in interpreting exactly what he meant. Through the ages men have taken six verses in particular to mean that all homosexuality was abhorrent to Christianity, 'men with men working that which is unseemly' being a phrase on which it is hard to put any other construction. Paul would have known of the importance of homosexuality in Greek thought where homosexual love was often glorified as superior to the heterosexual; he also knew that it was an abomination to the Jews which may be the reason for his harsh denunciations. Throughout his letters, though he comes to regard circumcision as unnecessary and certain dietary laws superfluous, and of course is confident that the Messiah has come, he otherwise holds fast to the Jewish Law. Certain authorities have sought to emphasise that his invective may be directed only against physical abuse in the kind of cult ceremonies Paul, coming as he did from Tarsus, would have been well acquainted with. Readers must draw their own conclusions.

The last four lines of the first chapter are interesting in a quite different way. They can be interpreted as meaning that those who watch, applaud and approve wrongdoing in others, though doing none themselves, are more guilty than those who commit it. An example would be that of the dictator who, rather than carry out torture himself, allows its use by his security forces and looks on with approbation.

He follows directly with a denunciation of hypocrisy. God will render to every man according to how he has behaved, for He cares nothing for rank, riches or status, and is no respecter of persons. Perhaps it is at this point that we should remind ourselves that Paul was not writing for believers living centuries after Christ. He had no doubt that the end of the world was at hand, as had all Christians of his day, and to him the Second Coming was a reality to be expected at any moment. Therefore repentance, amendment of behaviour and a full knowledge of God and Jesus are matters of urgency. Circumcision, he tells us, is of no use in itself, the physical act that is, but 'circumcision is that of the heart'. In other words, to have faith is most important of all, but being a Jew (i.e. a circumcised person) matters too, the rite of circumcision affecting the spirit as well as the flesh, because it was to the Jews originally that the oracles of God were sent by Moses. All men, however, Jew and Gentile alike, are sinners and Jews need not think themselves better than the rest of the world.

Inheritance of the world was promised to Abraham and his descendants, and this gift was made not on condition that it was merited through fulfilment of the law, but simply on the basis of the rightness of the faith they upheld. The relevance to all Christians is in Abraham's faith as the paradigm of their own. It was quite a new thought that Abraham was the father of all who believe, not only of the Jews. But if those who have a claim to the inheritance do so on the basis of their obedience to the law alone, they will be disappointed, since no one is truly obedient but Christ Himself. Against all hope Abraham continued to believe in God's promise that he would be the ancestor of many nations, even though he and his wife were old and childless. By the conception and birth of his son Isaac his faith was proved. Just as he never doubted God's promise, so we must never doubt it.

Man's parent-and-child relationship with God is integral to forgiveness and absolution, and his purpose for humanity is altogether merciful. We were enemies of God, but by the death of his son became his friends, thus atonement through Christ should be a source of joy. (In the next chapter Paul points out that while it is rare for someone to give his life to save even a good man, and not much rarer to do so for someone who has been his benefactor, Christ died for the wicked.) But at the very place where sin most outrageously abounded, in Israel's rejection of Jesus, there grace abounded more and triumphed gloriously. Certain people would draw the inference that we must go on sinning that grace may be multiplied, but this Paul rejects utterly.

At the moment someone receives baptism, the dying and rising again of Christ takes place in him without any cooperation or exercise of will on his part. Baptism is a pledge of that death which, in God's sight, the person concerned has already succumbed to and of resurrection through union with Christ. Martin Luther, in his commentary, said that it was as if Paul 'wanted to give us impressive proof of the fact that . . . every word in the Bible points to Christ.' Israel, says Paul, has misunderstood the law because it failed to comprehend that this was what it was all about.

Paul instructs the Romans on how to behave, and the Commandments not to kill, commit adultery, steal, bear false witness or covet are all summed up in the instruction to love one's neighbour as oneself. But one's enemy also must be loved. If an enemy is hungry, feed him, if thirsty, give him drink, for to do so is to heap 'coals of fire' on his head. The expression probably derives from the Egyptian ritual in which a man purged his offence by carrying on his head a dish containing burning charcoal on a bed of ashes. Paul goes on to speak of the imminence of the second coming, for the ministry of Jesus had ushered in the last days, the End-time. History's supreme events had taken place through Christ's life, death and resurrection.

Returning to one of his central themes, Paul has more to say about Judaism and Christianity. Dietary rules are no longer important. Now Christ's work on earth is done, the situation with regard to the ceremonial part of Old Testament eating and abstaining has been radically transformed. One obeys it by believing in him to whom it bears witness. Keep from hurting others with your dietary rules and remember that the Kingdom of God is not a matter of eating and drinking. But the strong Christian will not boast of his superior knowledge in this area. Paul explains that not everything which is delightful is to be avoided but one should not please oneself regardless of its effect on others.

He ends with greetings to a great many people and here women (Priscilla, Mary, Junia, Tryphena, Tryphosa, Julia, the sister of Nereus and the mother of Rufus) are accorded at least the same affection and admiration as men. Paul seems here to have tried to attach expressions of kindly commendation to all the individuals he mentions. At the end of this last chapter Tertius's declaration that he 'wrote this epistle' means not that he was its author but most probably that he wrote it from Paul's dictation.

What became of Paul? No one knows. The likelihood is that his fate was unknown even then, or Luke, who wrote the *Acts*, might have told us. What is known is that Paul came up for trial in Jerusalem and appealed, as he had the right to do, to Caesar. He was taken to the city to which he directed his letter and seems to have appeared twice before that Emperor whose very name causes a chill, Nero. In Rome he lived for two years under house arrest and the second of the letters to Timothy which bears his name sometimes includes the rather sinister note: '. . . written from Rome, when Paul was brought before Nero the second time.' Perhaps he died a martyr's death. No one can be sure. But if he did he would not have been thrown to wild beasts or made a human torch, but beheaded with a sword, as was prescribed for a Roman Citizen. He left behind him a book which is a blueprint for Christianity. Believers and non-believers alike cannot help but be stricken with awe by its temerity and Paul's genius.

THE EPISTLE OF PAUL
THE APOSTLE TO THE
CORINTHIANS

Though I speak with the tongues of men and of angels, and have not charity, I am become as sounding brass, or a tinkling cymbal. And though I have the gift of prophecy, and understand all mysteries, and all knowledge; and though I have all faith, so that I could remove mountains, and have not charity, I am nothing.

(1:13:1–2)
authorised King James version

Fay Weldon

It is hard to *like* Paul the Apostle. One is not out of sympathy when Ananias the Chief Priest of Jerusalem tries to get him thrown out of town for preaching the Christian gospel and remarks to the Roman authorities, 'We have found him a pestilent fellow'. There seems to be so little love flowing from Paul, other than 'in God' which sometimes seems a way of getting out of the need for it in person, and perhaps why so many cruelties get to be perpetrated in God's name. Certainly, all, at the time, were in awe of this slippery, preaching, threatening, cajoling young man, always one step ahead of his enemies: he who BC would have been a prophet but AD must be an apostle, he who has a hot-line to God and God to him (or so he says), but *like* him? No. Many at the time must have suspected that on the road to Damascus this turncoat Paul, once Saul the persecutor of the Christians, did not see God, but rather a path to personal power, twinkling and beckoning in the desert sun. Perhaps Paul the Apostle simply 'crossed the floor' in the political parlance of our own country, our own age. When all of a sudden it seems the other side is singing the best tunes, over you go. Why hang around? Enemy becomes friend, and vice versa.

Prating 'love', this Apostle Paul rants, rails, reproaches and leads others into mortal danger, preaching the forbidden gospel. Letters to the little groups of Christians, digging in here and there – Corinthia, Galatia, Ephesus, Rome itself – model for all revolutionary movements thereafter, confirming them in their dangerous belief. At the time, 'Behold, I see the heavens opened and the Son of Man standing on the right hand of God' was a statement sufficiently bold to get poor Stephen – 'a man full of faith and the Holy Ghost' – brought before Saul and stoned to death. That was our Saul before Damascus, that was, before he changed his name to Paul; our Saul in full scourging flight, 'breathing out threatenings and slaughter against the disciples of the Lord'. Does the leopard change his spots as he changes sides?

And doesn't Paul take up such an annoyingly large chunk of the Bible, after the romance and passion and savagery of the early days are all finished, after that death upon the cross, with his undramatic letters to here and letters to there? A very Mandelson of religious politics, demanding his united front? Listen to Paul in *Corinthians.* 'Now I beseech you, brethren, by the name of our Lord, that ye all speak the same thing, and that there be no divisions amongst you, but that you be perfectly joined together in the same judgement.' Oh, thanks! And it's to be *your* judgement, isn't it, because you have the hot-line to God? Or say you have. Don't smoke, don't own guns, don't be unrighteous, don't spit in church, let's have no dissension here! Don't, don't, don't. Put away our adulthood and submit – be as a little child. 'For now we see as in a glass, darkly, but then face to face.' How quickly the early church, under Paul's tuition, ceases to be visionary and turns respectable. How short are the days of miracle and wonder. Believe, behave! Consult, unite! We're under threat here, and how many divisions did the intellectuals ever have? Ignore them. 'For it is written I will destroy the wisdom of the wise.'

Judgement is nothing, you men and women of Corinthia, clustering together in your ochre landscape, your rough dwellings squatting low upon the burning land. The spirit is all, and the new faith. And what hope this new faith brings. Life is not so short, and brutish and hard as you thought: only believe and you are saved, the Kingdom of God is at hand: oh fortunate generation, with the marvel of the coming of the Son of Man still in living memory.

Though Paul your Apostle never actually met Him face to face he has talked to those who have, and God himself has appeared to Paul once or twice, and sent an Angel to free him from prison (the two gaolers were put to death as a consequence, which always seemed unfair). The Holy Ghost is a familiar visitor too, bringing with him the gift of tongues, the word of God (so long as you can un-garble it), that same gift which charismatic sects still experience today. Though not so terrifying as once it was, the descent of the Holy Spirit is diminished in these cosy days into something seen rather as a relaxing kind of psychotherapy – or else defined as glossolalia, the mere description of a medical condition.

Love is all, writes Paul, so long of course as it's 'in God' and not in the flesh. 'Marry or burn!' (What a master of the sound-bite is this Paul!) Spare us from fornication, for the flesh can only exist at the expense of the spirit, so the flesh must be subdued, a doctrine which has suited many ever since.

'It is good for a man not to touch a woman,' says Paul and can it be that as a result of these eleven words for near on two thousand years women have been seen as temptation, and blamed, and priests have been celibate, and miserable (or gay) and sex a source of so much shame and degradation? Are men and women so easily led? So easily persuaded to forgo pleasure for the sake of principle? It seems so. Better to be as he himself is, says Paul, and celibate, but if you can't help it, then marry and behave. At least Paul has this much mercy: perhaps he saw the impracticality of what he wanted to achieve: a world without sex. 'Let the husband render unto the wife due benevolence: and likewise also the wife unto the husband.' Well, that's okay. That's generous, that's civilised, that's better than many manage or preach today, let alone then. Kindness and good manners get us a long way.

And next to sex there's bad company. 'Adulterers and effeminates: revilers and abusers of themselves with mankind.' Abhor, abjure! 'A fornicator, or covetous, or an idolater, or a railer, or a drunkard, or an extortioner: with such a one, no, not to eat.' Well, that makes sense. My mother, aged ninety, assures me that the breakdown of family life began on the first occasion a person declared guilty in a divorce case was asked to dinner. Forget when they got allowed into the Royal Enclosure at Ascot. Yes, folks, there was a time when moral blame was levelled at those who erred in sexual matters: when the breakdown of a marriage meant one party was guilty and one was innocent and the Court was prepared to say which. Nowadays there's simply no time for any of that. But who is to say we were not happier then?

And yet because we today don't much like Paul, it does not mean God was not speaking to him. The ways of the Creator are very strange. Our contemporary judgement, our political, emotional and spiritual correctnesses are not His. The magic of the language of Corinthians must be our evidence as to the actuality or otherwise of revelation. Did the Paul we know write the words? Or did the angels, as he claimed, write through him? Write, not speak, I say advisedly, for every writer knows the moment when the words on the page seem driven not by the mind but by an understanding that they already exist and which the hand merely serves. Remember that these are actual letters, written on parchment rolls, laboriously. They are not, unlike the rest of the Bible, spoken words of myth, fable and history mixed, flowing through a dusty landscape, gathered together from a thousand doubtful sources and recorded by those who often had their own interest to serve. They come from the hand of the writer, and can of course change in translation but that's about all.

'Though I speak with the tongues of men and angels,' writes St Paul the poet, 'and have not charity, I am become sounding brass or tinkling cymbal. And though I have the gift of prophecy and understand all mysteries and all knowledge: and though I have all faith, so I could remove mountains, and have not charity, I am nothing . . . Charity suffereth long and is kind: charity envieth not: charity vaunteth not itself, is not puffed up . . . Doth not behave itself unseemly, seeketh not her own: is not easily provoked, thinketh no evil . . .' We all know the passage, and rightly, for it is part of our Christian heritage, even if only to be spoken to us warningly by teachers. (I suspect Kipling based his poem *If* upon 2 *Corinthians* 1:13.)

'Charity' is often translated as 'love', but that word too has become so misused it begins to lose grandeur. The original word derives from the Roman *caritas*, usually translated as 'affection' but that too in context lacks gravitas. Our new 'empathy' is probably nearer to the actual meaning, but who could use such a base and modern word for so magnificent a usage? What is meant, I think, by 'charity' is the unexpected lurch of the heart towards others which can take the soul by surprise. So that 'now abideth faith, hope and charity, and the greatest of these is charity,' and if Paul, apostate and poet, tells us so, we had better believe him. The timeless truths remain. Two millennia are just the twinkling of an eye in the sight of God, and/or the writer.

THE EPISTLE OF PAUL THE APOSTLE TO THE HEBREWS

Let brotherly love continue. Be not forgetful to entertain strangers: for thereby some have entertained angels unawares. Remember them that are in bonds, as bound with them; and them which suffer adversity, as being yourselves also in the body.

(13:1–3)

authorised King James version

Karen Armstrong

We are currently living in a time of religious transition. In many of the countries of Western Europe, atheism is on the increase, and the churches are emptying, being converted into art galleries, restaurants and warehouses. Even in the United States, where over ninety per cent of the population claim to believe in God, people are seeking new ways of thinking about religion and practising their faith. In our dramatically altered circumstances, the old symbols that once introduced people to a sacred dimension of existence no longer function so effectively. In the Christian world, some people are either abandoning the old forms, or trying to reinterpret such doctrines as the incarnation or the atonement in a way that makes sense to them at the beginning of the third Christian millennium.

The author of *The Epistle to the Hebrews* was writing at another pivotal moment in religious history, when the traditional symbols of the divine in Judaism – the Law of Moses, the Jerusalem Temple, and the old covenant between God and the people of Israel – seemed increasingly unsatisfactory to a significant number of Jews who were also struggling to find new ways of being religious. During the first century CE, there were a number of different sects, which were attempting to reinterpret Judaism. The most popular of these sects was that of the Pharisees, who based their spirituality on the Law; they were the most progressive and innovative Jews of the period and wanted to bring the Law up to date, by amending the Law as found in scripture by developing an oral or customal law, based on the actual practice of Jews. They enjoyed the support of most of the ordinary people. The Saducees were mostly members of the aristocratic and priestly classes; they were traditionalists, who wanted to stick to the letter of the Law as found in the Bible; their piety centred on the ancient cult in the Temple. The Essenes were more radical; they believed that the End of Days was nigh and that the Judaism of their day was corrupt, and had withdrawn from mainstream society to await the final battle between the powers of good and evil; some had retreated to Qumran beside the Dead Sea, and lived in a quasi-monastic community.

Christianity began as yet another of these Jewish sects. Until St Paul took the new faith to the gentile world, the original disciples of Jesus had no intention of founding a new religion. They believed that Jesus had been the Messiah and that he would shortly return in glory to inaugurate God's kingdom. They observed the Law and worshipped daily in the Temple, were regarded as devout and legitimate Jews, and were not eager to admit gentiles into their sect. The author of *Hebrews* was writing to a group of these Jewish Christians, but he was trying to persuade them to be more radical. He was almost certainly not St Paul, but was probably Paul's contemporary, writing during the 60s, some thirty years after Jesus's death. The Temple, whose rites he describes in such detail and which was destroyed by the Romans in 70 CE, was obviously still standing, but our author, like other Jews at this time, no longer felt that its rites and imagery yielded access to God. He and the Jewish Christians to whom he was writing were in a stage of transition; they were trying to decide what Jesus had meant to them and what his function was in their religious life. The recipients of his letter had various theories, but their roots were still in Judaism, whereas our author was beginning to break away from the traditional Jewish faith, and develop something new.

Our author is aware that he is being controversial, and that many of his readers still felt comfortable with the Temple liturgy. But he was not alone in discovering that these ancient rites, which had been profoundly satisfying to Jews for centuries and which had been crucial to their spiritual life, no longer spoke to him of God. The Qumran sect would have nothing whatever to do with the Temple; they believed that their community constituted a spiritual Temple and that when the Messiah returned at the End of Days, he would build a new Temple, not made by human hands but built miraculously by God himself. They denounced the Jerusalem priests as wicked and sinful, and looked forward to the arrival of a Messiah who would be a perfect priest of the House of Aaron. They clearly felt so uncomfortable with the Temple liturgy that they condemned it as perverse. The Pharisees were less extreme. They continued to worship in the Temple, but were also beginning to teach that charity and acts of loving kindness were just as effective a means of expiating sin as the old animal sacrifices. The loss of the Temple in 70 CE was a devastating blow, but Jews had already begun to retreat from it, and were thus able to make the transition to rabbinic Judaism with the minimum of fuss, encountering the divine presence in the sacred text of the Law rather than in a sacred building.

The author of *Hebrews*, like other Jewish Christians, shared many of the concerns of the Pharisees and the Essenes; like them, he was trying to find a new way to be Jewish, which put Jesus, the Messiah, at the centre of the picture instead of the Law and the Temple. The Temple liturgy seems to have died on him, and now left him cold. He was especially perturbed by the fact that the Jewish priests had to offer 'those sacrifices' 'continually', over and over again, 'year by year', and all to no avail, for these rituals 'can never take away sins' (10:1,11). He felt the same kind of frustration with the Temple as St Paul experienced about the Law, which, far from liberating Paul from his sins, had only made him more conscious of his sinfulness (*Romans* 7). Where the Pharisees and the Essenes found God in the Law and the sacred community, respectively, these Jewish Christians were making Jesus a symbol which brought them into the divine presence.

We should not underestimate the magnitude of this change. In almost every civilization in the ancient world, the Temple was one of the chief symbols of the divine. Indeed, religion was inconceivable without temple worship and animal sacrifice. When those Jews who had been deported to Babylon by Nebuchadnezzar in 586 BCE, when their Temple had been destroyed for the first time, asked how they could sing the Lord's song in an alien land (Psalm 137:4), they were not simply being maudlin or nostalgic about their ruined Temple on Mount Zion in Jerusalem. They were voicing a real theological difficulty. A deity was inaccessible to his worshippers if he did not have a shrine. Whereas today people feel they can encounter God and pray to him wherever they happen to be (in a field or a mountain-top, as well as a church), this was not so in the ancient world. A god could only meet his devotees in a place that he had chosen. The Temple was a replica of his home in the divine world, which mysteriously made him present here below. In pre-modern religion, the reproduction contained something of the original archetype and a symbol was inseparable from the spiritual entity to which it pointed. The effect of this was similar to the way the son of a dead friend brings the father into the room with him, because he reminds us physically of the deceased, and, at the same time, makes us feel his absence more acutely. The author of *Hebrews* takes this symbolic spirituality for granted; it is fundamental to his argument. The Jerusalem Temple, he explains, is a copy of God's spiritual Temple in the Heavenly Jerusalem; its rituals imitate the celestial liturgy in the Heavenly Sanctuary, and this process of *imitatio dei* (on which all premodern religion was based) brought something of that transcendent reality down to the world of men and women.

Our author understood the Temple symbolism, but, like other Jews, found that it no longer worked for him. The Temple and its cult seemed to him repetitious and pointless; these rites no longer yielded any sense of the divine. There are clear indications that Jews were not alone in this. In some parts of the Greek world, people were beginning to find Temple worship meaningless too, and had started to locate the divine in other symbols which did give them that sense of transcendance and ecstasy that human beings seem to need. Today those who do not find this enhanced life in religion, seek transcendence in art, music, literature, sport, or even in drugs. This shift from temple worship in late antiquity represented a major religious change. It would once have been considered the height of blasphemy to deny that the Temple gave men and women access to the divine, so essential had it been to the religious experience of humanity.

The Temple was an attempt to express an ineffable divine reality in human terms. Our doctrines (such as the Trinity, the Incarnation, the Atonement, or even the concept of a personal God) are also symbols, which attempt to give shape to our experience of the sacred. These doctrines cannot fully contain the reality of what we call 'God', any more than a building could. They can only point to a Reality which must surpass them, as it goes beyond all human categories and systems. Western Christians have tended to lose sight of the crucial fact that we can only speak of the divine in terms of signs and symbols. Since the scientific revolution of the sixteenth and seventeenth centuries, Western people have often assumed that 'God' was an objective but unseen reality (like the atom), and that our doctrines were accurate descriptions of this divine Fact. But theology should be regarded as poetry (Greek and Russian Orthodox Christians have always been aware of this). Theology is merely an attempt to express the inexpressible as felicitously as possible. But, as we all know, some of our poetic symbols lose their power and immediacy, as our circumstances change. Today many Christians feel that the ideas of a personal God or of the divinity of Jesus are absolutely essential to faith, but in the ancient world people felt just as strongly about the divine presence in the Temple. When a particular image of the sacred loses its valency, it does not mean that religion itself must die. The old symbol is often taken up and given fresh life in a new and different system.

That is what is happening in *The Epistle to the Hebrews.* Where once Temple worship gave all believers a direct experience of the numinous, our author clearly finds that the Temple is *only* a symbol. When the Prophet Isaiah had been able to see the divine presence and the heavenly sanctuary while he was worshipping in the Temple, seeing *through* the symbolism and the liturgy to the Reality behind it (*Isaiah* 6:1–4), our author can see no further than the physical rites. For him, they are simply rules about the outward life, and have no power to transform us interiorly; the Temple priests are obviously imperfect, since they are only human; the sacrifice of bulls and goats is messy and pointless; and the building itself clearly man-made. He can no longer see what Isaiah saw. In order to work effectively, a symbol has to be experienced as a direct link to the more elusive and transcendent reality to which it directs our attention, but our author can only see the Temple as a human artefact. Similarly, for many sceptics today, the conventional doctrines of Christianity, which for centuries gave people an immediate sense of God, seem nothing more than human constructs.

But instead of jettisoning the old symbol of the Temple, as the Qumran sect did, our author reinterprets it. He makes Christ the new High Priest. In the old cult, the High Priest entered the Holy of Holies (the innermost sanctum of the Temple, which represented [*sic*] the divine presence) once a year on the Day of Atonement. He alone could enter this most sacred place, and the people came into God's presence vicariously through this symbolic rite. The Holy of Holies was carefully designed to re-present God's Throne in the Heavenly Jerusalem. Now, by virtue of his sacrificial death, Christ had entered into the celestial sanctuary once and for all. He had bypassed the symbolism and introduced believers to the sacred Reality itself. For our author, the figure of Christ had become *the* new symbol that brought humanity to the divine; he was 'the express image of [God's] person' (1:3). (The Jerusalem Bible has been truer to the author's intention and to the old symbolic spirituality by rendering this 'a perfect copy of [God's] nature'). As a 'copy' of God in human form, Jesus gave our author a direct experience of the divine: when he contemplated the human figure of Jesus, he had a clear sense of what God was like. People had no further need of earthly symbols, therefore, since they had already gone directly into the divine presence with Christ; they had already passed over, in the person of their High Priest, into the next world:

> But ye are come unto mount Sion, and unto
> the city of the living God, the heavenly
> Jerusalem, and to an innumerable company
> of angels, to the general assembly and church
> of the firstborn, which are written in heaven,
> and to God, the Judge of all . . . (12:22–3)

Again, the Jerusalem Bible has preserved the original more forcefully than the King James version, by translating this last sentence: 'You have come to God himself.' In the person of their new High Priest, Christians have already come directly into the divine presence. They may feel that they are living a mundane life here below, but they are really with God in the Heavenly Jerusalem.

But, as with any religious symbolism, there were difficulties. Our author is poignantly aware that it is hard to live a religious life without any tangible replicas of the divine here below. Jesus had gone away, into another dimension, and Christians had to have faith in what was unseen. Their lives, as the author makes clear, were hard and full of suffering; how could they believe that they were already in Heaven? The epistle also makes it clear that the figure of Christ was by no means firmly established as the only symbol that gave Christians a sense of God. Some of the recipients of his letter thought that angels were more effective mediators than Jesus; others were still drawn to the figure of Moses and the Law. This reminds us that Christianity did not spring forth ready-made from the minds of the apostles after the Resurrection. Christians had to work hard to make Jesus a viable symbol of the divine, using all their creative expertise. They would continue to discuss who and what Jesus had been and what he had meant to them for centuries. Western Christians would finally accept the ruling of the Council of Chalcedon (451) that Jesus had both a divine and a human nature, something that neither Paul nor the author of *Hebrews* (who saw Jesus only as a human 'copy' of God) had claimed. The Greek Orthodox Christians were not satisfied with Chalcedon and went on discussing Christology for another two hundred years. They developed quite a different notion of Jesus. Maximus the Confessor (*c.* 580–662), the founder of Byzantine theology, believed that God would have become human even if Adam had not sinned; Jesus had not died to atone for our sins, but he was the first human being to be wholly deified; what he had been, all Christians could be.

The point is that people who call themselves Christians have had very different ideas about God and

Jesus over the years. Our theology has changed dramatically in the past, and can do so again. Today the old counciliar definitions about God or Jesus do not always speak to Christians or would-be Christians. They seem to belong to another age, and can appear to be as fabricated and arbitrary to many people as the old Temple and its liturgy had become for our author. *The Epistle to the Hebrews* reminds us that there is no need to repine if a rite, an image, or a doctrine dies on us. We can, like our author, use our imaginations to build on the past and create a symbol that will speak to us more eloquently and directly of the sacred.

THE GENERAL EPISTLE
OF JAMES

*Speak not evil of one another, brethren. He that speaketh evil
of his brother, and judgeth his brother, speaketh evil of the law,
and judgeth the law: but if thou judge the law, thou art not
a doer of the law, but a judge. There is one lawgiver, who is
able to save and to destroy: who art thou that judgest another?*

(4:11–12)

authorised King James version

His Holiness the Dalai Lama

As I read the lines of this *Epistle of James*, I am struck by the similarities between this beautiful letter in the Bible and some of the texts in my own Buddhist tradition, especially those that belong to a genre known as *lojong*, literally meaning 'training the mind'. As with *lojong* texts, I believe, this epistle can be read on different levels. On the practical level, however, it encapsulates many of the key principles that are crucial for learning how to be a better human being. More precisely, it teaches us how to bring our spiritual vision to life at the highest possible level.

I feel humbled to be invited to write an introduction to this important part of the Christian scriptures. As we enter a new millennium and Christians all over the world celebrate two thousand years of their tradition, I am reminded that this holy scripture has been a powerful source of spiritual inspiration and solace to millions of fellow human beings world-wide. Needless to say, I am no expert on Christian scriptures. I have, however, accepted the invitation to comment personally on the epistle from the perspective of my own Buddhist tradition. I will particularly focus on passages that evoke values and principles also emphasised in the Buddhist scriptures.

The epistle begins by underlining the critical importance of developing a single-pointed commitment to our chosen spiritual path. It says, 'A double minded man is unstable in all his ways' (*James* 1:8), because lack of commitment and a wavering mind are among the greatest obstacles to a successful spiritual life. However, this need not be some kind of blind faith, but rather a commitment based on personal appreciation of the value and efficacy of the spiritual path. Such faith arises through a process of reflection and deep understanding. Buddhist texts describe three levels of faith, namely: faith as admiration, faith as reasoned conviction, and faith as emulation of high spiritual ideals. I believe that these three kinds of faith are applicable here as well.

The epistle reminds us of the power of the destructive tendencies that exist naturally in all of us. In what is, for me at least, the most poignant verse of the entire letter, we read, 'Wherefore, my beloved brethren, let every man be swift to hear, slow to speak, slow to wrath: for the wrath of man worketh not the righteousness of God' (*James* 1:19–20).

These two verses encapsulate principles that are of utmost importance to a spiritual practitioner, and for that matter, any individual who aspires to express his or her basic human goodness. This emphasis on hearing as opposed to speaking teaches us the need for open-heartedness. For without it we have no room to receive the blessings and positive transformation that we might otherwise experience in our interaction with our fellow human beings.

Open and receptive, swift to listen to others, we should be slow to speak, because speech is a powerful instrument that can be highly constructive or profoundly destructive. We are all aware how seemingly harmless speech can actually inflict deep hurt upon others. Therefore, the wise course is to follow the advice of one well-known Buddhist *lojong* text: 'When amongst many, guard your speech and alone, guard your thoughts.'

The instruction that we should be 'slow to wrath' reminds us that it is vital to ensure some degree of restraint over powerful negative emotions like anger, for actions motivated by such states of mind are almost invariably destructive. This is something we must both appreciate and strive to implement in our everyday lives. Only then can we hope to reap the fruit of living a spiritual life.

The real test of spiritual practice lies in the practitioner's behaviour. There is sometimes a tendency to think of the spiritual life as primarily introspective, divorced from the concerns of everyday life and society. This, I believe, is plainly wrong and is also rejected in this epistle. Faith that does not translate into actions is no faith at all, as the text says:

If a brother or sister be naked, and destitute of daily food, and any of you say unto them, 'Depart in peace, be ye warmed and filled'; notwithstanding ye give them not those things which are needful to the body; what doth it profit? Even so faith, if it hath not works, is dead, being alone (*James* 2:16–17).

We find a similar principle in Buddhist texts as well. They advise that when helping others, giving material aid comes first, speaking words of comfort comes second, giving spiritual counsel comes third, while fourth is demonstrating what you teach by your own personal example.

I have long been an admirer of the Christian tradition of charity and social work. The image of monks and nuns devoting their entire lives to the service of humanity in the fields of health, education and care of the poor is truly inspiring. To me, these are true followers of Christ, demonstrating their faith in compassionate action.

The epistle addresses what a Buddhist might call 'contemplation of the transient nature of life.' This is beautifully captured in the following verse: 'Whereas ye know not what shall be on the morrow. For what is your life? It is even a vapour, that appeareth for a little time, and then vanisheth away' (*James* 4:24).

In the Buddhist context, contemplation of life's transient nature brings a sense of urgency to our spiritual life. We may be aware of the value of spiritual practice, but in our daily lives, we tend to behave as if we will live for a long time. We have a false sense of the permanence of our existence, which is one of the greatest obstacles to a dedicated spiritual life. More important, from an ethical point of view, it is the assumption of permanence that leads us to pursue what we see as the 'legitimate' desires and needs of our enduring 'self'. We ignore the impact of our behaviour on other people's lives. We might even be willing to exploit others for our own ends. So, profound contemplation of life's transient nature introduces a note of healthy realism into our life as it helps put things in proper perspective.

The epistle is passionate in its advocacy of respect for the poor. In fact, it presents a severe critique of the conceit and complacency of the rich and the powerful. Some of these criticisms may have a certain historical significance, but they underline an important spiritual principle, which is never to forget the fundamental equality of all human beings. A true spiritual practitioner appreciates what I often describe as our 'basic spirituality'. By this I am referring to the fundamental qualities of goodness, which exist naturally in all of us irrespective of our gender, race, social and religious backgrounds.

By criticising disdainful attitudes towards the poor, the epistle persuasively reminds us of the need to return to a deeper appreciation of our humanity. It reminds us to relate to fellow human beings at a level of basic humanity. I often tell people that when I meet someone for the first time, my primary feeling is that I am meeting a fellow human being. It does not matter to me, whether the person is considered 'important' or not. For me, what matters most is basic warm-heartedness.

Certainly, from the standpoint of mere humanity, there are no grounds for discrimination. In the language of the Bible, we are all equal in the face of creation. And in the language of Buddhism, we all equally aspire for happiness and shun suffering. Furthermore, we all have the right to fulfil this basic aspiration to be happy and overcome suffering. So if we truly relate to our fellow human beings with a recognition of our fundamental equality, considerations of whether someone is rich or poor, educated or uneducated, black or white, male or female, or whether he or she belongs to this or that religion naturally become secondary.

When we read this text from the Bible today, two thousand years after it was written, it reminds us that not only are many of our fundamental spiritual values universal, they are also perennial. So long as human beings' fundamental nature, aspiring for happiness and wishing to overcome suffering, remains unchanged, these basic values too will remain relevant to us both as individual human beings and as a society.

I would like to conclude by remembering my friend Thomas Merton, a Catholic monk of the Cistercian order, who opened my eyes to the richness of the Christian tradition. It is to him that I owe my first, real appreciation of the value of Christian teachings. Since we met in the early 1960s, I have dedicated a large part of my time and effort to promoting deeper understanding amongst the followers of the world's major religions. And it is to this noble objective that I dedicate the words I have written here.

THE REVELATION OF
ST JOHN THE DIVINE

And he said unto me, 'It is done. I am Alpha and Omega, the beginning and the end. I will give unto him that is athirst of the fountain of the water of life freely. He that overcometh shall inherit all things; and I will be his God, and he shall be my son.'

(21:6–7)
authorised King James version

Kathleen Norris

I love this unlovable book for many reasons. It's a pretty good description of the writing process – crazed angels directing you to write, and not write, and to eat words that taste sweet in the mouth but soon turn to gall. 'Make it new,' Ezra Pound said; 'Did that,' answers Jesus, and you write it out as best you can, letting the images and symbols fly, and then the fools interpret it literally, arguing over what everything *means.*

I am attracted to *Revelation* also because it was Emily Dickinson's favorite book of the Bible, and because it takes a stand in favor of singing. In fact, it proclaims that when all is said and done, of the considerable noises human beings are capable of, it is singing that will endure. A new song – if you can imagine – and light will be what remains. I find this a cause for hope, and am further buoyed to learn that the latter prediction, at least, is in tune with the conjectures of contemporary astrophysicists, who have yet to weigh in on the question of song.

Revelation is a casebook of visionary excess: a man

appears holding 'in his right hand seven stars: and out of his mouth went a sharp two-edged sword: and his countenance was as the sun shineth in his strength' (1:16); a beast rises out of the sea 'having seven heads and ten horns, and upon his horns ten crowns, and upon his heads the name of blasphemy' (13:1). Voices sound like thunder or trumpets, a throne sits in a sea of glass, surrounded by cherubim and lightning, four angels stand at the four corners of the earth, four horses – white, red, black, and pale – herald an apocalypse. But for all of this, the book is also an ordinary human vessel, a letter meant to be read aloud. It begins and ends with a blessing upon those who read it to others, and those who hear and heed it.

Emily Dickinson would have heard *Revelation* read aloud many times in daily family devotions and at the church she attended until she was in her mid-thirties. Chapter 21, or the 'gem chapter,' is known to be a favorite, and it is easy to see how its dense mouthfuls of imagery would have appealed to her, the walls of the holy city of Jerusalem vividly described as having twelve foundations, each one made of a different stone: jasper, sapphire, chalcedony, emerald, sardonyx, sardius, chrysolyte, beryl, topaz, chrysoprasus, jacinth, and amethyst.

Typically, Dickinson puts *Revelation* to personal use, writing a jaunty letter in the autumn of 1873 to a dear friend, Mrs Josiah Gilbert Holland: 'To live is Endowment. It puts me in mind of that singular Verse in *Revelation* – "Every Several Gate was of one Pearl".' But in more chilly weather, after the Christmas of 1882, just a month after the death of her mother, she wrote to the same friend:

> The Fiction of 'Santa Claus' always reminds me of the reply to my early question of 'Who made the Bible' –
> 'Holy Men by the Holy Ghost,' and though I have now ceased my investigations, the Solution is insufficient.
> Santa Claus, though, illustrates Revelation.
> But a Book is only the Heart's Portrait – every Page a Pulse.

As usual, Dickinson's whimsy is dead-on serious. Santa does illustrate a simple moral: act good (at least in front of those who matter) and you will get the goodies. John of Patmos is not so simple. Intent on apocalypse, which at its Greek root means 'uncovering,' he holds up a mirror to the human heart, and doesn't bother to ask if we like what we see there. As he speaks to the churches, we can see ourselves: how the youthful, earnest heart soon forgets its first fervor and grows lukewarm, distracted by the world, compromising faith and justice and love for comfort or gain.

And John's images do seem to pulse, the work of a visionary in prison on a windswept island, who has to struggle to say in words what those incessant winds have revealed to him. This is a poet's book, which is probably the best argument for reclaiming it from fundamentalists. It doesn't tell, it shows, over and over again, its images unfolding, pushing hard against the limits of language and metaphor, engaging the listener in a tale that has the satisfying yet unsettling logic of a dream.

Perhaps *Revelation* is best understood as prison literature, but not necessarily escapist, although many Christians use it for easy reassurance that 'when the roll is called up yonder' they'll find themselves securely placed on the list, and too bad about you. More than any other book of the Christian Bible, *Revelation* has suffered from bad interpretation: solipsistic, short-sighted, cruel. Cruelty is not a distinguishing feature of the book itself; rather, it describes in stark terms the world we have made and boldly asserts that our cruelties and injustices will not have the last word.

Like the Psalms, *Revelation* is a compendium of biblical images and themes, and it is clear that John has drunk deep from the prophets, who consistently warn us not to tip the scales of justice too far in our favor, lest God overturn our precious applecarts. The prophets are difficult for us to bear because they remind us that our measure of discomfort at apocalypse is the measure of our comfort with the way things are. Who really wants to hear about a doomed city, formerly great, where the wealthy fed on dainties and clothed themselves in finery, while the children of the poor begged on the streets for bread? If it sounds familiar, it should, for it is how a prophet sees the here and now:

And the merchants of the earth shall weep and mourn . . . for no man buyeth their merchandise any more: The merchandise of gold, and silver, and precious stones, and of pearls, and fine linen, and purple, and silk, and scarlet . . . and cinnamon, and odours, and ointments . . . and wine, and oil, and fine flour, and wheat, and beasts, and sheep, and horses, and chariots, and slaves, and souls of men.

And the fruits that thy soul lusted after are departed from thee . . . and thou shalt find them no more at all. (18:11–14)

The here-and-now import of *Revelation* is so consistently ignored that I was relieved to find the novelist Mary Gaitskill stating, in a recent essay, that the book no longer reads to her 'like a chronicle of arbitrarily inflicted cruelty . . . [but] like a terrible abstract of how we violate ourselves and others and thus bring down endless suffering on earth.' (As I write this, Serbs and Albanians are busy taking revenge on one another in Kosovo; by the time you read this the bloodshed will be somewhere else, the justifications for it somewhat different, though just as finely tuned.) There seems no end to it, but *Revelation* insists that there is. It is a healing vision, meant to give us hope. God's wrath is stirred by what we have done to the world he made, and that's the good news. God intends to take our mess and make it come out right.

The hope engendered by *Revelation* is as bitter and bracing as the hope one finds in an emergency room or ICU or hospice. All that seemed to matter, all competence, all status, all that was formerly of value is revealed as nothing compared to the beat of a pulse, that next breath. The book embraces a great psychological truth, that the crises and apocalypses of our lives are not meant to beat us into submission so much as to give us room to change and grow. But we usually don't rise to the challenge; we stick with the devil we know, and John is honest about that as well. Our 'blaspheming' and 'fornications' are not an intellectual game but, as Mary Gaitskill puts it, a blaspheming 'of life itself by failing to have the courage to be honest and kind,' an addiction to 'sex done in a state of psychic disintegration, with no awareness of one's self or one's partner, let alone any sense of honor or even real playfulness.'

Revelation uncovers the world as it is, and reveals to us our true condition. And John insists that, despite ourselves, God wills to restore this world to a beauty we can scarcely imagine. It is a city, not a solitude, an important distinction in the narcissistic din of American culture. It is a city as only God can envision it, without tears, which we are invited to envision as well, and by implication asked to strive for in the present, even if it means forgoing 'getting in touch with ourselves' in order to better constitute a community.

And the God who has been stirred to cataclysmic rage by our stubborn selfishness and lack of love surprises us after all. What is evil has been swept away, until only the good remains. And God desires to be with those who have suffered most in a cruel, unjust, and violent world. This God does not act at all like a vengeful dictator infatuated with power but comes to gently 'wipe away all tears from their eyes.' If, as the pop psychologists insist, imaging is half the battle, John is already there: 'and there shall be no more death, neither sorrow, nor crying, neither shall there be any more pain: for the former things are passed away' (21:4).

Will Self

My friend Ben Trainin died thirteen years ago of a heart attack, brought on by an asthma attack, brought on by the complications of a compressed, involuted life: a decoction of existence. He and his girlfriend were living in a shoe box-shaped flat just off the Commercial Road in Whitechapel. The bed – where he died – was crammed under a window, from which you could see the plastic-wrapped schmutter in the windows across the road. Ben was twenty-eight.

He was not a simple soul – he was complex. He came from a convoluted family with connections both bohemian and East End. He'd gone up to Nottingham University to read history, but after doing too much amphetamine he was found giving an extempore, *al fresco* sermon, from the pulpit of the roof of his digs. He served drinks at the Colony Room club in Soho for the next couple of years, courtesy of his – self-styled – 'godfather' Ian Board. Then he took the Oxford general entrance paper and scored an unprecedented result. Interviewed by Christopher Hill – then still Master of

Balliol – Ben was offered a place to read history. That's how we met.

Ben was fucking complex. Part of his act was to feign simplicity. Gap-toothed, tousle-haired, slack-jawed, he would gawp at me and intone 'Amazing!', 'No!', 'Really?' and 'Will!', before gurgling with giggles like an idiot. He walked with knees half bent, as if he were continually going downhill.

Ben was a giver of unexpected presents. I would be sitting in my room reading and Ben would silently tiptoe down on in. He'd deposit a book of Basho's poems, or a manual of Ch'an Zen teaching, then – still without speaking – he'd depart. From Ben I first heard the expression 'random acts of senseless generosity'.

He was brilliant and confused. One time he found me having a bad acid trip, prostrate on my bed, ensnared by a vision of an illimitable cathedral comprised entirely of screaming mouths. 'Bad trip,' he stated on seeing the state I was in. 'You need wine.' He poured two bottles of Burgundy down me, employing a furled magazine as a funnel. An hour later I was dancing to Edwin Starr's *Eye to Eye Contact*, at the Law Society disco.

Ben's maxim as far as drugs were concerned was 'little but often'. He constantly smoked tiny nuggets of hashish and snorted less than nugatory lines of amphetamine. With some like-minded souls we formed a rhythm and blues band. Ben loved Robert Johnson and might well have brokered a deal on his own soul in return for guitar-picking skill. Together we composed unlikely ditties. I loved him very much.

In the imbroglio of acid, speed, heroin, hashish, cocaine, philosophy, youth, literature, political protest, sex, friendship and dancing, Ben's mind frayed. The dissolution of our peer group seemed congruent with his own mind. When we left the university, Ben began to take day-returns from his own sanity. Then awaydays became bargain weekends. We pitched up in Brixton, squatting, in 1982. A very raw, very ragged time – especially for one who was frayed. One night Ben brandished a U-bend bicycle lock in my face and dared me to kill us both, batter us both to death. For someone who practised random acts of senseless generosity, the world had become a screaming, tight fist.

I saw Ben sporadically after that. He moved back to Kennington, a village a few miles outside Oxford. Initially he lived with a bizarre, obese character who was the local 'wise woman'. This was for real – I remember visiting him there and witnessing a sheepish young couple, who had come to consult her on the matter of fecundity. She was so fat she had a reinforced commode with an armchair of a seat. Ben said it was provided by the social services.

Then he moved in with a gay couple who were priests. They seemed caring men when I visited, and genuinely concerned for Ben's health and welfare, but there were nagging undertones – and even overtones – suggesting a less disinterested involvement on their part.

I was living in a borrowed flat in the Gloucester Road area during the hot, early summer of 1985. I had no money and expensive habits. One day Ben called and said he was coming over to see me for the first time in many months. In truth, I had begun to avoid him. The joint suicide attempt had been bad enough, but since then Ben had increasingly taken to interpreting the world through the dark glass of *The Revelation of St. John the Divine.*

He carried a pocket bible – leather-bound as I recall – with him wherever he went. In the midst of always turbulent, disconnected discourses, he would wrench the tome out and brandishing it cite the applicable prophecy and provide his own piece of exegesis, which constituted impossibly spidery marginalia. Disturbingly his references were always correct – the last piece of mental viability left to him. Montaigne said: 'In my part of the country we call a man who has no memory "stupid".' Ben was never stupid. He spoke of the sharp two-edged sword (1:16), and the utility of communion with he who has 'the keys of hell and of death' (1:18).

Like many people who are teetering on the edge of psychosis – one foot rammed hard in the door of perception lest it slam shut forever – Ben found in *Revelation* an awful, immanent level of identification; an apparently fixed point around which his own frail psyche could orbit and then fission. Ben didn't subscribe to any, one view of the meaning of *Revelation* – he subscribed to them all.

I'm not certain that Ben's illness was ever adequately diagnosed. I do know that he was receiving some kind of help or treatment at the time of his death, but I don't think they'd yet managed to hammer this beautifully rounded persona into a square hole of psychopathology. My hunch is that he was manic-depressive. Perhaps now, with improved drugs, better cognitive approaches, Ben might have been saved – but I doubt it.

For there was an anguished level of insight in this man's disintegration. Even as he ran over – for the nth time – the precise equations that decoded the numerological content of *Revelation* – four beasts times seven seals, times twelve tribes of twelve thousand – he would still find himself hectored by the furies of his own reason, and pulling himself up short expostulate 'Of course, it's all a load of superstitious bollocks really.'

So Ben paced around the spacious, unpaid-for flat on this hot, early summer day. He wanted us to do *this* together, and to go *there*. He thought we ought to consider becoming *such-and-such*, or dedicating ourselves to this *particular* cause. And all of it was derived from *Revelation*, all of it was coextensive with – and tantamount to – the determined, ordained, god-directed universe.

He wanted me to go to the Natural History Museum with him, but I wouldn't. He scared me. When someone you love is veering in and out of sanity it's straightforwardly terrifying. They may have their foot rammed in the door, but if they let go the draught could suck you out of rationality along with them; expel you into a screaming void of the id.

Ben said goodbye to me, or rather he said he had come to say goodbye to me. He pocketed the small book of no calm and he left. He died a week later.

He wouldn't have – didn't – want to be in the

condition he was. I believe he willed himself to death. On the despairing grapevine that sprang sand roots in the long hours immediately after his death, time and again I heard from other friends and lovers that Ben had been by that preceding week; that he had cropped up for the first time in months; that he had said he was coming to say goodbye – not simply said 'goodbye'.

A few months later I was ordering a takeaway in a fried chicken joint on Haverstock Hill when elements of a familiar litany came floating to me: an anti-prayerful, desperate incantation. It was the hulking man standing next to me in the queue, frayed jeans sagging open at the fly to reveal NHS issue pyjama bottoms underneath. We were – I internally acknowledged – within the crazily paved precincts of the Royal Free Hospital, that ziggurat of social hygiene. The man – who, non-pejoratively was clearly suffering from an array of schizoid symptoms – was speaking of that woman: 'And upon her forehead was a name written, MYSTERY, BABYLON THE GREAT, THE MOTHER OF HARLOTS AND ABOMINATIONS OF THE EARTH.'

His speech was Roman, then italicised, then capitalised. It was his own, private revelation.

I became, if not exactly fixated, at any rate intrigued by this seam of perverse Biblical exegesis, which was being squeezed out from the minds of the insane like variegated toothpaste ejected from a tube. I would lend an ear to any inapposite mutterer or street ranter I chanced upon, confident that in at least one out of three hits, there would be revelatory pay dirt.

I read *The Book of Revelation* once – I never wanted to read it again. I found it a sick text. Perhaps it's the occlusion of judgmental types, and the congruent occlusion of psyches, but there's something *not quite right* about *Revelation*. I feel it as an insemination of older, more primal verities into an as yet fresh dough of syncretism – the NeoPlatonists still kneading at the stuff of the messiah. The riot of violent, imagistic occurrences; the cabalistic emphasis on numbers; the visceral repulsion expressed towards the bodily, the sensual and the sexual. It deranges in and of itself, and sets the parameters, marshals the props, for all the excessive playlets to come. In its vile obscurantism is its baneful effect; the original language may have welded the metaphoric with the signified, the *logos* with the flesh, but in the King James version the text is a guignol of tedium, a portentous horror film.

I have read the exegetical texts on *Revelation* and I have read the book itself several more times. I feel no closer to understanding what it is about. Not in the obvious senses – I appreciate the status of Hebraic and early Christian prophecy as pure revelation, decoupled from the mere temporal causality, spatial contiguity – but in the sense that I cannot empathise with this piece of writing, I cannot feel what it might be like to feel it.

Last night I plugged into the internet and went looking for *Revelation*. Funny how the dead get deader. Ben was dead from the moment he died, but five years after his death he was deader, and now he's deader still. I know this because of the anachronistic quality of my vision of him: if he were to be resurrected now, he would look out of place next to my full colour VDU screen, with its weary emphasis that what you see is what you get.

I keyed it into a not especially vigorous search engine, keyed in the bald awfulness of it: *The Book of Revelation*. Hit the return key and waited. The screen departed as a scroll when it is rolled together and I was offered a choice of 2,666,896 web sites. And these were by no means all 'Top 10 Revelations in Marcia Clark's New Book'. Oh no, if only. No, they were the real McCoy: the apocalyptic visions visited on the wired generation in the here and now of Christian-defined 1998. They no longer have to mutter in fast food outlets, they no longer have to address themselves to bare precincts, their only witnesses scurrying fast in the opposite direction. Now they can make the screen depart as a scroll when it is rolled together.

Our sense of the apocalypse is steeped in the language of *Revelation*. In this century the star called Wormwood *has* fallen, and the sea has become as black as sackcloth of hair, and the moon has become as blood. We have heard the silence – about the space of half an hour – that accompanied the opening of the seventh seal, yet still we are here.

I have no truck with personal immortality – it is the dross of the opium of the people. I have no time for the conception of humans as born in sin, screaming for redemption. If *Revelation* conjures up one single feeling in me, as we stand on the cusp of a new millennium, awaiting television retrospectives that will occupy the space of many hours, it is one of superstitious awe, 'Look on my works, ye Mighty, and despair'. To think this ancient text has survived to be the very stuff of modern, psychotic nightmare.

Not only the good die young – but some do.

In memory of Benjamin Gregor Trainin, 1957–85

CONTRIBUTOR BIOGRAPHIES

Peter Ackroyd
The Book of Isaiah

Peter Ackroyd's books include the bestselling biographies *Dickens* (1990), *Blake* (1995) and *The Life of Thomas More* (1998), and the novels *Dan Leno and the Limehouse Golem* (1994) and *Milton in America* (1996). His book *Dickens: Public Life and Private Passion* was published in Spring 2002 to accompany a three-part BBC TV series. Another television series on London, screened in Autumn 2003, was accompanied by the tie-in book *Illustrated London,* which was shortlisted for the 2003 British Book Awards Illustrated Book of the Year. Most recently he has published a biography of Chaucer (2004), and he followed *The Clerkenwell Tales* (2003), set in the late-medieval world, with *The Lambs of London* in 2004. He is the winner of the Somerset Maugham Award, the Guardian Fiction Prize for Biography and the prestigious James Tait Black Memorial Prize. In 2003 he was awarded the CBE. He lives in London.

Karen Armstrong
The Epistle of Paul the Apostle to the Hebrews

Karen Armstrong's first book, the best-selling *Through the Narrow Gate* (1981), described her seven years as a nun in a Roman Catholic order. She has published numerous books, including *A History of God*, which has been translated into thirty languages, *A History of Jerusalem* and *In the Beginning: A New Reading of Genesis*. Her more recent works include *Islam: A Short History* and *Buddha*. Her forthcoming *A Short History of Myth* will be published later in 2005. She lives in London.

Louis de Bernières
The Book of Job

Louis de Bernières's first three novels are *The War of Don Emmanuel's Nether Parts, Señor Vivo and the Coca Lord* and *The Troublesome Offspring of Cardinal Guzman*. *Captain Corelli's Mandolin* has been a major best-seller worldwide and it won the Commonwealth Writers' Prize, Best Book, in 1995. Since then it has been translated into 11 languages, and was made into a film in 2001. Also in 2001 he published *Red Dog*, a collection of stories inspired by a statue of a dog encountered on a writer's expedition to Australia. The play *Sunday Morning at the Centre of the World* was broadcast on BBC 4 in 1999, and published in 2001. His latest novel is *Birds Without Wings* (2004).

Bono
The Book of Psalms

Bono (Paul Davis Hewson) was born in Dublin in 1960. At seventeen he joined the embryonic U2 with three school friends. U2 were signed to Island Records in April 1980 and released their first single the following month. They have gone on to sell over 125 million albums worldwide, gathering 14 Grammys and 12 MTV awards along the way. Bono has appeared on the cover of *Rolling Stone* twelve times in that period. Bono has used his fame to draw attenton to Africa and the crises of poverty and HIV/AIDS. The *New York Times* cited Bono's work as one of the reasons why President Bush promised to increase US aid by nearly $30 billion over five years, including a major new initiative to fight AIDS in Africa. In 2004, this promise resulted in the largest increase in US foreign assistance in forty years. Bono lives in Dublin, Ireland, with his wife and four children.

A.S. Byatt
The Song of Solomon

A.S. Byatt was born in Yorkshire. Her novels include *The Shadow of the Sun, The Game, The Virgin in the Garden* and *Still Life*. In 1990 her bestselling novel *Possession* won the Booker Prize and the Irish Times/Aer Lingus International Fiction prize, and was made into a film in 2002. Her other books include *Angels and Insects* and two short story collections, *The Matisse Stories* and *The Djinn in the Nightingale's Eye*. The third in the series based on a Yorkshire family, *Babel Tower*, was published to great acclaim in 1996, and the fourth and final instalment, *A Whistling Woman*, was published in 2002. As well as being a distinguished literary critic, she has served as a judge of various literary prizes, including the Booker Prize. AS Byatt was awarded the CBE in 1990 for her work as a writer. In 2002 she was awarded the Shakespeare prize by the Alfred Toepfer Foundation, Hamburg. Her latest book is *The Little Black Book of Short Stories*. She lives in London.

Thomas Cahill
The Gospel according to Luke

Thomas Cahill is the author of the bestselling *Hinges of History* series, which includes *How the Irish Saved Civilization, The Gifts of the Jews* and *Desire of the Everlasting Hills*. He has studied with some of America's most distinguished literary and biblical scholars at New York's Union Theological Seminary, Columbia University, Fordham University, and the Jewish Theological Seminary of America. His most recent title, *Sailing the Wine-Dark Sea: Why the Greeks Matter* (2003) was published to coincide with the Olympic Games 2004. Cahill was recently invited to address the US Congress on the Judeo–Christian roots of moral responsibility in American politics. The former director of religious publishing at Doubleday, he divides his time between New York City and Rome.

Nick Cave
The Gospel according to Mark

Nick Cave is best known as a musician. His first band, The Birthday Party, arrived in London from Melbourne, Australia in the early 1980s and stunned the United Kingdom with swaggering, raw-boned blues. Since their split in 1983 he has been the lead singer, songwriter and musician with Nick Cave and the Bad Seeds. He has also written a film script for the prison movie *Ghosts . . . of the Civil Dead* as well as a highly acclaimed novel, *And the Ass Saw the Angel* (1990). Cave's most successful album to date was 1996's *Murder Ballads*, followed by a productive few years that included *The Boatman's Call* (1997) and the piano-based elegies of *No More Shall We Part* (2001). His latest release is *Abattoir Blues/The Lyre of Orpheus*. He lives in London.

The Dalai Lama
The General Epistle of James

His Holiness the 14th Dalai Lama, Tenzin Gyatso, is the head of state and spiritual leader of the Tibetan people. He was born in 1935 to a peasant family and recognised as the reincarnation of the 13th Dalai Lama at the age of two. He began his monastic Buddhist education when he was six. 'Dalai Lama' is a Mongolian title meaning 'Ocean of Wisdom'. In 1959 he was forced into exile with the brutal suppression of the Tibetan National uprising in Lhasa by Chinese troops. For the last 39 years he has been living in Dharamsala, India. As leader of the Tibetan Government-in-Exile he advocates democracy and autonomy for the Tibetan people from Chinese rule. In his lectures and tours around the world he emphasises the importance of love, compassion and forgiveness. His publications in English include *Ancient Wisdom Modern World* and his autobiography *Freedom In Exile*. His Holiness was awarded the Nobel Prize for Peace in 1989.

E.L. Doctorow
The First Book of Moses, called Genesis

E.L. Doctorow's books include the novels *Ragtime, Billy Bathgate, Loon Lake* and *The Book of Daniel*. His work has won two National Book Critics Circle Awards, the National Book Award, the PEN/Faulkner Award, the Edith Wharton citation for fiction, and the William Dean Howells medal from the American Academy of Arts and Letters. In 2000 he published *City of God*, which questioned issues of religious schism through the figure of a writer who investigates the theft of a brass cross from a Manhattan church, and which the *Houston Chronicle* described as 'the greatest American novel of the past 50 years'. He lives and works in New York City.

Charles Frazier
The Book of Job

Charles Frazier is the author of *Cold Mountain*, which won the National Book Award and was made into a film in 2003. He, his wife, and their daughter have a farm in Raleigh, North Carolina, where they raise horses.

Francisco Goldman
The Gospel according to Matthew

Francisco Goldman is the author of the novels *The Long Night of White Chickens*, which won the Sue Kaufman Prize for First Fiction from the American Academy of Arts & Letters, and *The Ordinary Seaman*, which was a finalist for the IMPAC Dublin International Literary Prize. Both novels were short-listed for the PEN/Faulkner Award. He has also been awarded a Guggenheim Fellowship. His latest novel is *The Divine Husband*. He is currently the Allan K. Smith Professor of English at Trinity College in Hartford, Connecticut. He divides his time between Brooklyn and Mexico City.

Alasdair Gray
The Books of Jonah, Micah and Nahum

Alasdair Gray is an old asthmatic Glaswegian who lives by painting, writing and book design. His books include the novels *Lanark, 1982 Janine, The Fall of Kelvin Walker, McGrotty and Ludmilla, Poor Things, A History Maker;* short story collections *Unlikely Stories Mostly, Ten Tales Tall & True, Mavis Belfrage, The Ends of Our Tethers;* poetry *Old Negatives;* polemic *Why Scots Should Rule Scotland 1992, Why Scots should Rule Scotland 1997;* play *Working Legs (for people without them);* autobiography *Satire Self Portrait 4;* literary history *The Anthology of Prefaces.* His commentary on his paintings and drawings, *A Life in Pictures,* will be published by Canongate in 2006. His hobbies are socialism and liking the English.

David Grossman
The Second Book of Moses, called Exodus

David Grossman is one of Israel's leading writers. He is author of seven award-winning and internationally acclaimed novels including *See Under: Love, The Book of Intimate Grammar, The Zig Zag Kid* and *Someone to Run With.* He has also written three powerful journalistic accounts about his encounters with Palestinians, *The Yellow Wind, Sleeping on a Wire,* and *Death as a Way of Life,* as well as a number of children's books and a play. He was born in Jerusalem, where he now lives with his wife and three children.

Barry Hannah
The Gospel according to Mark

Barry Hannah is the author of eleven novels and several collections of short stories. His books include the novels *Geronimo Rex* (winner of the William Faulkner Award and a National Book Award finalist) and *Ray* (an American Book Award nominee), and the collection of stories *Airships,* which is regarded as a contemporary classic. His plaudits include recognition from the American Academy of Arts & Letters for achievement in fiction and the Robert Penn Warren Award from the Fellowship of Southern Writers. He lives in Oxford, Mississippi.

Thor Heyerdahl
The First Book of Moses, called Genesis

Thor Heyerdahl was a world famous ethnologist, zoologist and adventurer. He was famous for his numerous expeditions. These included a journey made from Callao, South America to the Raroia atoll, Polynesia on the *Kon-Tiki* raft; Morocco to Barbados on the *Ra I* and *Ra II* weed boats; and, Iraq to Djibouti on the weed boat the *Tigris*. He was particularly renowned for his work on Easter Island and Tenerife. Published extensively, he has received a number of international prizes and awards. In 1999 he received the *Peer Gynt* prize in Norway. He was a member of various scientific congresses, notably the International Congress of Americanists, the Pacific Science Congress, and the International Congress of Anthropology and Ethnology. He died in 2002.

Richard Holloway
The Gospel according to Luke

Richard Holloway is a well-known writer and broadcaster. He is a former Bishop of Edinburgh and Gresham Professor of Divinity. He is a Fellow of the Royal Society of Edinburgh. Author of twenty-five books, the most recent is *Looking in the Distance: The Human Search for Meaning*, published by Canongate.

P.D. James
The Acts of the Apostles

P.D. James has won many awards for crime-writing from Britain, America, Italy and Scandanavia, and has received honorary degrees from six universities. In 1983 she received the OBE and in 1991 she was made a life peer. In 1999 she received the Mystery Writers of America Grandmaster Award for long term achievement. Her novels include *An Unsuitable Job for a Woman, Innocent Blood, Shroud for a Nightingale, A Taste for Death, The Children of Men, Original Sin,* and *A Certain Justice.* Her novels include a series of books featuring the Scotland Yard policeman Commander Adam Dalgleish, the most recent of which are *Death in Holy Orders* (2001) and *The Murder Room* (2003). She lives in London.

Charles Johnson
Proverbs

Charles Johnson won the National Book Award in the USA in 1990 for his novel *Middle Passage.* A widely published literary critic, philosopher, cartoonist, screenwriter, essayist and lecturer, he is one of twelve African-American authors honoured in an international series of stamps celebrating great writers of the twentieth century. He is currently the Pollock Professor of English at the University of Washington. His novel, *Dreamer,* was published to great acclaim in October 1998.

Ray Loriga
The Gospel according to Luke

Ray Loriga (born 1967) currently lives in New York and Madrid. He made his debut with the novel *The Worst of Everything* (1992), which received an enthusiastic reception from critics, who immediately singled him out as a new talent. He established his reputation with *Heroes* (1993), which has gone into more than eight editions. He has also published *Strange Days* (1994), *Fallen from Heaven* (1995) and *Tokyo Doesn't Love Us Anymore* (1999). His latest book is *El hombre que inventó Manhatten,* and it was published in 2004.

Blake Morrison
The Gospel according to John

Blake Morrison was born in Skipton, Yorkshire. He is the author of two collections of poetry, *Dark Glasses* and *The Ballad of the Yorshire Ripper*, and has also written for theatre and television. His best-selling memoir *And When Did You Last See Your Father?* won the Waterstone's/Esquire/Volvo Award for Non-Fiction and the J R Ackerley prize for Autobiography in 1993. He has published *As If*, which explores the Bulger trial and its aftermath, and *Too True*, a collection of his stories and journalism written over the last five years. His first novel, *The Justification of Johann Gutenberg*, a ficitional portrait of the fifteenth-century printer and the inventor of movable type, was published in 2000. His latest book, *Things My Mother Never Told Me*, a memoir of his mother, was published in 2002. He lives in London, where he is currently Professor of Creative and Life Writing at Goldsmiths College.

Kathleen Norris
The Revelation of St John the Divine

Kathleen Norris is an award-winning poet and writer, and the author of *The Cloister Walk, Dakota: A Spiritual Geography*, and *Amazing Grace: A Vocabulary of Faith*, as well as seven books of poetry. A recipient of grants from the Bush and Guggenheim foundations, she has twice been in residence at the Institute for Ecumenical and Cultural Research at St John's Abbey in Collegeville, Minnesota, and has been an oblate at a Benedictine Monastery in North Dakota since 1986. Her recent work, *Virgin of Bennington*, traces her own life before Dakota. Other works include *Journey: New and Selected Poems, Little Girls in Church* (a poetry collection) and *The Holy Twins*, a children's book on St Benedict and St Scholastica in collaboration with author/illustrator Tomie de Paolo. She and her husband live in South Dakota.

Pier Paolo Pasolini
The Gospel according to Matthew

Pier Paolo Pasolini achieved fame and notoriety as a film maker, although he had written numerous novels and essays before his first screenplay in 1954. His first film *Accatone* (1961) was based on his own novel, and was a violent depiction of a pimp's life in Rome that caused a sensation. He was arrested after 1962's *Ro.Go.Pa.G.* for what was regarded as blasphemous content. Similar controversy was expected for *The Gospel According to Saint Matthew* (1964), but it was actually acclaimed as one of the few honest portrayals of Christ on screen. His career alternated between the political and the personal, expressing his views on Marxism, atheism, fascism and homosexuality. The notorious *Salo, or The 120 days of Sodom* (1976), fused Mussolini's fascist Italy and the work of the Marquis de Sade. Pasolini was murdered in mysterious circumstances shortly after its completion.

Benjamin Prado
The Book of Job

Benjamin Prado was born in Madrid in 1961 and published his first novel, *Strange*, in 1995. It was followed by *Never Shake Hands with a Left-handed Gunman*, and *Where Do You Think You Are Going and Who Do You Think You Are*, both published in 1996, and *Someone's Approaching* (1998). He is also the author of several books of poetry: *The Blue Heart of Enlightenment* (1991), *Personal Matters* (1992), *Shelter from the Storm* (1996) and *All of Us* (1998). His works have been translated into numerous languages.

Piers Paul Read
The Wisdom of Solomon

Piers Paul Read, the third son of the poet and critic Sir Herbert Read, is the author of fourteen novels and four works of non-fiction, among them *Alive: the Story of the Andes Survivors*. His novels have won a number of awards, among them the Hawthornden Prize, the Somerset Maugham Award and the James Tait Black Memorial Prize. *Alive* received the Thomas More Award for Catholic Literature in the US. He is a Fellow of the Royal Society of Literature and is vice-president of the Catholic Writers' Guild. His most recent book is *Alec Guinness: The Authorised Biography*. He is married with four children and lives in London.

Ruth Rendell
The Epistle of Paul the Apostle to the Romans

Ruth Rendell is the author of more than forty novels, among them the Inspector Wexford series, and six volumes of short-stories. She also writes under the pseudonym Barbara Vine. Many of her books have been adapted for television, and feature films based on her work have been made by Claude Chabrol and Pedro Almodovar. She has received numerous fiction prizes, including the Arts Council's National Book Award for Genre Fiction, four Gold Daggers and the Cartier diamond dagger (lifetime achievement award) from the Crime Writers' Association, the Edgar Allan Poe Award and the Angel Award for Fiction. Ruth Rendell received a CBE in 1996 and in the following year was made a Life Peer. Her most recent book is *13 Steps Down* (2004).

Mordecai Richler
The Book of Job

A renowned novelist, essayist and satirist, Mordechai Richler was one of Canada's most skilled and popular writers. He could be controversial too: his early novels outraged some in Montreal's Jewish community, and his later non-fiction work provoked a number of Quebec's nationalists. His tremendous talent was indisputable in books such as the *Apprenticeship of Duddy Kravitz* and *Barney's Version*. He died in 2001.

Steven Rose
The First Book of Moses, called Genesis

Steven Rose is Professor of Biology at the Open University and visiting professor at University College London. His research centres on the molecular and cellular mechanisms of memory formation, as well as writing on the social framework and repercussions of science. He is the author or editor of fourteen books, including *The Chemistry of Life* (1966) and *Not in Our Genes* (1984). In 1993 he won the Rhône-Poulenc Science Book prize for *The Making of Memory*. His latest book *The 21ˢᵗ Century Brain: explaining, mending and manipulating the mind* will be published in Spring 2005. He has published over 300 research papers and been awarded various honours including the Sechenov and Anokhin medals (Russia) and the Ariens Kappers medal (Netherlands). In 2002 he was awarded the Biochemical Society model for excellence in public communication of science.

Will Self
The Revelation of St John the Divine

Will Self is the author of *The Quantity Theory of Insanity*, short-listed for the 1992 John Llewellyn Rhys Memorial Prize, winner of the 1993 Geoffrey Faber Memorial Prize. His books include *Cock & Bull, My Idea of Fun, Grey Area, Junk Mail, The Sweet Smell of Psychosis, Great Apes* and *Tough, Tough Toys for Tough, Tough Boys*. His novel *How the Dead Live* describes how the dead simply move to duller parts of London, and it was shortlisted for Whitbread Book of the Year. His latest book is the collection of short stories *Dr Mukti and Other Tales of Woe*. He lives in London.

Meir Shalev
The First and Second Books of Samuel

Meir Shalev, one of Israel's most celebrated novelists, is the author of *Four Meals, Esau, Roman Russi* and *Alone in the Desert*, all of which have been literary and commercial successes. His latest novel, *Fontanelle*, has enjoyed best-seller status in Israel and Holland. His books have been translated into eighteen languages. He has written a book of biblical commentaries, *The Bible for Now,* and a book of literary criticism, *Mainly about Love*. He also writes children's books, and is a columnist with the Israeli daily newspaper, *Yediot Ahronot*. He lives in Jerusalem with his wife and children.

Darcey Steinke
The Gospel according to John

Darcey Steinke is the author of three novels. *Up Through Water* and *Jesus Saves* were *New York Times* Notable Books of the Year. Her Novel *Suicide Blonde* has been translated into eight languages. Her short fiction has appeared in *The Heretic's Bible, Story Magazine,* and *Bomb*, and her non-fiction has been featured in the *Washington Post,* the *Chicago Tribune,* the *Village Voice, Spin,* and the *New York Times Magazine*. Her web project, *Blindspot,* was included in the Whitney Museum's 2000 Biennial. She currently teaches at New School University and lives with her daughter in Brooklyn.

Joanna Trollope
The Books of Ruth and Esther

Author of eagerly awaited and bestselling novels often centred around the domestic nuances and dilemmas of life in contemporary England, Joanna Trollope has also written a number of historical novels and a study of women in the British Empire, *Britannica's Daughters*. In 1988 she wrote her first contemporary novel, *The Choir,* followed in 1989 by *A Village Affair,* and she has published a book almost every year since. Her novels have been translated into 25 languages, and her most recent is 2004's *Brother and Sister,* a story which explores themes of adoption, loyalty and the nature of identity. Awarded the

OBE in 1996, she divides her time between London and Gloucester-shire, for which county she was made a Deputy Lieutenant in 2002.

Fay Weldon
The Epistle of Paul the Apostle to the Corinthians

Fay Weldon was born in England and raised in New Zealand. She took degrees in Economics and Psychology at the University of St Andrews in Scotland and then, after a decade of odd jobs and hard times, began writing fiction. She is now a well-known novelist, screenwriter and cultural journalist. Her novels include *The Life and Loves of a She-Devil* (the TV version of which is available on DVD), *Puffball*, *The Cloning of Joanna May*, *Affliction* and *Worst Fears*. Her autobiography *Auto da Fay* and her latest novel, *Mantrapped*, have recently been published. She has four sons and lives in Dorset.

A.N. Wilson
The Gospel according to Matthew

A.N. Wilson is an award-winning novelist and biographer. He is the author of the bestselling *Jesus* (1992) and *Paul: The Mind of the Apostle* (1997). His novels include *The Healing Art* (Somerset Maugham Award), *Wise Virgin* (WH Smith Award) and the five books in the *Lampitt Chronicles*. His biographies include studies of Sir Walter Scott, John Milton, Tolstoy, CS Lewis and Hillaire Belloc. He lives in north London.

Copyright Information